Looking Backward, 1988—1888

62

DATE DUE

D011778

Looking Backward,

1988–1888

Essays on Edward Bellamy

Edited by Daphne Patai

The University of Massachusetts Press

Amherst, 1988

Copyright © 1988 by
The University of Massachusetts Press
All rights reserved
Printed in the United States of America
LC 88-10621
ISBN 0–87023–633–4 (cloth); 634–2 (pbk.)
Designed by Edith Kearney
Set in Linotron Plantin
Printed by Thomson-Shore, Inc.
and bound by John H. Dekker & Sons

Library of Congress Cataloging-in-Publication Data

Looking backward, 1988–1888 : essays on Edward Bellamy / edited by
   Daphne Patai.
      p. cm.
   Bibliography: p.
   ISBN 0–87023–633–4 (alk. paper). ISBN 0–87023–634–2 (pbk. : alk.
paper)
    1. Bellamy, Edward, 1850–1898—Criticism and interpretation.
   2. Utopias in literature. 3. Social problems in literature.
   I. Patai, Daphne, 1943–
   PS1087.L66 1988
   813'.4—dc19   88–10621
                                           CIP

British Library Cataloguing in Publication data are available.

Contents

Chronology

SYLVIA E. BOWMAN

1850   Edward Bellamy born, 26 March, to Rev. Rufus King and Maria Putnam Bellamy in Chicopee Falls, Massachusetts.

1864   After a profound religious experience, Edward is baptized on 13 April.

1867   Fails to pass physical examination for West Point; becomes independent reader and student at Union College, Schenectady, New York. Interested in Comte and Socialism.

1868–1869   With his cousin, William Packer, lives and studies in Germany.

1868   Begins study of law in Springfield, Massachusetts.

1871   Passes bar examination with distinction; opens law office in Chicopee Falls and closes it after one case. Publishes "Woman Suffrage" in *Golden Age*.

1872   To New York City to be free-lance journalist. Publishes "Railroad Disasters" and "National Education" in *Golden Age*.

1872–1877   Works for the Springfield *Union* as editorial writer and book reviewer; presents two lyceum speeches containing basic concepts later used in *Looking Backward*.

1873   Writes "Religion of Solidarity," his basic lifelong belief.

1875   First short story, "The Cold Snap" (September).

1876   "A Providence" and "The Old Folks' Party" (stories).

1877   "Lost," "A Summer Evening's Dream," "Taking a Mean Advantage," "Superfluity of Naughtiness," "A Mid-Night

Adapted from Sylvia Bowman, *Edward Bellamy*, © 1986 and reprinted with the permission of Twayne Publishers, a division of G. K. Hall & Co., Boston.

Dream," "Hooking Watermelons," and "Extra Hazardous" (stories).

1877–1878   Leaves Springfield *Union;* tours Hawaiian Islands and elsewhere with brother Frederick.

1878   "Two Days' Solitary Imprisonment," "Pott's Painless Cure," "Deserted" (stories). First novel: *Six to One: A Nantucket Idyl.*

1878–1879   *Dr. Heidenhoff's Process* serialized in Springfield *Union;* published as book in 1880.

1879   Stories "Jane Hicks" and "Taking a Mean Advantage"; novel *The Duke of Stockbridge* serialized in *Berkshire Courier.*

1880   Charles and Edward Bellamy found the *Penny News* in Springfield (February); by 13 May, it becomes the *Daily News.* "That Letter" and "A Tale of the South Pacific."

1882   Marries Emma Sanderson, 30 May.

1884   Son Paul born, 26 December; Edward retires from economically troubled *Daily News* to write fiction. *Miss Ludington's Sister,* serialized in *Literary World* and published as a book.

1886   Daughter Marion born, 4 March. "The Blindman's World" and "Echo of Antietam."

1887   "At Pinney's Ranch."

1888   Publication of *Looking Backward.* "A Love Story Reversed."

1889   First meeting of the Boston Bellamy Club, 8 January; February, club decides to publish the monthly magazine the *Nationalist;* "To Whom This May Come" and "A Positive Romance."

1891   Bellamy founds the *New Nation,* 31 January. The *Nationalist* ceases publication with March-April issue.

1891–1894   Bellamy and Nationalists deeply involved with Populism; Bellamy ceases publication of the *New Nation,* 1894.

1897   *Equality* published. Bellamy and his family leave in the fall to reside in Denver because of his ill health.

1898   Returns to Chicopee Falls. Dies, 22 May. *The Blindman's World and Other Stories.*

1900   *The Duke of Stockbridge.*

Looking Backward, 1988—1888

Introduction:
The Doubled Vision of
Edward Bellamy

DAPHNE PATAI

When Julian West, the proper Bostonian hero of Edward Bellamy's most famous novel, awoke in the year 2000 after a sleep lasting more than a century and began to contemplate his old world in light of the new, a whole generation of Americans woke up with him to the possibilities of change in their country. One hundred years after the publication of *Looking Backward 2000–1887*, Bellamy continues to be a controversial figure, as the essays in this volume, commemorating the novel's appearance in 1888, attest.

Bellamy (1850–1898) was a cultural critic in the broadest sense of the word, and his work touches on a vast range of concerns. Virtually no aspect of late nineteenth-century life went unrecognized in his utopian novels, *Looking Backward* and its 1897 sequel *Equality*, and in his extensive journalism. As social reformer and creative writer, Bellamy combines in his work aspects of life too often treated as opposites: imagination and practicality. More than this, a good deal of Bellamy's scathing attack on the capitalist excesses of his time came from his deep-rooted conviction that ordinary human beings, condemned to a life of labor in conditions of the utmost insecurity and ill health, were thereby prevented from realizing their true potential as creative beings possessed of both intellect and imagination. Avoiding the allocation of personal blame, Bellamy saw the roots of the problem as inherent in social and economic structures that pitted capital against labor for the sake of private profit. He did not flinch from pronouncing a moral judgment upon the system that made rapacious accumulation and indifference to one's fellow beings perfectly rational responses. But in the industrial forces that were rapidly changing American life, he saw the possibility of a massive transformation. While clearly a product of his time, as is evident in many of his ideas, Bellamy was nonetheless capable of going beyond the cherished rationales for inequality that were advanced in his own day—as they still are in ours. Life begins with its material base, he argued again and again, and without economic equality, political equality—that is, democracy—is a mere pretense. The struggle for a better world based upon radical egalitarianism became the main project of Edward Bellamy's maturity.

Through *Looking Backward* and Bellamy's subsequent writings and agitation on behalf of Nationalism (as his brand of socialism, and the political movement that arose from his writing, was called), Edward Bellamy tried to make visible the not-yet-visible. In order to do so, he invited his readers to dwell on, as well as dwell in, his image of a conflict-ridden past containing within itself the seeds of transformation into a better future. Evoking the familiar, he proposed change; evoking the new, he made it familiar. To look forward, he insisted, we must look backward. This is the ironic implication contained in the very title *Looking Backward*.

Certainly it invites playfulness, this notion of looking forward by looking backward. Oscar Ameringer, the radical humorist quoted by Franklin Rosemont in his essay on Bellamy's multifaceted contributions to American radicalism, toyed with these possibilities in his recollection of having read *Looking Backward* at the turn of the century: "Yes, yes, *Looking Backward*. A great book. A very great book. One of the greatest, most prophetic books this country has produced. It didn't make me look backward, it made me look forward, and I haven't got over looking forward since I read *Looking Backward*." How much more complicated the notion becomes in our time, as we commemorate this anniversary and indeed look backward at Bellamy's achievement and forward toward his vision of a different world. For Bellamy's future is now nearly our past, and we look at him and his work from the perspective of an additional 100 years since he first published *Looking Backward*. What was 112 years into the future in the year the novel appeared is a mere 12 years away from us, and Bellamy himself has been dead for nearly 90 years. But the problems he dealt with are still with us: the tyranny of an industrialism run for private profit, poverty in the midst of plenty, economic inequality that mocks the concept of political equality, the monopolistic concentration of wealth and power, the lack of cooperation and waste of productive forces in competition, the denigration of labor and adulation of wealth that allows the well-off to monopolize not only the material goods but also the moral goods, the perpetual insecurity and limited horizons of lives defined by boring and unhealthy work and frightened by the perpetual possibility of its absence, since it alone entitles one to a livelihood.

We are peculiar creatures, equipped to look backward but unable to see into the future, hence living in a "blindman's world," as Bellamy called it in one of his short stories. But if we cannot see into the future, at least we can envision it through acts of imagination that in their turn become elements in the shaping of that future. Bellamy tried to bring a better future into existence by his imaginative evocation of it, for he understood the power of a vision that grants, through acts of imagination, material form to an unpeopled, not-yet-existing time. From his day to ours, however, his vision has generated controversy and disagreement. The essays that follow, written by literary critics and historians, approach Bellamy's complex work from a variety of perspectives. Details about Bellamy's life and career, about his book and its impact, will emerge throughout this volume and there is no need to summarize them here.

Milton Cantor, in "The Backward Look of Bellamy's Socialism," sets the stage for a reexamination of Bellamy's work by presenting a vivid portrait of Chicopee Falls, Massachusetts, in Bellamy's youth. He traces Bellamy's nostalgia for a world already disappearing even as he was growing up, a prefactory world based on a rural society moving at a leisurely pace and living in harmony with nature. Class lines were imprecise in this pre-1840s Chicopee, and those willing to work could make a fair living, something that became ever less likely as Chicopee developed into an ugly factory city with tenements. Bellamy constantly reaffirmed the small-town virtues of this Chicopee of days gone by and held them up against the urban society that was extinguishing them. Cantor argues that Bellamy envisioned Boston in the year 2000 along lines consistent with his prejudices against an industrial age. Lacking confidence in working-class activism, Bellamy is, from this perspective, a genteel reformer in the mold of the Mugwumps, holding elitist views of the worker, and possessed of an anti-democratic cast of mind and deep reservations about politics, even labor politics. Thus Cantor exposes Bellamy's deviations from revolutionary socialism and the great European tradition.

Going still further back, to an exploration of the conjunction of real and ideal that shaped earlier utopian works such as Plato's *Republic* and Thomas More's *Utopia*, Lee Cullen Khanna, in "The Text as Tactic: *Looking Backward* and the Power of the Word," finds this opposition replicated in the two main contemporary approaches to utopian fiction— that of the social sciences and that of literary criticism. Emphasizing that these two different disciplinary perspectives reflect and are a natural outgrowth of tendencies existing in the utopian genre itself, Khanna points out the ways in which utopian speculation pulls readers in contrary directions even as it simultaneously denies any permanent dichotomy between theory and praxis, the abstract and the concrete. Seen from this point of view, Bellamy was able in a singular fashion to sustain the polarities inherent in the genre and make them work toward the end of transformation of both self and society, the intertwining themes of *Looking Backward*. Examining Bellamy's earlier writings, Khanna identifies transformation as his constant concern, evident in novels and short stories alike. The pervasive duality of Bellamy's turn of mind became a fundamental structure of *Looking Backward*—but expressed with such clarity and force that the book bridged the gap between contemplation and action, text and life, and triggered creative energies in the form not only of further utopian texts but of political action as well. Thus did Bellamy demonstrate "the power of the word."

Jean Pfaelzer's "Immanence, Indeterminance, and the Utopian Pun in *Looking Backward*," begins with a rich accounting of the material conditions that fostered the writing of Bellamy's novel. Like Khanna, Pfaelzer then focuses on the utopian duality, the space between reality and possibility, that is opened by utopian fiction. She examines the fantastic or nonmimetic mode that coexists in Bellamy's novel alongside a realistic or mimetic mode and sees the real meaning of the novel as emerging from the tensions inherent in the depiction of a good place that is no place—utopia. Pfaelzer suggests a complex reading of *Looking Backward* that does not reduce it to a social planning text. Instead, she examines Julian West as a symbolic creation characterized by an indeterminacy that challenges the reader. She notes the tension produced by the text's contrasts between the utopian present and the nonutopian past, a tension that engages the reader even as, in the end, it confronts Julian West with an insoluble dilemma. And she explores the conservative subtext expressed through the novel's typical traits of a conventional romance. Ultimately, Pfaelzer argues, the novel exists as an expression of longing that cannot be resolved by the utopian text.

In "Gender, Class, and Race in Utopia," Sylvia Strauss, like Milton Cantor, explores the limitations of Bellamy's writings and of any politics deriving from them. Strauss concentrates on women's struggle for the vote in nineteenth-century America and Bellamy's response to it, arguing that his apparent feminism was actually part of his larger strategy of winning women's support for the reorganization of society that he proposed. But Bellamy's is a corporate state and his industrial army a model of patriarchal thinking. With an opportunism that Strauss considers characteristic, Bellamy was willing also to countenance continued racial discrimination in an effort to make his vision palatable. His middle-class bias, evident in his limited goal of converting the educated and cultured classes, was repeated in the Bellamy clubs that sprang up to propagate his ideas. Thus Bellamy rates no better in relation to class—the very issue he purported to be addressing. Indeed, his models for the future citizens of Boston were precisely people of his own class and station. On all three counts, then, Bellamy's vision fails, Strauss argues, for he was unable to challenge the racial, class, and gender hierarchies of his time.

Between the viewpoint held by Cantor of Bellamy as a figure indulging in nostalgia for a bygone era, and that presented by Warren Wagar (discussed below) of Bellamy as a "scientocrat," falls Howard Segal's appraisal of an aspect of *Looking Backward* that is too seldom examined closely. In "Bellamy and Technology: Reconciling Centralization and Decentralization," Segal describes the tensions introduced and in some measure resolved in Bellamy's work between industrialism and agrarianism, between centralization and decentralization. Technology is both principal cause of and solution to the problems Bellamy addresses in *Looking Backward*, but, Segal argues, technology is no one thing, nor even is decentralized technology; rather, it is a multifaceted term, amenable to use for purposes of liberation or enslavement. Such tensions are evident in *Looking Backward*, in which technology leads to both centralization and decentralization. Bellamy sought to strike a balance between a whole series of terms that are usually presented as dichotomous: collectivism and individualism, homogeneity and heterogeneity, industrialism and agrarianism. Segal suggests that the novel's popularity may well have come precisely from the more balanced vision of community-and-cooperation and technological advances that it presents and that few of its imitators attained. Bellamy was aiming at a middle ground; he transported the garden of rural America into the city itself, transforming the entire landscape and healing this split. *Looking Backward* thus anticipates many later attempts to use technology to create such a balance, attempts such as Henry Ford's nineteen "village industries" in southeastern Michigan. Despite the failure of Ford's experiment, Segal asserts, decentralized technology is more popular and practicable today than ever before and *Looking Backward* depicts a middleway between the extremes of the antitechnology and the protechnology positions.

Segal makes the important observation that decision making and control are issues separate from matters relating to a society's physical location, scale, and size. And it is precisely this former matter, of control and decision making, that is the focal point of W. Warren Wagar's essay "Dreams of Reason: Bellamy, Wells, and the Positive Utopia." Wagar views scientocracy—the rule of science as implemented by experts—as the key feature of Bellamy's text and argues that this is the dominant twentieth-century ideology with seeds clearly discernible in nineteenth-century utopian writers. Utopias can never provide models of good political life, Wagar

writes, because conflict and uncertainty are inherent in politics. Hence the
sole element distinguishing one utopia from another is the source of authority. Bellamy's utopia is a positive one—based on reason and empiricism—
as were the utopian and dystopian novels of H. G. Wells, with whom Wagar
compares Bellamy. Wagar objects to the equation of democracy with equality and concentrates his discussion on the former. An undemocratic and
dangerous belief in the power of modern science and its experts lurks in
Bellamy's vision of the proper organization of labor. The overarching
conviction that wisdom is embodied in correct social design, Wagar argues,
causes the design itself to become the real ruler of positive utopian societies.

Two subsequent essays, by Kenneth Roemer and Franklin Rosemont,
attempt to synthesize and address the kinds of issues raised by older
writings on Bellamy (and, equally, by other contributors to this volume).
Roemer does this from the point of view of a literary critic, exploring the
charge of stasis so often leveled at utopian fiction, while Rosemont's perspective is that of a historian of radical ideas and movements. In both
essays, the dynamic nature of utopian speculation emerges and is affirmed,
dialectically responding to and creating new realities.

In his "Getting 'Nowhere' beyond Stasis: A Critique, a Method, and
a Case," Kenneth Roemer uses reader-response theory to explore how
readers perceive stasis and dynamism in a utopian text. Like Khanna and
Pfaelzer, Roemer argues for a more complex reading of utopias, one that
goes beyond the traditional sociohistorical content analyses based on assumptions about the text as a fixed entity. Roemer recognizes the continuing utility of traditional approaches, which may help us note inconsistencies and problematic features of a utopian text—for example, between the
dynamic promise and the static delivery of many utopias. But he urges that
this "stuckraking," which too easily leads to the detection of static, even
totalitarian, intents in any utopian speculation, be complemented by textual analyses and biographical and historical studies that illuminate the
potential or actual responses of readers confronting utopian texts. Thus
Roemer proposes a three-dimensional approach, comprising (1) content
analysis; (2) textual analysis based on reader-response theory, which explores the networks of invitations to readers that exist in any utopian text;
and (3) examination of documented responses of actual readers. For each of
these dimensions Roemer uses his own concern with the stasis-dynamism
problem in utopian fiction and, in particular, *Looking Backward*, as a test
case. Bellamy's own responses, as first reader of *Looking Backward*, are
analyzed in Roemer's final section on documented readings, which focuses

on the intriguing process of opening and closing a text that makes it impossible to see the text as a fixed entity to be mined for its content alone.

As if following Roemer's suggestions, Franklin Rosemont's essay, "Bellamy's Radicalism Reclaimed," explores the full panoply of Bellamy's ideas as manifest in writings from adolescence to the end of his life and traces their extraordinary impact on several generations of American radicals. No other American has inspired so many to become socialists, but, Rosemont argues, Bellamy was first of all an imaginative writer, in whose work there recurs a double critique—of the mind and of society, each at war with itself. In different ways, Bellamy's writings attempt to work through these joined problems, and the popularity of his *Looking Backward*, Rosemont states, attests to the book's emancipatory impetus. Rosemont shows that every significant current of labor radicalism in the late nineteenth century and early twentieth century was affected by Bellamy's vision of the future. Bellamy criticized the labor movement for stopping at half-measures rather than attacking wage slavery at its roots. But Bellamy's influence not only was felt in the mainstream labor movement, it was also pervasive in the emerging socialist movement, which received its momentum from Bellamyism, not from Marxism. Eugene V. Debs and Daniel DeLeon, leaders of the two socialist parties of the period preceding World War I, were both initially inspired by Bellamy, as was the feminist writer and activist Charlotte Perkins Gilman. In the period between 1895 and 1915, Rosemont writes, most of those who contributed an original vision to the cause of working-class emancipation began with Bellamy's ideas. "One man's revolutionary imagination," says Rosemont, "ignited many others"—the phenomenon Khanna alludes to in her essay when she speaks of Bellamy's "generativity." In tracing the evolution of Bellamy's thought, Rosemont depicts a Bellamy not at all the militaristic high-tech statist he is often accused of being. Like Roemer, Rosemont sees Bellamy as ever in the process of reconsidering and refining his ideas. His was a socialism nourished, Rosemont says, by poetry and the imagination, responsive to what went on around him and also to others' responses to his own ideas. In his nonviolence, his radical environmentalism (a theme usually ignored in writing about Bellamy), and his powerfully eros-affirmative, feminist, and socialist commitments, Bellamy speaks to our time.

Nancy Snell Griffith concludes the volume with a selected annotated bibliography of Bellamy's major works and of the most important secondary studies of Bellamy and of *Looking Backward* in particular. It is culled from her recent book *Edward Bellamy: A Bibliography*.

All the essays in this volume reveal the doubled vision of Bellamy held by critics and readers. They also speak to the doubled vision held by Bellamy himself. For Bellamy is not merely controversial; he is a complex figure whose earliest writings reveal a psychologically probing and even metaphysical turn of mind. Especially illuminating in Bellamy's early fiction is his fascination with the theme of the doubling effect itself. Long before *Looking Backward*, but also in that work, Bellamy is preoccupied with time, with the fragility of identity, and with the constant shifting of perspectives that makes new visions possible. In the story "The Blindman's World" (1886), for example, looking at another world provides a vantage point from which one can better see one's own. As he questions ordinary assumptions and circles around his themes, Bellamy sees the tragic aspect of being able to look only backward, not forward. This dovetails with his perspective in *Looking Backward*, which is, of course, a history of the future—a contradiction in terms unless one makes this mental shift and sees as past what may lie in the future because nothing else will make it accessible to us now.

As he looks through his telescope pointed at Mars, the narrator of "The Blindman's World" describes the effort required in order to see: "Every atom of nerve and will power combined in the strain to see a little, and yet a little, and yet a little, clearer, farther, deeper" (Bellamy, 1968 [1898], 5). The Martian he addresses mentions the sadness of a literature "written in the past tense and relating exclusively to things that are ended" (p. 23). As opposed to this: "We [Martians] write of the past when it is still the future, and of course in the future tense" (p. 24). It needs to be stressed that Bellamy's interest in this theme does not signify a fatalistic sense of life inexorably unfolding beyond the control or intervention of human beings, for such a view would be incompatible with the energy that went into writing *Looking Backward* and its sequel, *Equality* (1897), the very title of which proclaims Bellamy's primary concern.

The theme of overcoming the ordinary boundaries of our experience of time is apparent in Bellamy's other early fiction as well and is frequently connected to reflections on writing and to an awareness of how our very grammar betrays our limitations. In the story "The Old Folks' Party" (1876), the young people who dress up as the selves they will be in fifty years discover that in a sense they are indeed already aged, their young selves dead and gone. At different phases of life we are to all intents and purposes different persons, says one character in this story, "and the first person of grammar ought to be used only with the present tense. What we were, or shall be, or do, belongs strictly to the third person" (Bellamy 1968 [1898], 64). Bellamy depicts the young people's confrontation with a genuinely old woman, a meeting in space and time of individuals at different points in their lives and to whom past and future have quite different meanings. He thus casts into doubt not only the belief in a persistent identity, but also the conventional notion of a shared present. Again we encounter the doubling effect, and the sense of pathos as we contemplate people connected to the past and future through a misperceived notion of "self." Appearing to share the present, we are merely co-occupants of a moment whose meaning differs from person to person. It is this ability to make individual distinctions, to not subsume human experience into the usual gross generalizations, that served Bellamy well as he went on to contemplate the diverse positions occupied by individuals within a class society.

In the Kafkaesque story "Two Days' Solitary Imprisonment" (1878), the main character, through imagining the horrors of guilt and the inability to prove one's innocence, finds his life enmeshed in precisely the nightmare he has imagined. Again, dream and reality interpenetrate. In "A Summer Evening's Dream" (1877), the theme of the passage of time and one's forgotten self, in this case recaptured, also appears. And in "A Love Story Reversed" (1888), the change of perspective brought about by reversal is demonstrated as Bellamy explores the consequences of women speaking their love to men instead of playing out their conventionally passive role. The point of convergence in these varied texts is the different view, of oneself and one's world, that results from a change of focus, a break in the smooth surface of experience. Revelations emerge from these shifts in perspective.

The culmination of Bellamy's fascination with such shifts is *Looking Backward*, a story about our past told from the point of view of our future and about our future as experienced by a man from our past. All utopian fiction works with devices for producing estrangement, but what is interesting in Bellamy is that, judged by the evidence of his writing, he was intrigued by these devices, and the philosophical problems they evoked, long before he put them to work in the cause of social reform.

We each read with our own optic, of course, and this means that very often what one reader sees as central will be, to another reader, peripheral. This fact should not, however, cast us into irresolvable relativism. As Warren Wagar has written in another context, "a writer must be judged not only by what he says, but by what he says most effectively, and with the greatest conviction" (Wagar 1984, 194). In Bellamy's case, it seems to me that his most effective and impassioned writing was on the issue of economic equality, and it is to this issue that I now wish to turn.

If Bellamy wanted to free people from the weight of their personal past, as his 1880 novel *Dr. Heidenhoff's Process* and some of his short stories suggest, he had nonetheless an unusually strong sense of the impersonal past—the past of which all, equally, are heirs, and it was in this common human heritage that he found an ethic. He called this ethic the "religion of solidarity" and it provides the simple and relentless rationale of his absolute economic egalitarianism. By envisioning a separation of "income" from "work," by proposing the abolition of wage slavery through the equal distribution (in the form of credit to be dispensed as one desired) of society's overall wealth among its citizens, all to be joint and equal owners of the nation's resources and enterprises, and by advocating that work, utilizing technological advances, be drastically reduced and shared by all, Bellamy opens the way for a redefinition of work, leisure, and social relations.

The moral basis of this nonviolent transformation is spelled out in *Looking Backward* when Dr. Leete explains to Julian West that "the title of every man, woman, and child to the means of existence rests on no basis less plain, broad, and simple than the fact that they are fellows of one race—members of one human family" (Bellamy 1960 [1888], 100). No individual is "self-made," Bellamy repeatedly asserted. The common history linking members of the human family was more important to Bellamy than the "personal" achievements, however glorious, of an individual's life story.

Bellamy addressed this issue in his "Talks on Nationalism" published in *The New Nation,* the journal edited by him and published weekly from 1891 through 1894 and that served as organ of the Nationalist movement. "Mr. Smith," Bellamy's Nationalist spokesman, explains to a "seeker of definitions" why the formula "To each according to his deeds" does not justly represent the views of most socialists, for it suggests that "men's only duties are to themselves." Mr. Smith proceeds to make an interesting, typically Bellamyesque argument:

> . . . a law awarding to each the value of his deeds or work, as a matter of
> absolute right would be fraudulent, because it would assume that an individual
> owns himself and has a valid title to the full usufruct of his powers without
> incumbrance or obligation on account of his debt to the past and his duties
> toward the social organism of which he is a part and by virtue of which only he is

able to work more effectually than a savage. This assumption is wholly false. "No man liveth to himself." The powers he has inherited from the common ancestry of the race measure his debt to his contemporaries, not his claims upon them. The strong are the rightful servants and debtors of the weak, not their masters. (Bellamy 1969 [1938], 26–28).

Rejecting the two predominant schemes for distributing wealth—the haggling of the market place, on the one hand, and the arbitrary edict of the state, on the other—Mr. Smith expounds the third, the Nationalist way: "From each equally to each equally." This is already the principle enacted by all modern states, he argues; it underlies the political, judicial, and military institutions of national solidarity, in which citizens have equal duties to the nation and the nation recognizes an equal duty toward all citizens. All that is needed is for this principle to be extended to the nation's economy. "The demand of the nation upon all is equal, but where there is inability, either partial or complete to fulfill the demand, the nation does not, therefore, diminish its service of protection toward the citizen. The army fights for him though he cannot fight, and the taxes are spent for him though he can pay none. It is not possible that any other law should prevail under a national organization of industry" (p. 30). This argument is the basis for Bellamy's repeated claim that his Nationalism was merely a further development of the already existing idea of the nation.

In his 1894 introduction to the American edition of *The Fabian Essays*, Bellamy succinctly stated his differences from the Fabians: "Now Nationalists are socialists who, holding all that socialists agree on, go further, and hold also that the distribution of the cooperative product among the members of the community must be not merely equitable, whatever that term may mean, but must be always and absolutely equal" (Bellamy 1984, 126).

Again and again in his writings Bellamy spoke of the sham of democracy when it is unaccompanied by economic equality. In the first chapter of *Equality*, Julian West realizes the limitations of what he took to be the democracy of his day. Campaigning and voting are shown to be controlled by and subordinated to the needs of capitalists, while "the people" play no role at all in "the so-called popular system of government in your day," as Edith Leete points out (Bellamy 1968 [1897], 13). Julian West summarizes the reality of the situation: "Undoubtedly the confusion of terms in our political system is rather calculated to puzzle one at first, but if you only grasp firmly the vital point that the rule of the rich, the supremacy of capital and its interests, as against those of the people at large, was the central principle of our system, to which every other interest was made subservient, you will have the key that clears up every mystery" (p. 13).

Here Bellamy does indeed indicate the "key" that explains his dissatisfaction with the suffrage as an independent issue. And in one ironic sense, events seem to have borne out his view that the vote, without economic equality, was of limited value. The women's movement of the past two decades of our own time has been severely undermined by the absence of a thoroughgoing commitment to economic equality. Too easily can its feminism be reduced to the sort of liberal "feminism" that thinks itself fulfilled once privileged women ascend to equality with men of their class. No doubt Bellamy was limited in his ability to move out of a patriarchal framework of awareness; clearly he paid insufficient attention to the more subtle operations of the gender hierarchy and even more so to racial oppression. Nonetheless, he went to the heart of the matter by unceasingly proclaiming economic equality—by which, as his two utopian novels show, he meant a radical and absolutely equal sharing of the total wealth of the society—as the indispensable prerequisite for any pursuit of justice and political equality. For all his lack of attention to the myriad ways in which women's subordinate status vis-à-vis men is articulated (the documentation of which is a major achievement of contemporary feminism), Bellamy noted that this status rested first and foremost on an economic dependence that must be abolished.

In Mr. Smith's talk with a Woman's Rights Advocate, he signs her petitions for woman suffrage, representation on factory inspection boards, and equal pay for the same work, but then goes on to urge her to join a Nationalist club. He explains that he supports the suffrage "merely as an entering wedge for obtaining the economical equality of women with men which nationalism proposes," for " . . . the equality of women with men can never be anything but a farce so long as the mass of the feminine sex remains dependent upon the personal favor of men for the means of support" (Bellamy 1969 [1938], 80). It is a mockery of the suffrage, Mr. Smith contends: "You might as well give it to a race in a state of partial or complete slavery. It is only when considered as a step towards women's economical independence that woman suffrage can be intelligently advocated" (pp. 80–81). Urging women to press greater claims upon society, Smith reiterates Bellamy's view of the past:

> The human inheritance comes down to us as the result of innumerable ages of
> labor, struggle, achievement and martyrdom on the part of a common and
> blended ancestry. It is absolutely an estate in common. Hitherto this most

obvious fact has been utterly disregarded. There has been no attempt at an organization to administer the estate in the common interest, but the strong heirs have seized what they could get and keep, the weak heirs being downtrodden. This ancient, immeasurable, wrong, nationalism proposes to remedy, by making the nation assume the trusteeship of the common estate for the common and equal benefit of all the heirs, whether men or women, strong or weak. If they have inherited weakness, that measures their claim upon the estate; if they have inherited strength, that is their debt to the estate. If their weakness be owing to womanhood, it is a twice sacred title. (P. 83)

This is not, Smith goes on, a matter of benevolence, but of justice.

The denial to women of an equal and independent share in the world has been, up to this time, the greatest crime of humanity. But nobody was to blame for it, in particular, and it could never be remedied to all eternity so long as particular women could only appeal for their rights to particular men, however generous the latter might be. Their claim, like that of all the weaker heirs, was upon the estate and against society collectively, and could never be met until society should be collectively organized. (P. 84)

Under Nationalism, a woman's "means of support will be an income equal to that of all citizens, and whether she be married or unmarried, will be her personal right, and received through no other person. She will, that is to say, through life, be not only economically equal with every man, but absolutely independent of any man" (pp. 84–85). All women, Smith argues, are bound to be Nationalists once they realize what it means. "Ours is the cause of the oppressed and of those who have no helper, everywhere, whether men or women, but it is particularly and emphatically the cause of women. The program of nationalism is woman's Declaration of Independence" (p. 84). That Bellamy depicted the abolition of women's economic dependence within the context of a general commitment to absolute economic equality does not diminish the benefits that would accrue to women from such a policy. What Bellamy failed to envision was the depth of the transformation of male and female behavior that would ensue.

During the final year of *The New Nation*'s existence, every issue began with the following paragraph entitled "Economic Equality," summarizing what Bellamy meant by Nationalism:

The exercise of irresponsible power, by whatever means, is tyranny, and should not be tolerated. The power which men irresponsibly exercise for their private ends, over individuals and communities, through superior wealth, is

essentially tyrannous, and as inconsistent with democratic principle and as
offensive to self-respecting men as any form of political tyranny that was ever
endured. As political equality is the remedy for political tyranny, so is economic
equality the only way of putting an end to the economic tyranny exercised by the
few over the many through superiority of wealth. The industrial system of a
nation, like its political system, should be a government of the people, by the
people, for the people. Until economic equality shall give a basis to political
equality, the latter is but a sham. (*NN* April 8, 1893)

In contrast to Bellamy's vision, we have today so thoroughly absorbed
the atomized responsibility and extreme privatization of all aspects of life
that despite news, day after day, of fraud and corruption at the highest levels
of finance and government, national and international policy making, we
treat each case as a separate delinquency, ever focusing on individuals gone
wrong. In this situation, Bellamy's indictment of nineteenth-century capitalism—his attack on both the wage and the dole—applies even more to
our own time than it did to his. In present-day America, social services are
reduced while expenditures on military research and hardware soar. War
and perpetual preparation for it are good for business. "Welfare chiseler" is
a familiar term, while "plutocrat"—one of Bellamy's favorite words—is
virtually unheard, for extreme contrasts of poverty and wealth are now
accepted as the way things are and should be. Levels of unemployment that
a few decades ago were deemed a crisis now hardly evoke protest. Instead,
they are accepted, even touted as achievements compared to the still higher
rates that seem imminent from worker "redundancy" through technological innovation and crises of "overproduction" and "underconsumption,"
crises that many people take to be inevitable features of life. Bellamy
described this very situation in his "Parable of the Water Tank" in *Equality*.
 But to study Bellamy is not to invoke authority in support of one's own
protest. It is, rather, to explore the work of an imaginative writer who raises
possibilities for us. His texts, as he well knew, are far from perfect and self-
contained monuments. It would be ridiculous to pretend otherwise. What
they are in abundance is an impassioned critique of an unjust society made
in the name of the very values professed by that society, a critique not afraid
of being tarred by the brush of "moral passion." They are also, importantly, a vision of a different kind of future. Bellamy's writings are a
reminder of human potentiality beyond the mere acquisition of material
goods in exchange for the sale of one's labor; they are an evocation of a more
autonomous life in which human beings need not forever fight over re-

sources that conventional methods of production and distribution, out of the control of most people, turn into objects avidly desired.

Though life depends on material means, Bellamy understood that human life is not thereby reduced to the production of the means of existence. Economic well-being, education for life (as opposed to merely for work), and the cultivation of autonomous activities all are necessary if people are to realize their individual potentialities. Bellamy's vision is grounded in reality; he calls for a change not in human nature but in human institutions. In his scheme there is no production that is not directly related to use, no private profits to motivate the production of unwanted items for which a market must then be created. Work is to the measure of human beings, and it is their self-regulation that determines the amount of time it occupies. "If any particular occupation is in itself so arduous or so oppressive that, in order to induce volunteers, the day's work in it had to be reduced to ten minutes, it would be done. If, even then, no man was willing to do it, it would remain undone" (Bellamy 1960 [1888], 60).

Bellamy never lost sight of the intellectual and creative possibilities of all individuals, and it was for the sake of the greater realization of these possibilities that he fought for a new economic organization, capable of integrating his doubled vision. He naturally spent much time on the industrial organization of his society—the question that seemed most pressing in his historical milieu. But Bellamy's concern was first of all with the quality of life and the individual's opportunities for personal development in harmony with the natural and social world. In his early fiction, as several essays in this volume indicate, Bellamy focused on psychological and existential questions; in response to his own creation in *Looking Backward*, however, as Kenneth Roemer shows, Bellamy himself became more politicized. The doubled vision—inward and outward, toward past and toward future—took on a more single-minded political purpose: to win adherents to the cause of economic equality. But the orientation toward the inner life was never lost; it is present in *Looking Backward* and further explored in *Equality*.

Certainly Bellamy did not worship the working class; he was not vulnerable to any mystique of manual work or of the working class as the true subject of history. Rather, he envisioned a society in which everyone works a small part of the time, with the result that the "working class" has in effect disappeared. He does not distinguish between manual and mental labor; he states that in his future society no hierarchical division is associated with these activities. He points to the absurdity of ever more con-

formist and undifferentiated individuals, interchangeable worker-pieces to
the capitalist owners, clinging to an illusory "freedom" that keeps them
from taking control of economic production and distribution, the very
activities their labor makes possible. But though his emphasis was on the
organization of production—the "plan" without which his book would
have been dismissed—it should not be forgotten that his essential objective
was the development of free human beings. This is why, as Franklin
Rosemont shows, Bellamy listened to critics from the left, especially anarchists and feminists, and incorporated many of their suggestions into his
writings following the publication of *Looking Backward*. The "industrial
army" was a metaphor designed as a means to an end, not a concept to
which Bellamy was chained.

It is intriguing to note that ideas very similar to Bellamy's have, in recent
years, been set forth by a leading French social thinker, André Gorz,
former co-director, with Jean-Paul Sartre, of the journal *Les Temps Mod-
ernes*. Like Bellamy, Gorz attempts to reconcile the visionary and the
practical. His books, now available in English, are, again like Bellamy's, a
critique of industrial society and an image of a different future. In *Farewell
to the Working Class* (1982) and other writings, Gorz analyzes the nature and
organization of work in advanced industrial societies and argues that work
has a limited future in societies in which full-time waged work is simply no
longer available for everyone and will become increasingly less so. Gorz's
focus is on the kind of alternative society this material fact allows to come
into existence: a "dual society" in which such fragmentary work as is
necessary to produce durable essential goods (the realm of heteronomy,
Gorz calls this) would be reduced and redistributed, while self-determined
and creative activities (the realm of autonomy) would increase and become
the dominant factor in life. Both wages and welfare must be eliminated and
a universal "social income" set in their place—again, ideas very similar to
Bellamy's.

Gorz analyzes the rise of what he calls a "non-class of non-workers"—
those who, far from having a class-consciousness as workers, experience
their work "as an externally imposed obligation in which 'you waste your
life to earn your living.'" The abolition of workers and work, as these are
now structured and understood, is the goal of this "non-class," for the
personal character of work is inevitably eroded as standardization and
formalization occur (pp. 7–8). Gorz's discussion of how the industrial
system in itself results in subjugation goes beyond Bellamy's, but both men
share an emphasis on the primacy of subjective needs and desires in opposition to the logic of capitalism. As unemployment inevitably rises due to

technological advances, people must fight not for the "right to work" but for the right to an income regardless of work, and for a sharing of the work that remains to be done. Such a struggle is already under way in various parts of the advanced industrial world, as the numbers grow of those who are more or less permanently unemployed. But, in a duplication of the demand that society's problems be resolved by lone heroes, Gorz, like Bellamy, is regularly criticized by reviewers for not providing all the answers, for not showing us clearly how to get from here to there.

Lacking illusions that all work could be turned into a creative act, Bellamy, unlike William Morris, felt that a certain amount of socially indispensable and possibly pleasureless labor was inescapable. He did not argue that such labor could ever cease to be onerous. Instead, he saw that the balance between work and leisure needed to change—an argument entailing radical revisions in the very understanding of each. "Work" would cease to be an individual's principal source of identity. Rather, the major part of a person's life would take place outside the parameters of work—and this would no longer merely be "leisure," the period of recovery necessary in order to assure the return to alienated labor. The radical egalitarianism of his vision would keep the two spheres from splitting apart. Domination, always necessary to maintain inequality, would disappear. Unpleasant work would be only that: unpleasant work occupying a small part of an individual's life. The overall organization of society (again with no pretense that economic organization could be totally eliminated) would by its radical economic equality and effective utilization of industrial capacities make possible as never before a flowering of individual development for all. This is why Bellamy considered his Nationalism to be the most radical form of socialism.

Integrating the visionary and the concrete: this was Bellamy's concern. It is the emancipatory impulse he can strengthen in us today. The shape of the problems we now confront of course differs somewhat from Bellamy's configuration. But the answer, as in Bellamy's day, is never merely a technical one; it must, rather, always be cast in terms of human control over our common destiny. Bellamy's limitations belong to his time. His vision far transcends it and has much to say to ours.

Works Cited

Bellamy, Edward. 1960 [1888]. *Looking Backward, 2000–1887*. Reprint. New York: New American Library.
———. 1968 [1898]. *The Blindman's World and Other Stories*. Reprint. American Short Stories Series Volume 4. New York: Garrett Press.

————. 1968 [1897]. *Equality.* Reprint. Upper Saddle River, N.J.: Gregg Press.

————. 1969 [1938]. *Talks on Nationalism.* Reprint. Freeport, N.Y.: Books for Libraries Press.

————. 1984. *The Religion of Solidarity.* London: Concord Grove Press.

Gorz, André. 1982. *Farewell to the Working Class: An Essay on Post-Industrial Socialism.* Translated by Michael Sonenscher. Boston: South End Press.

Wagar, W. Warren. 1984. "George Orwell as Political Secretary of the Zeitgeist." In *The Future of "Nineteen Eighty-Four,"* edited by Ejner J. Jensen, 177–99. Ann Arbor: University of Michigan Press.

The Backward Look of
Bellamy's Socialism

Milton Cantor

Edward Bellamy, born in 1850 of a long line of Connecticut and Vermont
ancestors, was the frail and precocious son of a New England country
parson in Chicopee Falls, Massachusetts. The father, a Baptist minister,
was amiable, indolent, good-natured, of a more liberal religious bent than
his strong-willed wife. Maria Bellamy was a religious zealot whose spirit
burned with the fires of an uncompromising Calvinism. Possessed of the
unbending qualities of seventeenth-century Puritan New England, she
dominated the Bellamy household, pressed books—but never useless fiction!—upon her son, and made sure that the daily family prayers, twice-
a-day Sabbath devotions, and Sunday school educational requirements
were observed. In a sense Bellamy personified the clash between a rigid
Calvinism and a Puritanism gone secular and tolerant. This is not to suggest
parental conflict. The Bellamy household remained deeply religious. It
offered a sense of comfort and security, a warm, affective, nurturing family
life. Small wonder Bellamy later observed that love of home "is one of the
strongest, the purest, the most unselfish passions that human nature
knows"; and he understandably confessed to a "deep-seated aversion to
change" (Bellamy 1873, "Home"). Having a deep-rooted sense of place,
Bellamy, notwithstanding sojourns in New York City and abroad, was a
man who never left home. Nor did he possess a divided religious vision.
Calvinism largely won out. He enjoyed "an indescribably close and tender
communion with what seemed to him a very real and sublime being . . .
[and] took a deep and awful pleasure" in prayer (Bellamy Folder 19).[1]

And yet Bellamy lived in an age of watered-down religion, one increasingly resorting to moralistic strictures and bromides, and his was,
as John Thomas aptly termed it, "a profoundly dislocated sensibility"

For some important ideas in this esssay, I am greatly indebted to R. Jackson Wilson. His
article, "Experience and Utopia: The Making of Edward Bellamy's *Looking Backward*,"
Journal of American Studies 11, no. 1 (April 1977): 45–60, is thoughtful, compelling, and
scrupulously researched.

(Thomas 1983, 28). But this dislocation owed much to the age itself. A child of post-Jacksonian America, Bellamy came to maturity not only in an era of religious declension, but also in a region and a nation that remained over-whelmingly rural, a land dominated by farm-sized plots and farm family households. His home was not far from the Connecticut River, surely similar to the Charles that Julian West, the fictional hero of *Looking Backward*, described as a "blue ribbon winding away to the sunset." A half-day's ride from Chicopee Falls, Bellamy writes in another account, "the Housatonic crept with many a loving curve . . . and many a lake and pond gemmed the landscape" (Bellamy 1962 [1900], 3). He described "a smil-ing, peaceful landscape," where men wisely left "everything as Nature left it" and where the White Mountains or the Berkshires had shaggier slopes, wilder torrents, loftier forests than in Julian West's own age a hundred years earlier, for the ravages of the late nineteenth century had been corrected (Bellamy 1970 [1897], 296, 297). Idealizing the "changeless frame of nature," Bellamy's prefatory rural society provided the ecologi-cal model for the utopian world of the year 2000.

But in contrast to Julian West's utopia of *Looking Backward*, and Bel-lamy's pastoral ideal, there was Chicopee Falls, the first section of his hometown to become industrialized (Shlakman 1935, 48). Here the Belcher factory turned out iron castings, and a paper and cotton mill was built, and the Irishmen who built them and dug the canal moved into the rows of tenements that arose alongside the mills. These were not ordinary homes inhabited by proper Protestant citizens and surrounded by respectable-sized green plots, but stark, yardless block-long buildings pressed closely together into which Irish families were crowded. The first mill operatives were women, some coming out of Springfield, where their fathers worked as skilled mechanics in the Armory, and some arriving in wagons from farms and rural hamlets north and west of Chicopee (Shlakman 1935, 49). This new industrial army entered a rural community in the 1820s and 1830s and transformed it, with the cotton mills becoming the town's economic heart and with many small manufacturers dependent on continuous mill operations. By the late 1840s, Irish women began to replace the Yankee operatives, and in the 1850s, a time of economic slump, complaints of rowdyism in the streets began to be heard.

For farmers, merchants, and professionals, those long familiar with Chicopee's landscape, a marked transformation was underway and usually the Irish were blamed for civic tumult, cholera outbreaks, intemperance—the "rum shop in every fourth house" was noted—and Sabbath desecra-tion, the last further offending Yankee sensibilities (Shlakman 1935, 96).

Additional charges occurred when French Canadians began to replace the Irish mill operatives in the late 1850s. By now a permanent factory labor force had been established. Intermittent depression characterized the decade, which produced severe work conditions and, after 1860, very considerable ferment in the ranks of labor. By then the old order had completely changed. Polish Catholics were coming into Chicopee. No longer were there only Yankee workers, speaking the same language, sharing the same cultural traditions as merchant and craftsman, worshipping in the same churches, and holding to a common lingua franca—all of which had lent solidarity and homogeneity to the community. Now the ranks of labor were divided, Catholic churches had been erected, and rising living costs led to strikes and resentment.

Bellamy grew to maturity in the midst of this mounting social and economic crisis. He watched Chicopee Falls shift, as he recalled, from a "thriving village" to an ugly factory city crowded with industry, tenements, and Catholic millhands struggling to survive (Bellamy 1968 [1889]). The Bellamys' unpretentious frame house with its picket fence—a symbol of the besieged old Yankee—was located near the grimy mills, rows of brick tenements, and mansions of factory owners and agents who, Bellamy later observed, shaped the destiny of Chicopee's work force, controlled the churches, and determined the shape of every social and public development in the city. In one direction he could see the smokestacks and hard-scrabble life of factory workers and, closing in upon him, industrial ugliness, labor strife, and social disorder; in the other, an older America that was disappearing under the machine and that he increasingly longed for and idealized. He became aware of "half-clad brutalized children" who "filled the air with shrieks and curses as they fought and tumbled among the garbage that littered the courtyards" (Bellamy 1926 [1888], 323). And understandably, and much like the Unitarians and transcendentalists of a generation earlier, he was repelled by the developments transforming America—this urban disorder, the new materialistic ethos, and the greed of the commercial classes. In contrast to it all, he advised readers to "make the most of these few perfect spring days" or to "go afishing" (Bellamy 1874, "Spring Days"; 1873, "Go Afishing"). Also like the transcendentalists, Bellamy found "in observation of nature play alike for the intellect and the heart of a God" (Bellamy, "Unpublished"). Or, in another instance, he conveys the wonder of climbing "these mighty hills," sleeping "at noon on a sunny sward," lying "beneath the pines and listen [ing] to the song of eternity in their branches" (Bellamy, "Eliot Carson"). It follows that Bellamy grew nostalgic for the old ways of the New England gentry and the preindustrial small town, wishing to retain the latter's leisurely pace, to be reassured by its quiet routines and order, and to be sustained by its proximity to the world of nature.

As he later recalled, Bellamy grew up in a simple mill village "where there were no rich and very few poor, and everybody who was willing to work was sure of a fair living" (Bellamy 1968 [1889], 1). This idealized memoir, similar to many descriptions of small-town rural America, was not greatly overdrawn. Class lines of course existed in such communities but, except perhaps in the South, they were never rigidly fixed and were of necessity often ignored. So, too, was special privilege, which, for those living in the nineteenth-century rural community, was invariably considered a European phenomenon. Composed largely of Protestant, reasonably well-educated, English-speaking, churchgoing families with impeccable Anglo-Saxon credentials, such a town was an organic community, a moral island in a rising sea of strange faces, changing values, and peculiar cultural mannerisms.

For the moment, in Bellamy's youth, this community still stood on the edge of America's industrial revolution. Though social and religious complexity had begun to overtake Chicopee, the town's traditional culture continued to exert great influence and power. For its high-minded and professional citizens, a genuine sense of community remained. The growing city still suggested the small town of a half-century earlier rather than the bustling industrial center to come. Contrasting the old and the emergent, Bellamy continually reaffirmed small-town virtues in an urban society that seemed to threaten values he held dear. He yearned for a time when a feeling for a community prevailed, the spirit of cooperation, not competition, existed, the pandemonium of commerce was remote, class lines were less rigid, moral values were unquestioned, and the beneficent effects of nature were close by. That was the traditionally homogenous society he knew as a child and young adult. His editorials in the Springfield *Union* understandably deplored the crime and moral corruption of his age, the commercialism that worshipped primitive accumulation and predatory acquisition. "Snobbery and shoddy toadyism and venality, have made such public characters as Franklin and Washington and Lincoln almost an impossible conception, so far," he wrote, have Americans "drifted from their fast anchorage in unimpeachable integrity" (Bellamy 1877, "Burning"). Although the American yeoman was incorruptible, he could never successfully contend against the forces of degeneracy. Thus Bellamy shared the apprehensions of the respectable elements who were most familiar to him. Like him, they watched the changing world fearfully, the modern industrial city materializing in the mill towns springing up around them. They sympathized with his "feelings of disgust" at urban sights and sounds, the factory "stenches and filth," "the perpetual clang and clash of machinery," "the interminable rows of women, pallid, hollow-cheeked, with faces vacant and stolid," the "festering mass of human wretchedness" (Bellamy 1926 [1888], 323, 324; 1970 [1897], 54–55). And while their reactions were not unmixed, they showed greater concern than compassion toward those around them.

In Bellamy's late adolescence, then, the factory system, its technology and work force, became realities. The future of Chicopee Falls was now ordained. So was his own scenario. Hostility to private capitalism and the competitive system, to the "imbecility of private enterprise," which—at least on a large scale—had produced an "inferno of poverty beneath civilization," would have centrality to his two published utopian novels, *Looking Backward* and *Equality* (Thomas 1983, 169).[2] But the anxieties catalyzed by the new industrial system and its emergent proletariat prompted him to avert his eyes when imagining the future society. Hence Boston in the year 2000 was much like pre-1840 Chicopee. Nothing could be seen of 1888 mill towns, the sweatshops, substandard wages, child labor, dreadful home and work environments, or even the "aggressive" and "ubiquitous" drummers. Indeed Boston was much like the Chicopee of his youth—before the mills, before it became a grimy, sprawling city invaded in turn by Irish, French Canadian, and Polish workers, and before the rows of grim tenements in which they lived. It had "miles of broad streets, shaded by trees," landscaped parks and squares on which fronted homes and cottages with little footpaths and gardens with rustic bowers.

Looking Backward, it comes as no surprise, lacks any description of a factory or workbench. Julian West, Bellamy's autobiographical invention, visits a restaurant, a retail store, and a warehouse, but spare and antiseptic comments about the work force are all that one finds (Bellamy 1926 [1888], 153–57). Utopia's workers in *Looking Backward* are faceless, having the depersonalized and automatic qualities of soldiers on duty and, whether waiter or clerk, not interacting with those they serve. Those described in *Equality* are similarly drawn. They may work in "palaces of industry" and have "strong, cultured faces, prosecuting with the enthusiasm of artists their self-chosen tasks of use and beauty," but they otherwise lack personality or specific characteristics. When Julian West visits one such "palace," a textile factory, no workers are even present or described. He talks to the factory manager and later in the novel to a woman at a plow rather than to a man at a lathe. In neither book did he meet a male industrial worker

(Bellamy 1970 [1897], 155–61). His encounters, instead, are almost always with professionals of one kind or another: doctors, ministers, teachers, or managers.

Bellamy's imaginative projections—people, buildings, and society itself—are unsurprising. After nearly a year in New York City, within the "four walls of his Brooklyn apartment," where he engaged in a "profound" spiritual meditation, he had withdrawn to Chicopee in 1872, thereby tacitly admitting defeat in the big league world of Manhattan journalism. Recoiling from the failed adventure, he would never again confront the new urban order for any length of time. In 1894, over twenty years later, he did visit New York, where, witnessing a strike, he reacted with considerable repugnance—hardly the response of a loyal soldier in the cause of socialism (Wilson 1977, 53). Bellamy, in effect, returned to his home town, married the girl next door (or, more accurately, in the next room, for she had been raised in his parents' home), and softened and glossed over his recent urban failure, transforming it into something of a success. For in lieu of defeat he substituted loyalty to a calling higher than mere self-serving careerism. "Let others count gold," he rationalized, "Let others number the tongues that echo their name. For me, I prize more the vague and wavering images that visit my soul in hours of revery than any other excitations of the mind. Every one to his taste. Mine runs rather to dreaming than dollars, rather to fancy than fame" (Wilson 1977, 52).

Back in Chicopee, Bellamy also took on the pose of young Werther. Convinced of the insufficiency of the ideals in which he was raised,

> the young man . . . casts them aside and with soul wide open goes through dry places seeking everywhere to find God. He carries his loyalty in his hand anxious only to find some fitting shrine where he may lay it down and be at rest. Then, indeed, as the hopelessness of his search is borne in upon him come days and nights full of bitterness and blasphemy, of recklessness and at last of profound life weariness. (Bellamy Notebook 1, 38–39)

But world weariness and spiritual malaise were merely the ephemeral posturings of a young man. Bellamy would soon replace them with a "religion of solidarity." It was, in effect, a self-denying ethic that sought, in the Emersonian sense, to recover a communion with "eternity," that fashionable romantic conceit that ran riot in New England from the days of Jonathan Edwards and that was not far removed from the oversoul, the Wordsworthian landscape of Tintern Abbey, or Thoreau's experiences at Walden Pond. Emphasis on the individual, which he brooded upon in New York, had, like Minerva's owl, taken flight at the dusk of his urban days, being replaced by an escape from the "prison" of self into the transcendence of personality.

These transcendental resonances have saliency to Bellamy's responses to nature. "The Religion of Solidarity," for example, at times reads like a transcendental tract: the "desire after a more perfect communion" with the landscape, the "lust after natural beauty amounts to a veritable orgasm," "under its [nature's] influences that senses are sublimed to an ecstasy" (Schiffman 1955, 3). Bellamy's references to the "All-Soul" and the "universal," his feeling " 'most intimately, tenderly' the presence of the universal spirit in all things in the Spring" inevitably call up the oversoul and that saturnalia of feeling that the Concord group had aspired to (Bowman 1958, 28–30).[3]

Out of the New York year came the "Eliot Carson Notebook," a rough draft that, internal evidence suggests, was written shortly before *Looking Backward* (Bellamy Notebook 3, 4; "Eliot Carson"). A fictional vehicle for the religion of solidarity, this unfinished autobiographical novel suggests that Bellamy himself considered living the solitary life in the manner of Thoreau, whom he much admired. This novel also depicted the pastoral landscape as the beneficent foil for the evil city. But it was more. Nature was also the agency that awakened "the desire for a more perfect communion" and prompted man to identify with the oversoul, the cosmos, infinity, that is, those vague spiritual forces that, in the lexicon of the pantheists and transcendentalists, underlay the universe. In effect, nature—with or without reference to the growing industrialization—had centrality in Bellamy's thought. His fictional hero, Eliot Carson, it is also instructive to note, had been a disillusioned lawyer and journalist who abandoned his position as mill superintendent in Hilton, a factory town, and chose a Thoreau-like withdrawal into nature. Thus Bellamy's reclusive hero reflected his creator's vocational crisis, equally intent upon a life of reading, philosophizing, walking in the woods, and seeking, like Thoreau, the rock-bottom essentials of existence. In successive drafts, Bellamy first placed Eliot Carson in the family home on the town's outskirts, then at a "farmhouse" outside of Hilton, later in a forest "cabin," and finally in the forest, "with the free swing of a hunter, carrying a rifle" (Bellamy, "Eliot Carson").

Carson's escape into nature as relief from urban society differed from the romantics' search for paradisiac fulfillment, from seeking submission in nature, from Thoreau's theme of renewal and Edenic return, and from Emerson's pantheism, which offered an escape from the gloomy framework of history or of contemporary life. Bellamy, after all, did project a highly developed social and economic order, a golden age of industrial technology and future social harmony that the Emersonian man never contemplated. Yet for them all there was a reach after the infinite, and Bellamy had something of the transcendentalist yearning for a monism of soul and nature in the dream of his "spirit as something interfused in the light of the setting suns, broad oceans, and the winds" (Bellamy, "Eliot Carson"). For them all, the untrammeled beauty of the landscape served, at a minimum, as counterpoint to the marked factory and urban growth, and to the corruption and materialism that came in the wake of such grim developments. Nature offered relief to those apprehensive about the social dislocations produced by these changes and longing for the freshness of an earlier and greener world. Such a world was predictably one in which there were no banks and the farmers had abundance.

For Bellamy, the yeoman, living close to the soil, was the last defense against the materialism and selfish individualism then overtaking the republic. To be sure, the yeomen of *The Duke of Stockbridge* were "uneducated, . . . wholly lacking in social vision, and capable of being mean spirited and surly," as well as possessed of "inherited instincts of servility." But "they had felt much and keenly," were a "simple, true-hearted people," and existed in an age when men were their own masters and the better for it (Bellamy, "Eliot Carson"; 1962 [1900], 63). Identifying with the yeomen, though in guarded fashion, Bellamy urged—in one Springfield *Union* editorial—that young men remain at their rural firesides where they might yet attain a true independence. He also endorsed their causes, those of an older agrarian America and of the Populism to come: opposition to monopolies and the "great wastes" of competition, suspicion of trade and banking, faith in the work ethic, and the producerist ideology (Bellamy 1926 [1888], 230).[4]

Similar sentiments were attributed to craftsmen, whether in towns or rural communities, and they received a like-minded sympathy and idealization. Recalling the prefactory era when artisans dominated, Dr. Leete, in conversation with Julian West, provides an appealing reminder of a past simplicity, when "commerce and industry were conducted by innumerable petty concerns with small capital," when "the individual workman was relatively important and independent in his relations to the employer, . . . when a little capital or a new idea was enough to start a man in business for himself, . . . and there was no hard and fast line between the two classes" (Bellamy 1926 [1888], 52). Bellamy here echoed the Mugwump line, the elite nostalgia for an older America and for the small manufacturer and businessman, the groups "suffering quite as much and [having] quite as much to dread from monopoly as has the poorest class of laborers" (Bellamy 1937, 56). He lamented the obvious decline of the "businessmen with moderate capital" who had conducted the nation's trade before the emergence of the corporation and the trust. "There is now almost no opportunity left for starting in business in a moderate way; none, indeed," he deplored, "unless backed by large capital" (p. 57).

Dr. Leete, continuing, fondly reminisces about the good old days: "labor unions were needless then, and general strikes were out of the question." Regarding the latter, Bellamy's views were known long before his alter ego rejected working-class militance. Strikes were another instance of social disorder. Bellamy, to be sure, had supported the 1892 strikers at Homestead, Pennsylvania, and two decades earlier acknowledged the right to strike when it was the only way to "redress . . . [a] crying injustice." But it always produced a growing unease: it was a "blundering instrument" and it "injures society for the sake of individuals." Advising "strikers to act with much circumspection," Bellamy admitted that "strikes may be justifiable, but the presumption is against them" (Bellamy 1875). And unlike his response to 1892, he had condemned the bloody violence of 1877, called for its "crushing" and assailed the destruction of railroad property (Bellamy, 1877, "Who Has"). And in an attendant observation, he generally found that unions were of little use (Bellamy 1892, "Homestead Tragedy").[5] He had always maintained that "no mere organization of labor . . . will alone solve the problem of securing permanent employment on favorable terms" (Bellamy 1892, "Trade Unionism").

In contrast to the sturdy yeoman and proud artisan, there were Chicopee's textile operatives. Eliot Carson's escape into nature was also an escape from those who worked in the mills. Returning from one of his many forest strolls at the end of the day, he watched Hilton's mill hands pass by: "Some with stolid, godless, patient faces, mere human oxen, others flippant, exchanging coarse jests, voluble with vulgarity. 'To think,' said Carson, ' . . . each of those narrow foreheads is a prison to the dark soul within it, and what a prison, what a dungeon dark' " (Bellamy, "Eliot Carson"). The snobbishness and elitism of Julian West, limned as a wealthy Brahman, is obvious. At the outset of *Looking Backward*, he exhibits the conventional attitudes of his type: holding a loathing for workers, perturbed that the nation is drawing into the vortex of class war and chaos, and fearful that society trembles at the abyss. Likewise, Dr. Leete later affirms as much. Julian West, he recounts, had once lived in an era troubled by strikes, lockouts, slums, and starvation. Both men share Carson's mix of pity, contempt, and fear of the Hilton mill hands. Julian West scornfully dismisses both workers who would "follow anyone who seemed likely to give them any light on the subject" of how to obtain better wages, hours, and working and living conditions and their "many would-be leaders" (Bellamy 1926 [1888], 16). Discussing "The Strikers," a sculptured group of bareheaded laborers of "heroic size" on a pedestal in the Boston Common, he tells Dr. Leete that the strikers of his era, the 1880s,

> had not the slightest idea of revolting against private capitalism as a system. They were very ignorant and quite incapable of grasping so large a conception. They had no notion of getting along without capitalists. All they imagined or desired was a little better treatment by their employers, a few cents more an hour, a few minutes less working time a day, or maybe the discharge of an unpopular foreman. The most they aimed at was some petty improvement in their condition, to attain which they did not hesitate to throw the whole industrial machine into disorder. (Bellamy 1970 [1897], 208)

And the latter occurrence, almost needless to add, would produce that social turbulence which left the upper class disquieted and distraught. Dr. Leete confirms his observations: "Look at those faces. Has the sculptor idealized them? Are they the faces of philosophers? Do they not bear out your statement that the strikers, like the workingmen generally, were, as a rule, ignorant, narrow-minded men, with no grasp of large questions?" (p. 208).

Bellamy leaned toward environmentalism as explanation of human behavior. He believed the unspeakable conditions of workshop and tenement shaped the brutalized workers who walked the city streets. Human nature was inherently good, he was convinced, or, as Dr. Barton sermonized, "men in their natural intention and structure are generous, not selfish, . . . godlike in aspirations, instinct with divinist impulses of tenderness and self-sacrifice . . . " (Bellamy 1926 [1888], 287–88). Nonetheless, as Julian West notes with distaste in *Looking Backward*, workers' aspirations were "chimerical," their "bodies were so many living sepulchres," and "on each brutal brow was plainly written the *hic jacet* of a soul dead within" (p. 324). As Dr. Leete laments in *Equality*, "the masses of mankind" in the late nineteenth century "accepted servitude to the possessing class and became their serfs on condition of receiving the means of subsistence" (Bellamy 1970 [1897], 80). Circumstances, then, made workers what they were, but such recognition hardly mitigates the responses of these upper middle-class observers.

Mingled disdain and pity, hostility and sympathy find voice in Bellamy's writings. Edith Leete, who is invariably depicted in affectionate terms, asserts, "Those who tamely endure wrongs which they have the power to end deserve not compassion but contempt" (Bellamy 1970 [1897], 15). Her creator understandably expressed an antidemocratic bias, one common to a raft of genteel Christian reformers across the nineteenth century. Like such Mugwumps, reformers, and contemporaries as George Ticknor Curtis, Thomas Bailey Aldrich, Charles Eliot Norton, Richard Watson Gilder, and Henry Demarest Lloyd, Bellamy also worried over the entry of new immigrants into the political culture and held serious reservations about the efficacy of labor parties. About the latter, and speaking through Dr. Leete, he asserted that they "never could have accomplished anything on a large or permanent scale" (Bellamy 1926 [1888], 253).

Bellamy also looked at reformers with a critical eye. The "self-styled 'reformer' of this day," he charged, "is everywhere recognized as a politician who relies upon slander and hypocrisy as his sole weapon" (Bellamy 1970 [1897], 80). The nation had sunk into a morass of "low principles," he grieved, much as had such Mugwump reformers as Norton, Curtis, Gilder, Aldrich, and, belatedly, Henry Adams, with bribery, deceit, and "traditions of dissimulation worthy of a Metternich" (p. 15). Typical of this circle of genteel reformers, Bellamy felt personally violated by the innumerable strikes, mass organizations of labor, and class conflict. Workers, he concluded, were not fit to govern, themselves or society, and would make "a sad mess of society" were they in a position to do so (Bellamy 1926 [1888], 170).[6] Bellamy thus shared Mugwump elitism, its paternalistic view of the workingman, its antidemocratic cast of mind and doubts about representative government. Even the *Duke of Stockbridge*, which also sympathized with the downtrodden yeomanry, was hedged in by a cautionary lesson designed to avoid the emergence of a rural organization of protest. *Looking Backward* makes it indisputably clear that "the fittest may lead and rule" and that a new elite of skill and talent would administer society (Lipow 1982, 77).[7] Elsewhere Bellamy noted that the "men of education and position" would run things (Schiffman 1955, 139). "We shall take this subject," he wrote, "out of the hands of the blatant blasphemous demagogues and get it before the sober morally minded masses of the American people"—code words for the respectable middle class rather than the "population of ignorant, boorish, coarse, wholly uncultivated men and women" whom Dr. Leete derided (p. 138).

Bellamy thus echoed the genteel reformers' disconsolate criticism of political corruption and unscrupulous competition in the Gilded Age. Typical of them, he attacked the "monstrous grab game . . . the clutching fist . . . thrust into the spoils," with "the worst feature of this whole matter," referring to the Grant era scandals, being "that a class of men has come to the front with whom office holding is a profession—a means of support and enrichment" (Bellamy 1874, "Serbonian Bogs").[8] Condemnation of their artifice and amoral moneymaking was inextricably enmeshed with antagonism toward their political loyalties, which flowed into reservations about politics, even about labor parties, and which sought a substitute for them, as *Looking Backward* implicitly discloses (Bellamy 1926 [1888], 253).

Though ideologically related to these civil service and political reformers, Bellamy usually dismissed them, because they were limited to monotonously voiced jeremiads about "these dreadful days," the current civilization and its discontents. Indeed he confessed that before publication of *Looking Backward* he had no affiliations with or "any particular sympathy" toward industrial or social reformers (Bellamy 1968 [1889], 1). Naysayers and one-idea men, they were roughly equivalent to millennialists and Marxists in their inconsequential effect upon American life. Bellamy wanted meaningful reform, finding its possibility limited, given the terms of contemporary debate. Such reform was understood only by a saving remnant of the reform movement that recognized that a benevolent solidarity, or nationalism—"the express doctrine of Jesus Christ"—offered the only effective and long-term solution.

Bellamy had even less ambivalent feelings about radicals and revolutionaries than about reformers; he recoiled from the disorderly and destructive possibilities that they offered. "There is a vague discontent with the present state of affairs," he observed worriedly, "a chafing under the restraints of society and a disposition to disregard the rights of others that is neither American nor manly and that too often finds expression in indiscriminate acts of violence and crime" (Bellamy 1874, "Crime and Its Causes"). The timing and inclusiveness of these sentiments warrant mention. Written in 1874, in the midst of a protracted depression, they appeared three years before the bloodiest strikes in our history and fourteen years before publication of *Looking Backward*, and they attacked meliorists as well as revolutionaries. For the "discontent," Bellamy observes, "is largely the outcome of pernicious communistic teachings" of demagogues and so-called social reformers, whose chief object is to tear down the present fabric of society (Thomas 1983, 93).[9] In a letter to William Dean Howells, his literary mentor, he also dismissed socialists. Admitting to an inability to "stomach" the word "socialist," he asserted: "It smells to the average American of petroleum, suggests the red flag, with all manner of sexual novelties, and an abusive tone about God and religion" (Bellamy to Howells, July 17, 1888). In notes written after *Looking Backward,* he reaffirmed the conservative provenance of his collectivism and anticapitalist bias: "When I came to consider what could be radically done for social reorganization, I was helped by every former disgust with the various socialist schemes" (Bellamy, "Notebooks"). Believing revolution to be invariably unsuccessful—witness the Shaysites!—he argued that its followers had no moral foundation on which to build a better world (Thomas 1983, 100).[10] The new society would, for him, unfold in an epiphany of moral revelation that made drastic social upheaval unnecessary. Revolutionary change, moreover, was inevitably accompanied by violence and hence would be un-Christian. Rejecting such means, Bellamy considered socialism an ideal of eternal peace. It could only be achieved by nonviolent means, since means devolved into and were inseparable from ends (Bellamy 1891).[11] In sum, public ownership and control of industry was attainable by nonviolent change. The new social order, he affirmed, would evolve out of that "most bloodless of revolutions" (Bellamy 1926 [1888], 57, 285).

Likewise, as observed, Bellamy feared the "yawning" chasm between labor and capital, rejected class appeals as futile, abhorred the idea of class war, and obliquely attacked German socialists, who "lay undue stress on Socialism being a class movement" (Thomas 1983, 93).[12] He editorialized:

> The cure-all for our labor and capital frictions and smash-ups seems, then, to be this, to put into the hands of government all the carrying, transfer, exchange, productive industry of the country, its manufactures, agricultures, trade and its entire use of capital; permitting no private employment of this for personal profit. . . . Now go to, ye dreamers. . . . For a man to neglect his business and his family to study up such a scheme as this, is lunacy or worse. (Bellamy 1877, "Communism Boiled Down")

Equally suggestive of Bellamy's antipathy to socialists, as his contemporaries understood them, Dr. Leete also alludes to the "followers of the red flag," the revolutionists, and claims they had no role in "the new order of things": all they did was "hinder it" and "their talk so disgusted people as to deprive the best considered projects for social reform of a hearing." Bellamy even asserted, again speaking through Dr. Leete, that "the great monopolies" subsidized radicals "to wave the red flag and talk about burning, sacking, and blowing people up, in order, by alarming the timid, to head off any real reform" (Bellamy 1926 [1888], 252). So much for Bellamy as a revolutionary socialist.

Finally, Bellamy's nationalism, like his utopian state, depended upon a central unitary government, which was yet another deviation from the orthodox Marxist view of the state as withering away. Yet this government, as projected, was founded on traditional agrarian values consistent with the small-town heritage in which he had been raised. On virtually every count, therefore, Bellamy's socialism, insular, parochial, Christian, uniquely nineteenth-century American, was far removed from the conventional definition and the great theoretical graybeards of European revolution.

Notes

1. All Bellamy's original writings, notebooks, manuscripts noted below are deposited in the Bellamy collection of the Houghton Library, Harvard University. Cited as Notebook, "Unpublished," "Eliot Carson," "Memorandum," "to Howells," Folder.

2. For differences and similarities between *Looking Backward* and *Equality*, see Arthur Lipow (1982, 279–82 and passim). *Equality*, Lipow believes, reflected marked changes in Bellamy's views, especially the departure from the authoritarian and antidemocratic perspective of *Looking Backward*.

3. Bellamy, however, rejected any appeal to individualism—whether transcendental or entrepreneurial. Rather he sought to eliminate personality, to subordinate selfish individualism to some all-inclusive social order (see Lipow 1982, 43, 161). Further rejecting emphasis on the worth of the individual, he would join personality to "impersonal consciousness": "Spread your wings . . . the higher universal life is at once realizable" (Bellamy, "Religion of Solidarity," in Schiffman 1955, 11).

4. On the "imbecility of private enterprise," see Bellamy 1926 [1888], 240.

5. On labor and labor unions, see Bellamy 1892, "Trade Unionism"; "The Homestead Tragedy"; "Labor, Politics and Nationalism"; "A Nationalist View of the Homestead Situation"; and "The Trials of the Homestead Men." By 1891 Bellamy urged readers to "forget . . . what class you belong to," and spoke of the "common ancestry and inheritance" that emphasize each individual's status as "coheir and brother of all other men" and sees "true patriotism" as "an enthusiasm for humanity" (Bellamy 1891).

6. Although admittedly sympathetic to the struggle of labor, Bellamy nonetheless asserted that workers "knew nothing of how to accomplish" the changes needed by society: "The result of their efforts would be a descent into chaos." Bellamy denied that he advocated socialism (Quint 1953), and his cautious anti-capitalism and his nonviolent collectivist solution were the primary reasons for his appeal to a traditional middle-class readership. Here was an alternative to the violence of the 1871 Paris Commune, the bloody railroad strikes of 1877, the violent class conflict inherent in the doctrines of the First International, and the anarchist values of the Haymarket defendants of 1886.

7. See also Bellamy 1899.

8. See also Bellamy 1874, "The Head and the Tail Changing."

9. See also Bellamy 1892, "Some Questions Answered," 499, and "The Progress of Nationalism," 743; "Memorandum on Nationalism" (1889), manuscript, Bellamy Papers; and Morgan (1944, 87).

10. John Thomas's wise observations on Bellamy in *Alternative America* (1983) are reflected here and elsewhere in this essay and have influenced me.

11. See also Bellamy 1938, 190; and 1889, "Looking Forward," 4.

12. See also Bellamy 1892, "Some Questions Answered" and "The Progress of Nationalism," 743; "Memorandum on Nationalism" (1889), manuscript, Bellamy Papers; and Morgan (1944).

Works Cited

Bellamy, Edward. 1873. "Go Afishing." Springfield *Union*, May 20.

———. 1873. "Home Sweet Home." Springfield *Union*, September 27.

———. 1874. "Crime and Its Causes." Springfield *Union*, February 19.

———. 1874. "The Head and the Tail Changing." Springfield *Union*, April 3.

———. 1874. "Serbonian Bogs." Springfield *Union*, April 7.

———. 1874. "The Spring Days." Springfield *Union*, May 28.

———. 1875. "The Ethics of the Strike." Springfield *Union*, April 15.

———. 1876. Untitled Editorial. Springfield *Union*, November 17.

———. 1877. "Burning the Candle at Both Ends." Springfield *Union*, April 8.

———. 1877. "Communism Boiled Down." Springfield *Union*, August 3.

———. 1877. "Who Has Got to Pay." Springfield *Union*, July 25.

———. 1889. "Looking Forward." *The Nationalist* 2 (December).

———. 1889. "Memorandum on Nationalism." Manuscript, Bellamy Papers, Houghton Library, Harvard University, Cambridge, Mass.

———. 1891. "Several Questions Answered." *The New Nation* 1 (July 11): 374.

———. 1892. "The Homestead Tragedy." *The New Nation* 2 (July 16).

———. 1892. "Interview with Edward Bellamy." *The New Nation* 2 (July 16).

———. 1892. "Labor, Politics and Nationalism." *New York Herald*, August 28; reprint, *The New Nation* 2 (September 10): 568.

———. 1892. "A Nationalist View of the Homestead Situation." *The New Nation* 2 (July 16).

———. 1892. "The Progress of Nationalism in the United States." *North American Review* 154 (June): 742–52.

———. 1892. "Some Questions Answered." *The New Nation* 2 (August 6): 499.

———. 1892. "Trade Unionism: A Bird with One Wing." *The New Nation* 2 (October 1).

———. 1892. "The Trials of the Homestead Men." *The New Nation* 2 (October 8).

———. 1899. "Brief Summary of the Industrial Plan of Nationalism Set Forth in *Looking Backward* for Class Study." *The Dawn* (September 15).

———. 1926 [1888]. *Looking Backward*. Reprint. Boston: Houghton Mifflin.

———. 1937. "Nationalism—Principles, Purposes." In *Edward Bellamy Speaks Again!* Kansas City: Peerage Press.

———. 1938. *Talks on Nationalism*. Chicago: Peerage Press.

———. 1962 [1900]. *Duke of Stockbridge: A Romance of Shays' Rebellion*. Reprint. Cambridge, Mass.: Harvard University Press.

———. 1968 [1889]. "How I Came to Write 'Looking Backward.'" *The Nationalist: A Monthly Magazine* 1. Reprint. Westport, Conn.: Greenwood.

———. 1970 [1897]. *Equality.* Reprint. New York: AMS Press, Inc.

Bowman, Sylvia E. 1958. *The Year 2000: A Critical Biography of Edward Bellamy.* New York: Bookman.

Lipow, Arthur. 1982. *Authoritarian Socialism in America.* Berkeley: University of California Press.

Morgan, Arthur. 1944. *Edward Bellamy.* New York: Columbia University Press.

Quint, Howard H. 1953. *The Forging of American Socialism.* Columbia: University of South Carolina Press.

Schiffman, Joseph, ed. 1955. *Edward Bellamy: Selected Writings on Religion and Society.* New York: Liberal Arts Press.

Shlakman, Vera. 1935. *Economic History of a Factory Town: A Study of Chicopee, Massachusetts.* Northampton, Mass: Smith College Studies in History, vol. 20, nos. 1–4.

Thomas, John L. 1983. *Alternative America.* Cambridge, Mass.: Harvard University Press.

Wilson, R. Jackson. 1977. "Experience and Utopia: The Making of Edward Bellamy's *Looking Backward*." *Journal of American Studies* 11 (April): 45–60.

The Text as Tactic:
Looking Backward and the
Power of the Word

LEE CULLEN KHANNA

Utopian fiction is a hybrid genre, and Edward Bellamy, one of the great utopists, worked its inherent contradictions into a text of surprising social and political power. Although modern readers are likely to dismiss *Looking Backward,* citing its systematized solutions to social problems, stereotypical characters, and static society, its very clarity in these areas may well have contributed to its remarkable success.

A fuller appreciation of Bellamy's achievement should emerge from a consideration of two contexts: the tradition of utopian discourse and the tradition of Bellamy's own fiction, his early writings. With these two contexts more firmly in mind, modern readers may better understand Bellamy's exploration of archetypal utopian polarities and his evolution as utopian artist.

The problematic character of utopian speculation can be readily ascertained by turning to definition, as well as by recalling important texts. In naming the genre, Thomas More evoked opposition by means of a Greek pun: outopia—no place; eutopia—good place. Even before More's etymological enclosure of generic paradox, however, the conjunction of ideal and real sustained such major texts as Plato's *Republic.* As the ideal polis took shape in that dialogue, it was intended to clarify the just life for the individual citizen. Thus, such oppositions as public and private, imaginary and real, philosophical and political, contemplative and active, tested and troubled the characters who talked with Socrates.

When Thomas More took up these conflicts in the sixteenth century, his debt to Platonic thought was clear; yet the tension between contemplative and active energies became even more pronounced. In the dialogue that is the first book of *Utopia,* "Thomas More" and Raphael Hythloday discuss practical social and economic reforms, but the debate centers on the issue of public service. Although Hytholoday claims, citing classical precedent, that a philosopher in government will only drive himself mad, the argument remains unresolved at the end of the first book. As a result, the continued opposition between contemplation and action—or theory and praxis—frames the vision of utopia presented in the second book of More's *Utopia*. It is as if More suggests, by way of his open-ended dialogue, that the tension created by such sustained opposition is necessary in order to "see" utopia.

A recognition that the utopian tradition depends on a balance difficult to sustain may illuminate contemporary scholarly differences. Modern commentary on utopia diverges into two broad disciplinary areas: social science, including, importantly, political theory; and literary criticism. Social scientists have doubted the value of utopian speculation, because it is too unscientific. Indeed, Marx and Engels criticized utopian thought as escapist and detrimental to the practical work of social change. Those scholars of the social sciences who do admire utopian thought still tend to value it in proportion to its practical suggestions for change. They see utopian fictions as blueprints for such change, proposals for "perfect" or "ideal" societies.[1] From such a perspective utopian works are useful in proportion to the viability of the institutions they propose. Raymond Williams has suggested a further index of utility for utopias: their inclusion of methods for transition to a better society. Thus he praises Morris's *News from Nowhere*, because it contains "the crucial insertion of the *transition* to utopia" (Williams 1979, 59). Since *Looking Backward* exhibits no such transition, based as it is on a theory of natural economic evolution, Williams thinks the book less useful. Ironically, however, *Looking Backward* sparked many reform movements, while *News from Nowhere* had far less political impact.

Unlike political theorists who look for pragmatic results, literary theorists value hermeneutical complexity. Imaginative inventiveness, subtlety of plot and character, and "openness" of both text and social paradigm have attracted praise from recent critics. This group, too, tends to devalue *Looking Backward*. Here the reasons are its sentimental plot, one-dimensional characters, and didactic intent. Only very recently have some literary theorists called into question the hermeneutical emphasis of much twentieth-century criticism.[2]

What I would like to emphasize, however, is not the relative lack of exchange between these disciplines (several utopists do make use of both intellectual traditions), but the way in which this kind of apparent opposition in judging utopian thought reflects, and is perhaps a natural outgrowth of, opposing tendencies within the genre itself. I have suggested the opposition of theory and praxis, but nomenclature varies with fashion and may include contemplative and active, philosophical and historical, abstract and concrete, imaginative and empirical, strange and familiar, or, even, synchronic and diachronic. The key point is that utopian speculation pulls its participants in contrary directions.

Yet a permanent disjunction between theory and praxis, literature and politics, art and life, or text and body is exactly what the utopian enterprise denies. In other words, although readers must confront such oppositions when they engage in utopian speculation, they can come to rest "nowhere." It is the mental exercise of sustaining images of the "real" and imaginary, the pragmatic and the possible, that allows us to travel beyond binary intellectual habits to utopia.[3]

The reader of utopian fiction is asked to integrate different planes of experience in order to move from conception to execution in effecting changes that must be both personal and political. If defined by function, utopian literature always aims at transformation. The importance of recognizing utopian fiction as an agent of change is suggested by Williams when he says, "the element of transformation, rather than the more general element of otherness, may be crucial" (Williams 1979, 53). Although I believe he confines this insight too narrowly to the discussion of transition within a work, the observation itself is provocative. This is true despite the prominence of the "element of otherness" in the discussion of utopia in much modern criticism.[4] The estrangement or "defamiliarization" that Shklovsky saw as imperative in the functioning of all art is more relevant to science fiction and utopian fiction. The other world proposed in such fiction not only stretches the imagination of what is possible in social organization, but also makes us see our present society with new eyes— "defamiliarizing" our "real" world. The "cognitive estrangement" so achieved allows us to see problems in our society that we were able to ignore before.

After this experience of defamiliarization, however, the next step is movement from private response to public action.[5] Although "otherness" is a crucial element in the utopian process, without agency the utopian enterprise fails. Imaginative experience may lead to new insights, but since the altered vision involves public issues, the solitary reader needs to move towards community. Therefore, more than any other literature, utopian fiction invites holistic responses.

If the power of the word, the transformative function, is particularly important to the utopian genre, novels that provoke political action deserve particular attention. *Looking Backward* is just such a work. It moved thousands of readers to action, both nationally and internationally, as Sylvia Bowman's useful study, *Edward Bellamy Abroad,* amply documents. Bowman notes that the work was rarely mentioned in literary histories, but a survey of the international pattern of influence shows that Bellamy was, "if not the greatest literary artist the United States produced, certainly its most influential one from the ideological standpoint." She adds the following telling observation: "Although *Looking Backward* has been condemned and praised as a work of art, its artistry was sufficient to present a message about the future which inspired and moved the hearts and minds of men" (Bowman 1962, 436).

I would contend that Edward Bellamy's artistry as a utopist was of a high order, because he was uniquely able to sustain the polarities of the genre and work them toward the end of transformation, both of self and of society. He was well suited in terms of his personality and professional interests and because altered states, experiments with psychic and social transformation, had fascinated him for years before he wrote *Looking Backward*.[6] Even a cursory review of Bellamy's life reveals an unusual combination of the practical and romantic. The son of a preacher, young Edward wrote about intense early religious experiences. Although he later rejected traditional Christianity, his mystical bent remains important in his essays, particularly the *Religion of Solidarity,* his journal entries, and his fiction. Yet he undertook the practical profession of law, where, after distinguishing himself as a brilliant student, he began practice with a prestigious firm. When his first case required him to evict a widow, however, he abandoned this lucrative career forever. His subsequent profession as a writer involved practical journalism and romantic fiction, a fiction comparable to both Hawthorne and Poe in its imaginative extremes. Bellamy's friend and fellow writer William Dean Howells testified to this dual strain: in "Edward Bellamy we were rich in a romantic imagination surpassed only by that of Hawthorne" (Howells 1898, xiii). Yet in the same essay Howells observes of the man himself, "No one could see him, or look into his quiet gentle face, so full of goodness, so full of common sense, without perceiving he had reasoned to his hope for justice. He was indeed a most practical, a most American man, without a touch of sentimentalism in his humanity" (p. xii). The combination of practical and romantic in both his nature and career prepared Bellamy to sustain the comparable polarities of the utopian genre. The transformative effects of such a combination were seen first of all in Bellamy's own life. After he completed his utopian masterwork, Bellamy himself changed from romancer to reformer. The power of his own fictional vision turned him into political activist.[7]

Before this change, however, Bellamy had honed his skills with oppositional modes in his earlier fiction. His stories revolved around issues of altered states, or transformation, and his technique centered on what I shall call the interaction of the fabulous and the familiar. When examining his early fiction, one discovers not complex characters—nor indeed any real concern with characterization, ambiguity, or irony. Rather one meets again and again an inquiry into the nature of reality and its relative stability. By evoking unlikely situations or perspectives, these stories challenge our comfortable assumptions. For example, in "The Cold Snap," sudden climatic changes test moral strength and familial loyalties. The happy resolution of another story, "At Pinney's Ranch," depends upon fantastic telepathic powers. The "fabulous" element in each tale not only illuminates but also changes reality.

Brief précis of two stories, "The Old Folks' Party" and "The Blindman's World," and two novels, *Dr. Heidenhoff's Process* and *Miss Ludington's Sister*, should illustrate Bellamy's fascination with processes of transformation and his effort to gain control over change—to direct it—through his own imaginative power. In "The Old Folks' Party" a group of young people propose a surprising idea for a costume party. When Henry Long suggests they all dress as they expect to look in fifty years' time, one character exclaims, "You mean a sort of ghost party, ghosts of the future instead of ghosts of the past" (Bellamy 1898, 61). Henry adds, "Apparitions of things past are a very unpractical sort of demonology compared with apparitions of things to come" (p. 61). This focus on the future is complicated by Henry Long's (and Bellamy's) belief in shifting identities. Because we are all many selves in a lifetime, Long advocates a new linguistic system to represent these changes. Impatient with grammar, however, his friend Jessie Hyde returns the group to planning their costumes. Interestingly, she asserts the value of imagination over logic in dealing with the issues of discreet identities in time.

When the party is held a week later, the power of imagination and art are indeed proved as the young group thoroughly depresses itself with its convincing costumes and assumed mannerisms of old age. Just when melancholy threatens to destroy the whole evening, Henry springs to his feet, tears off his wig, and declares this glimpse of the future only a "nightmare." His arousal from illusion here anticipates the feeling of relief that floods Julian West as he wakes from his nightmare of the old Boston. In the 1876 story, of course, reality and the present seem to triumph over the future and the visionary. More important, however, for Bellamy's approach to utopian fiction, is the focus on transformations and the effort to gain control over both time and change. That such control is gained through the sudden reversal of a nightmare in the conclusion nicely foreshadows the most effective literary device of *Looking Backward*.

In another short story, "The Blindman's World," transformation and the control of time become public issues as well as private games. In that story a utopian society is presented through the dream travel of one S. Erastus Larrabee, professor of astronomy. He has fallen asleep at his telescope on a clear night, with Mars in view, and wakes to find himself on that planet. There Larrabee learns that the one thing distinguishing Martians from earthlings is the gift of foresight. This gift makes Mars utopian, because it can cope so much better with the future, including planning for death. In contrast, earth is dubbed the "blindman's world."

After this vision Larrabee wakes at his telescope and remembers nothing. Again, only by way of the dreaming state can he regain access to his experience of utopia; when sleepwalking one night he writes down the tale of his travel to Mars. Discovering the papers the next day, Larrabee is astounded both at the experience and his conscious unawareness of it, and queries, "when will man learn to interrogate the dream soul of the marvels it sees in its wanderings? Then he will no longer need to improve his telescopes to find out the secrets of the universe" (Bellamy 1898, 11). Interrogating the dream soul or exercising the imagination may lead to altered states—to utopia. "The Blindman's World" anticipates the utopian impulse more fully realized years later in *Looking Backward*. In the intervening years, Bellamy came to credit the power of vision over reality. The short story ends with a nostalgic wish for a lost Eden, which may have included foresight. By the time he wrote *Looking Backward*, Bellamy was not content with nostalgia.

If "The Blindman's World" focused on control of future time, an early novel, *Dr. Heidenhoff's Process* (1880), focused on the power of the past. Its hero, Henry Burr, loses his beloved, Madeleine Brand, because she cannot shake off the guilt of an early sexual transgression. Although Henry forgives her and urges their marriage, Madeleine bears her scarlet letter with even more dire effect than Hester Prynne. The novel hinges on a technological innovation, a machine that removes unwanted memories. When Burr reads of its invention, he takes Madeleine to the inventor, Dr. Heidenhoff, for treatment, and she forgets her sin. Their marriage plans seem a testimony to technology, but all is suddenly transformed when Henry wakes up to discover that the entire episode with Heidenhoff was a dream. While he slept, his "branded" love committed suicide. The sudden reversal of a dream here again anticipates the device that so effectively concludes *Looking Backward*, but with what different outcome. Dwelling on the past, the paralysis induced by guilt, and the static acceptance of things as they are lead to tragedy.

It is hard to know whether writing *Dr. Heidenhoff's Process*, with its exploration and rejection of the possibility of altered states, or the actual alteration of Bellamy's single state in 1882, when he married Emma Sanderson, accounts for the optimistic treatment of the theme of personal transformation in his next two novels. In any case, *Miss Ludington's Sister* (1884), with its bizarre exploration of discreet identities within the individual personality and of transformations from dream to spiritual vision to earthly happiness, prepares for the much more surehanded execution of such wonders in *Looking Backward* several years later. In the 1884 novel Bellamy suggests his theme of altering individual identities in the first few pages, as he presents the transformation of beautiful young girl to ugly crone, because of a scarring illness. In contrast to the permanent psychological damage done to the young Madeleine Brand, however, Ida Ludington finds new life through the power of art. Her portrait preserves her past beauty and inspires her young ward, Paul, with such devotion that he finally believes he has realized his ideal love in the flesh. Although the physical recuperation of the past is shown to be a fraud by the end of the novel, Paul is able to move into the future and a satisfying complete relationship by means of his loyalty to Ida Ludington's youthful identity. Working through this unwieldy plot, a reader may yet discover Bellamy's attempt to effect practical transformation by way of the protagonist's obsessive pursuit of an ideal and his faith in multiple identities.

Bellamy's literary apprenticeship, then, was dedicated to varied explorations of alternative selves and realities, and an ever freer experimentation with the relationship between the practical and the ideal, the familiar and the fabulous. The triumph of fully realized utopian vision is accomplished so persuasively in *Looking Backward* because transformation, both personal and public, was always Bellamy's concern. Howells again recognized the brilliance of Bellamy's achievement when he said of him that his art is "so singular that one might call it supremely his. He does not so much transmute our everyday reality to the substance of romance as make the airy stuff of dreams one in quality with veritable experience" (Howells 1898, vi).

Edward Bellamy succeeded in making the "airy stuff of dreams" so real in his great utopian novel that many Americans tried to transform his ideas into the stuff of "veritable experience." In that work he accomplished the utopian aim explicitly in his persistent assertion of the tensions of the genre. The fabulous and the familiar, new Boston and old, are amplified by means of a duality of metaphor, character, narrative stance, and reader response throughout the work. In other words, the paradoxical nature of utopian discourse found expression in every important aspect of Bellamy's narrative in *Looking Backward*. The very neatness and simplicity, the sharp outline, of Bellamy's dualistic paradigm does much to forward the universal utopian agenda: transformation of readers.[8]

Bellamy's genius in conceiving alternative modes of seeing expresses itself dramatically in the key metaphoric contrasts throughout the book.[9] No one who has read *Looking Backward* can forget his likening of nineteenth-century capitalism to a stagecoach on which the comfortable few sit at the expense of the straining masses who struggle to push the coach up the hill. This metaphor for the familiar economic reality is opposed later to the image of the new Boston, a stable pyramid secure on its base of economic equality for all. The dark underground chamber in which Julian West falls asleep sets off the sunny domes of utopia. Perhaps most memorable of all, the shrivelled and moldy-leaved rosebush of a starved people becomes the glowing perfect rosebush transplanted into the light and air of a just society.

The contrast between alternative realities in the utopian city and nineteenth-century Boston is amplified as well by the altered identities of its characters. Realism and complexity are not pertinent to Bellamy's purposes, since the aim of this fiction is not "fully rounded" characters, but rather the fostering of transformation of the self. To this end the reader encounters two Julian Wests, two Ediths, and even the reader's own identity is doubled. In each case the ideal wins out over its lesser alternative, with the most dramatic struggle illustrated in Julian West's crisis upon waking to his first morning in the new world. After clasping his temples to keep them from bursting, West falls prone upon the couch and wildly fights for his sanity. Then "the idea that I was two persons, that my identity was double, began to fascinate me with its simple solution of my experience" (Bellamy 1967 [1888], 141). A dual vision of society follows fast upon this crisis. West rushes out into the Boston streets, but "The mental image of the old city was so fresh and strong that it did not yield to the impression of the actual city, but contended with it, so that it was first one and then the other which seemed the more unreal. There was nothing I saw which was not blurred in this way, like the faces of a composite photograph" (p. 142).

The "composite photograph" is a striking image for the conjunction of fabulous and familiar that is the crux of utopian fiction. Bellamy's art springs in part from his ability to visualize this opposition, as in this metaphor of photographic double exposure. The two poles of utopian thought alternate in Julian West's vision here, as they must be juxtaposed in the reader's response.

Julian West's moment of identity crisis reveals the dualism of both individual and society that pervades the book. The connection between the two is critical, because only when the individual realizes a greater potential can society be changed. The apparent confusion between the attitudes of the old/new West is seen to be, like the contrasts in metaphor, an expression of dual possibilities. In fact, such a dualism not only perfectly suits the tension of metaphor and character in the rest of the book, but also makes the reader conscious of possible reform in self and society.

To read *Looking Backward* is to experience a tension in one's own nature as the pragmatic, "realistic" self strains against the reader one "ought" to be. Although this dichotomy might appear first in terms of illusion and reality, the book tends to reverse preliminary patterns of perception. This is nowhere more powerfully illustrated than in the dramatic conclusion.

Julian West eventually obtains his new Edith (and with her the old), and is about to enjoy the romantic peace and social harmony so long denied, when he is suddenly awakened by his former servant to the "reality" of the nineteenth century. Utopia was only a dream, after all. He and the reader are returned to familiar scenes, including the breakfast newspaper with its catalog of social injustice. Later, West, in a remarkable reprise of his walk in the new world, wanders about old Boston. Regarding the people around him, he says:

> I saw in them my brothers and sisters, flesh of my flesh, blood of my blood. . . . Presently, too, as I observed the wretched beings about me more closely, I perceived that they were all quite dead. Their bodies were so many living sepulchres. On each brutal brow was plainly written the *hic jacet* of a soul dead within. As I looked, horror struck, from one death's head to another, I was affected by a singular hallucination. Like a wavering translucent spirit face superimposed upon each of these brutish masks I saw the ideal, the possible face that would have been the actual if mind and soul had lived. (Pp. 305, 306)

As in his earlier crisis of identity, West views a "composite photograph" of old and new Boston. Yet here his perception of reality and illusion are reversed, as the familiar turns to nightmare.

However, with a final daring risk of verisimilitude, Bellamy describes a third awakening. Testing reader agility in the balance of generic polarities, Bellamy shifts the weight of utopian tensions once more. Instead of leaving protagonist and reader in a "defamiliarized" return to the "real" world, he sets both loose in utopia. Groaning and pleading, West suddenly finds himself sitting bolt upright in bed—in Dr. Leete's house. The morning sun shines through the open window into his eyes. Yet another metaphor, echoing the contrasts in the images we have come to know, seals the final

surprise: "As with an escaped convict who dreams that he has been recaptured and brought back to his dark and reeking dungeon, and opens his
eyes to see the heaven's vault spread above him, so it was with me, as I
realized that my return to the nineteenth century had been the dream, and
my presence in the twentieth was the reality" (p. 310).

In this final exercise of the dream reversal technique he had so long
practiced, Bellamy reached one of the most effective explorations of the
generic tension between fabulous and familiar in utopian discourse. Not
only is the old world defamiliarized, but the dream becomes real. Indeed,
the entire narrative strategy—metaphoric contrast, character doubling,
confusion of identities, dream travel—is geared to this alteration of perception. No doubt the timing of the final awakening contributes to its special
power, but one cannot underestimate the drama created by the consistent
and clear-cut demonstration of polarities throughout the work.

The apparently simple oppositional design that frames Julian West's
conversion to a society of economic equality shattered the stasis of many of
Bellamy's contemporaries. When readers closed the book they turned to
political action, founding hundreds of Nationalist clubs across the country
to try to change their society. Within three years *Looking Backward* had
been translated into four major languages, and it sold nearly a half million
copies in the first decade after publication. The book's program for reform
became the platform for the Populist Party, and even as late as 1935, such
disparate thinkers as John Dewey, Thorstein Veblen, and Eugene Debs
acknowledged its profound influence.

Bridging the gap between contemplation and action, text and life, Bellamy's book not only spurred early readers into reform efforts, but also
spawned dozens of new utopian works. Although often criticized for its
lack of aesthetic concerns, *Looking Backward* triggered creative energies in
many subsequent writers. Its generativity on many levels testifies to the
power of Bellamy's oppositional techniques.

In our own time the utopian agenda is no less urgent. Our best contemporary utopian novels seem to have progressed beyond direct juxtaposition,
however. In the work of Ursula LeGuin (1975; 1985), Marge Piercy (1976),
and Doris Lessing (1979–1983), we discover multiplicity instead of duality,
ambiguity instead of superior social systems, and complex characters instead of "types."[10] These novels do afford modern readers a valuable
inclusiveness and complexity of vision, and they reflect our familiar preference for relativity in assessing values. As more "open" and "dynamic"
worlds, they appeal to us; we analyze their subtleties. Yet I wonder if any
one of these intriguing books will achieve the power of the much simpler,

starker text written one hundred years ago by Edward Bellamy. In its unequivocal advocacy of absolute economic equality, as well as in its almost diagrammatic structural oppositions, *Looking Backward* still has much to teach us about the power of the word.

Notes

1. See, for example, the definition of utopias as "models of the perfectly constructed, perfectly functioning society" in Goodwin (1978, 2). For more recent discussion of utopia and political theory, see Goodwin and Taylor (1982).

2. For example, see the important recent work of Jane Tompkins on the cultural "designs" of popular nineteenth-century American fiction. She boldly challenges the notion of literary "greatness" and the possibility of an objective aesthetic. Her redefinition of literature makes the entire discipline more receptive to utopian fiction, for she sees "literary texts not as works of art embodying enduring themes in complex forms, but as attempts to redefine the social order" (Tompkins 1985, xi). Her revision of "value" in literature leads her to embrace, among other literary devices, stereotyped characters, because "they convey enormous amounts of cultural information in an extremely condensed form" (p. xvi). Such a perspective differs substantially from much twentieth-century criticism and its preference for mimetic fiction. This predilection colors the judgments of even such a fine Bellamy scholar as John Thomas. In his introduction to *Looking Backward*, for example, Thomas calls Bellamy a "moralist rather than an artist" (Bellamy 1967 [1888], 23). He goes on to say that in *Looking Backward*, "action and character function chiefly as devices for explicating ethical problems which Bellamy's village types carry about with them like so many placards" (p. 24). On the same issue of flat characters or types, however, Bellamy's contemporary, William Dean Howells, acknowledges that *Looking Backward* presents "types rather than characters; for it is one of the prime conditions of the romancer that he shall do this" (Howells 1898, x). Far from condemning such placard-bearing "types," however, Howells commends their use as necessary to Bellamy's purposes. It is, in fact, the prejudice of modern criticism that complex characterization and "realistic" action constitute superior fiction, and it is this bias that leads readers to deny the "literary merit" of *Looking Backward* and, indeed, most utopian discourse.

3. Arguments about generic precedents to utopia often resolve themselves into similar oppositions. R. C. Elliott in *The Shape of Utopia* (1970) emphasizes the debt to classical satire, while Northrop Frye (1965) defines utopia as "speculative myth"; others note the utopian debt to romance (Pfaelzer 1984, 20). While Frye emphasizes the primacy of "city" in utopian thought, Suvin (1979) claims that the genre has a natural affinity to pastoral. Such discussion underscores the necessarily mixed nature of utopian speculation, which must be both satiric and romantic if it is to fulfill its critical and creative functions.

4. Both Darko Suvin (1979) and Daphne Patai (1983) stress the value of seeing Victor Shklovsky's "ostranenie" as crucial to utopian fiction and demonstrate the usefulness of the concept of defamiliarization in their interesting analyses and applications to that fiction.

48 LEE CULLEN KHANNA

5. Both Williams (1979) and Pfaelzer (1984) discuss the importance of historicity in utopian texts and speculate about what may account for the relative stimulus to action provided by different kinds of utopian paradigms. Interestingly, in a recent paper, Darko Suvin (1986) has corrected his emphasis on utopian fiction as "verbal construct" because he wishes to see a connection between "utopian texts" and "utopian practices." Although his hypotheses about the varied connections conceivable between "locus" (text or signifier) and "horizon" (the variability of the signified that he calls "possible worlds") seems somewhat schematized, his discussion is provocative and underscores the crucial tensions of the utopian enterprise. Elizabeth Hansot's (1974) study of classical and "modern" utopian thought underscores the different emphases on contemplative or active, private or public responses, according to historical period. Her distinction is surely correct in terms of relative emphases, but the private and public reactions cannot be severed, finally, from each other.

6. Interestingly, even Bellamy's handling of alcohol seems to reflect his enjoyment of altered states. In her biography of Bellamy, Bowman notes that he varied periods of inebriation with total abstinence for the intense opposition of experiences. When he wrote *Looking Backward*, she says, he approached his desk with a cup of coffee in one hand and a glass of whiskey in the other (Bowman 1979 [1958], 14.).

7. I am indebted to Ken Roemer for making this point with particular force in his paper, "Perceptual Origins: "Preparing Readers to See Utopian Fiction" (1986).

8. Ernst Bloch suggests the value of such clarity to utopian fiction generally when he says, in a discussion of the meaning of utopia, "Action will release available transitional tendencies into active freedom only if the utopian goal is clearly visible, unadulterated and unrenounced" (Bloch 1970 [1963], 92).

9. For further discussion of the handling of metaphor in *Looking Backward*, see Khanna (1981, "The Reader and *Looking Backward*") and Roemer (1983).

10. Differences in gender perspectives may well account for some of this change, since these new utopias are written by women in large part. Recent feminist theory in a variety of disciplines has suggested that women tend to question binary oppositions and affirm multiplicity. The resurgence of positive utopian fiction in the last fifteen years may also owe much to the women's movement. In other words, women's renewed attention to the need for social and political reform may have found imaginative expression in the many new novels depicting the good society. This recent burgeoning of utopian fiction, including novels by Bryant, Bradley, Elgin, Gearhart, and Russ, as well as those of LeGuin, Lessing, and Piercy, has generated considerable interest. For bibliographies and analyses, see the following anthologies: *Alternative Futures: The Journal of Utopian Studies* 4 (Spring and Summer 1981); Marleen Barr and Nicholas Smith, eds., *Women and Utopia: Critical Interpretations* (New York: University Press of America, 1983); Ruby Rohrlich and Elaine Hoffman Baruch, eds., *Women in Search of Utopia* (New York: Schocken Books, 1984). Additional scholarship includes, importantly, the introduction and bibliography in *Daring to Dream* by Carol Farley Kessler (1984) and the bibliography by Daphne Patai (1981). Also see DuPlessis (1979), Khanna (1981, "Women's Worlds"), Pearson (1977), Russ (1981), Sargent (1983), and Somay (1984).

Works Cited

Bellamy, Edward. 1891 [1880]. *Dr. Heidenhoff's Process.* Reprint. London: Frederick Warne & Son.

———. 1891 [1884]. *Miss Ludington's Sister.* Reprint. London: Frederick Warne & Son.

———. 1898. *The Blindman's World and Other Stories.* London: A. P. Watt & Son.

———. 1940. *The Religion of Solidarity.* Edited by Arthur E. Morgan. Yellow Springs, Ohio: Antioch Bookplate Co.

———. 1967 [1888]. *Looking Backward.* Edited by John L. Thomas. Cambridge: Harvard University Press.

Bloch, Ernst. 1970 [1963]. *A Philosophy of the Future.* Translated by John Cumming. New York: Herder and Herder.

Bowman, Sylvia E. 1979 [1958]. *The Year 2000: A Critical Biography of Edward Bellamy.* Reprint. New York: Octagon Books.

——— et al. 1962. *Edward Bellamy Abroad: An American Prophet's Influence.* New York: Twayne.

DuPlessis, Rachel Blau. 1979. "The Feminist Apologues of Lessing, Piercy, and Russ." *Frontiers: A Journal of Women's Studies* 4, no. 1:1–8.

Elliott, Robert C. 1970. *The Shape of Utopia.* Chicago: University of Chicago Press.

Frye, Northrop. 1965. "Varieties of Literary Utopias." *Daedalus* 94: 323–347.

Goodwin, Barbara. 1978. *Social Science and Utopia.* Atlantic Highlands: Humanities.

Goodwin, Barbara, and Keith Taylor. 1982. *The Politics of Utopia: A Study in Theory and Practice.* New York: St. Martin's Press.

Hansot, Elizabeth. 1974. *Perfection and Progress: Two Modes of Utopian Thought.* Cambridge: MIT Press.

Howells, William Dean. 1898. Introduction to *The Blindman's World and Other Stories,* by Edward Bellamy. London: A. P. Watt & Son.

Kessler, Carol Farley. 1984. *Daring to Dream: Utopian Stories by United States Women, 1836–1919.* Boston: Pandora Press.

Khanna, Lee Cullen. 1981. "The Reader and Looking Backward." *Journal of General Education* 33: 69–79.

———. 1981. "Women's Worlds: New Directions in Utopian Fiction." *Alternative Futures* 4, no. 2–3: 47–60.

LeGuin, Ursula. 1975. [1974]. *The Dispossessed.* New York: Avon.

———. 1985. *Always Coming Home.* New York: Harper and Row.

Lessing, Doris. 1979–1983. *Canopus in Argos: Archives.* 5 vols. New York: Alfred A. Knopf.

Patai, Daphne. 1981. "British and American Utopias by Women (1836–1979): An Annotated Bibliography." *Alternative Futures* 4, nos. 2–3: 184–206.

———. 1983. "Beyond Defensiveness: Feminist Research Strategies." *Women's Studies International Forum* 6, no. 2: 177–80.

Pearson, Carol. 1977. "Women's Fantasies and Feminist Utopias." *Frontiers: A Journal of Women's Studies* 2, no. 3: 50–61.

Pfaelzer, Jean. 1984. *The Utopian Novel in America 1886–1896*. Pittsburgh: University of Pittsburgh Press.

Piercy, Marge. 1976. *Woman on the Edge of Time*. New York: Fawcett.

Roemer, Kenneth M. 1983. "Contexts and Texts: The Influence of *Looking Backward*." *Centennial Review* 27: 204–23.

———. 1986. "Domestic Nowheres and Androgynous Voices: The Sentimental Origins of *Looking Backward*." Paper delivered at the 2nd International Conference for Utopian Studies, Rome, Italy.

———. 1986. "Perceptual Origins: Preparing American Readers to See Utopian Fiction." In *Utopian Thought in the U.S.*, edited by Arno Heller. Innsbruck: Austrian Assoc. of American Studies.

Russ, Joanna. 1981. "Recent Feminist Utopias." In *Future Females: A Critical Anthology*, edited by Marleen Barr. Bowling Green, Ohio: Bowling Green State University Press.

Sargent, Lyman Tower. 1983. "A New Anarchism: Social and Political Ideas in Some Recent Feminist Eutopias." In *Women and Utopia: Critical Interpretations*, edited by Marleen Barr and Nicholas Smith. New York: University Press of America.

Somay, Bulent. 1984. "Towards an Open-Ended Utopia." *Science Fiction Studies* 11: 25–38.

Suvin, Darko. 1979. *The Metamorphoses of Science Fiction*. New Haven: Yale University Press.

———. 1986. "Locus, Horizon, and Orientation: The Concept of Possible Worlds as a Key to Utopian Studies." Paper delivered at the 2nd International Conference for Utopian Studies, Rome, Italy.

Tompkins, Jane. 1985. *Sensational Designs: The Cultural Work of American Fiction 1790–1860*. New York: Oxford University Press.

Williams, Raymond. 1979. "Utopia and Science Fiction." In *Science Fiction: A Critical Commentary*, edited by Patrick Parrinder. London: Longmann.

Immanence, Indeterminance, and the Utopian Pun in *Looking Backward*

Jean Pfaelzer

When Edward Bellamy wrote *Looking Backward* (1888), he clearly understood Thomas More's pun: *eu*topia—good place; *ou*topia—no place. *Looking Backward* is a text constructed and locked within the paradoxes of this pun. Originally Bellamy did not intend to create a recipe for real world praxis. Rather, he sought to deconstruct assumptions about social inevitability and replace them with an image of history that extrapolated the hopeful tendencies of the present. Critics who debate the technocratic, authoritarian, and vapid image of life in the year 2000 are evaluating *Looking Backward* as a mimetic representation of a possible society. Here I want to read *Looking Backward* as a text that provokes a cognitive dissonance between the present, as lived, and the potentialities hidden within it. I believe that *Looking Backward* has endured because it unearths radical tendencies in industrial capitalism, revealing potentials in nineteenth-century technology, monopolies, and social reform movements that have little to do with the industrial army, radio sermons, or a telltale locket.

Bellamy would have understood Ernst Bloch's comment "The future is always concealed in that which exists" (Bloch 1970, 87), for an important part of Bellamy's argument was that *Looking Backward* "seized on currents already present in society" and made no speculations that were "greatly in advance of public opinion" (Bowman 1958, 74). Bellamy's project thus had two aspects: first, to reveal that the economic and political configurations of industrialism prefigured a Nationalist future; and, second, to reveal that a socialist impulse lurked in the heart of Gilded Age individualism. Human consciousness could overcome fear, guilt, and even sin because it was society that determined a person's capacity for good and evil. Accordingly, Bellamy wrote the future history of the twentieth century, a history that would pull humanity out of the troubled present into its own anticipations. He located the utopian drive in both the positive and the negative aspects of the last quarter of the nineteenth century, years that capped an era of unprecedented and unregulated economic growth.

Edward Bellamy's utopia, in other words, defines the space between reality and possibility. Written in 1887, *Looking Backward, 2000–1887* identified for a distraught public—alarmed by a severe economic recession, violent strikes, and stranglehold monopolization of railroads and mining—the latent remedies residing in both the problems and the solutions of industrial capitalism. Fredric Jameson, following Ernst Bloch, locates such drives toward the future in contemporary needs as well as in their fantasized fulfillments: "It is this essential dissatisfaction at the very core of hope which drives time forward and which transforms each contingent wish into a figure of the Utopian wish itself, each contingent present into a figure of that ultimate presence of Utopia" (Jameson 1971, 138).

In defining motivation in his *Utopia*, Thomas More spoke only of the essential dissatisfaction: "Who be more desirous of new mutations and alterations than they that be not content with the present state of their life? Or, who be bolder-stomached to bring all in a hurly-burly (thereby trusting to get some windfall) than they that have now nothing to lose?" (More 1966). Bellamy, however, was aware of the function of the "contingent present," and it is hard not to suspect that one explanation for the extraordinary popularity of *Looking Backward* was its answer to the problem of what to do with the "bolder stomached." That is to say, Bellamy was careful to promise equality without class conflict. Throughout the book Julian West wonders what forestalled the violence of the 1880s: "All I can say is that the prospect was such when I went into that long sleep that I should not have been surprised had I looked down from your housetop today on a heap of charred and moss-grown ruins instead of this glorious city" (Bellamy 1888, 69). But Dr. Leete reassures him that Nationalism arrived peacefully: monopolies grew and consolidated automatically, evolving into "the one capitalist in the place of all other capitalists, the sole employer, the final monopoly . . . The Great Trust" (p. 78).

The economic process that signaled utopian redistribution was, paradoxically, an extension of the current trend toward incorporation (in trusts, pools, holding companies, and monopolies) that represented the developing concentration of wealth and power. Bellamy saw Nationalism concealed in capitalism. By 1893, according to U.S. Census Bureau estimates, 9 percent of the nation's families owned 71 percent of American wealth through monopolies controlled by such families as the Vanderbilts, Harrimans, Goulds, Carnegies, Rockefellers, and Morgans. Laissez-faire theory notwithstanding, monopolization depended on an explicit partnership between business and branches of a growing national government. When the

Supreme Court essentially invalidated the Sherman Anti-Trust Act in 1895, it further stimulated economic consolidation.

Looking Backward also absorbed and abstracted current theories of social cooperation and amalgamation, which sought to replace private property with social property, private ownership with public ownership, and competition with various forms of cooperation. A rhetoric of communalism had appeared in the labor movement, the women's movement, and the farmers' movement, as well as in attempts to preserve the antiracist legislation of the Reconstruction years. The period of the 1870s to the 1890s marks the first major success in the organization of American labor, through the Knights of Labor and later through the American Federation of Labor. Influenced by the activities and goals of abolitionism and by the restructuring of women's economic roles in an industrial society, women formed assemblies in the Knights of Labor and organized the largest collective activity for social reform through the suffrage movement. Farmers constituted a third group seeking collective redistribution of the national wealth, in the formation of the Populist Party.

Thus the imposition of the unknown on the known in utopian fiction functions as a palimpsest: the familiar seeps through the new. In his discussion of science fiction, Darko Suvin calls the innovation that is superimposed on the familiar reality "the novum," a term borrowed from Ernst Bloch (Suvin 1979, 63–84). I believe that in *Looking Backward,* as in all utopian fiction, however, the novum, the "postulated innovation," must refer to the entire alternative and redeemed society and that a new society must develop from historical actualities. Hence, Boston in the year 2000 refers to political premises that are internally logical, despite the magical illogic of Julian West's hypnotic voyage. The reader of *Looking Backward,* as a result, experiences a cognitive split: reincarnated Boston has an empirical history that Julian's visit lacks. In this sense, *Looking Backward* relies on a narrative sleight-of-hand; it has both a nonmimetic or fantastic mode, and a mimetic or realistic mode that reproduces familiar experiences by extrapolating from historical tendencies. Paradoxically, the futurist devices of *Looking Backward* negate the central axiom of its represented history: change itself.

Why was Bellamy so vague and imprecise about the transition to utopia, when he provided so many other details about the new society? Why did he refuse to tell us how to get to utopia? One answer is that he always understood the real meaning of *Looking Backward* to come from the contrasts and interplay of environments that are metaphors for history. Like a sundial, utopian space represents the passage of time. In other words, the real meaning of the tale is not programmatic, but comes from the tension between no place and the good place.

Bellamy has given us two alternative explanations for the genesis of *Looking Backward*, both of which ignore the process of transition from the present to the future. In the May 1890 issue of the *Nationalist*, Bellamy wrote: "In undertaking to write *Looking Backward*, I had at the outset no idea of attempting a serious contribution to the movement of social reform. The idea was of a mere literary fantasy, a fairy tale of social felicity. There was no thought of contriving a house which practical men might live in, but merely of hanging in mid-air, far out of reach of the sordid and material world of the present, a cloud palace for an ideal humanity." But, he recalls, as the story grew he realized that he had "stumbled over the destined cornerstone of the new social order," and he changed the romance from "a mere fairy tale of social perfection" to "a vehicle of a definite scheme of industrial reorganization" (Bellamy 1890, 202). Bellamy's explanation bears out Engel's famous critique of utopian socialism as an ahistorical "accidental discovery of this or that ingenious brain" (Engels 1935, 59). In 1894, seven years after writing *Looking Backward*, Bellamy provided a more autobiographical account. Here he says that concerns for his children's future motivated his decision to address in literature the national economic problem: "In the fall or winter of 1886 . . . I sat down to my desk with the definite purpose of trying to reason out a method of economic organization by which the republic might guarantee the livelihood and material welfare of its citizens on a basis of equality corresponding to and supplementing their political equality." He denied that the romantic fable was to "command greater attention" and explained that he used fiction for "the working out of problems, that is to say, attempts to trace the logical consequences of certain assumed conditions" (Bellamy 1894, 217, 223–24). Through narrative, Bellamy tested the social and psychological implications of political theory. In his view, the fable of Julian and Edith represents a historical analysis.

Bellamy, it would seem, never told us how to find utopia because the original goal of *Looking Backward* was critical rather than normative. Darko Suvin has aptly defined how the dialectic between the novum, which promotes estrangement, and the familiar details, which promote cognition, enhance a critical stance in the world of science fiction: optimally, "a sufficiently large number of precisely aimed and compatible details draw out a sufficiently full range of logical implications from the central [science fiction] novum and thus suggest a coherent universe with overall relationships that are—at least in respect of the thematic and semantic field associated with the novum—significantly different from the relationships assumed by the text's addressees." He adds that in order to bring about the most effective estrangement, the narrative details will "slyly enlist the reader's imaginative activity to fill in the gaps in the paradigm and create an 'illusion of reality,' analogous to that of the historical or 'realistic' novel, by a wise balance of the posed and the presupposed. In such best cases, the balance or shuttling allows the [science fiction] estrangement to feed back into the reader's own presuppositions and cultural invariants, questioning them and giving him/her a possibility of critical examination" (Suvin 1982, 6–7).

But even such card-carrying utopians as Ernst Bloch have been circumspect about the critical potential of the literary utopia (Bloch 1971, 136). Tom Moylan, in his excellent reading of Bloch, observes that Bloch finds an impoverishment when the utopia is "directly imagined," due to the reduction of the multiple levels of the utopian idea to the single, relatively abstract field of social planning (Moylan 1982, 160–61). For Bloch, the utopian moment should never be mimetically represented. Indeed, its power resides in its tentative state: "Since it does not yet exist, it must always speak in figures, which always call out structurally for completion and exegesis" (Jameson 1971, 142). According to Bloch, the literary utopian fills in the space that should reside in the imagination. Thus, Bloch falls into the same trap that ensnared Marx and Engels, who read the literary utopia as a blueprint, and judged it by its realizability (Moylan 1982, 161)—another confusion between *ou*topia and *eu*topia.

For Bloch, the utopian figure is latent and anticipatory. It designates elements in the present that indicate a tendency toward change. These signs of potential transformation are located in religion, philosophy, and art. Within these areas, Bloch distinguishes symbols from ideals: ideals have a definite content, whereas symbols have intimations of various possibilities. In this regard, Eugene Hill has observed, "Bloch identifies three levels on which (as he puts it) the present is illumined by the light of the future: the psychic level, with its wish-images projected forward; the moral level, with its ideals; and the aesthetic level, with its symbols—the last of these being, for Bloch, the richest of the three" (Hill 1982, 170).

I suggest that while the social and political manifesto in *Looking Backward* may land on the psychic or moral levels of Bloch's ladder, the representation of Julian West has the richness, intimation, and ambiguity of the symbolic, and it is through the hero's developing consciousness that we adhere to the latent potential for a redeemed society within industrial capitalism. *Looking Backward* does not simply designate certain political rearrangements as perfect. Rather, through the narration of Julian West, the text enfolds the reader in the question of how to envision the future, of how the present is "illumined" by the light of the future. Because a nineteenth-century aristocrat narrates the tale, purportedly written in the year 2000, to a twentieth-century socialist audience, Bellamy's presumed reader does not occupy the space of West's fictive reader but is forced to dislocate or disjar real assumptions from the narrator's assumptions. Hence the reader occupies a fictional space in utopia as well, which suspends his or her normal presuppositions about time, space, and history, which now exist nowhere except in the text. This narrative stance, in which historical contradictions remain and are resolved at once (that is to say, they remain in Julian but are resolved in the new society), persists even through the frustration and indeterminacy of Julian's final dream/return. Our function as readers is not to put Julian back together again, but to participate in and analyze the contradictions as if they were our own. It is safe to do this because we are not reading ourselves as Bellamy's gentle readers, but as Julian's socialist readers.

Thus, Bellamy's tale is both mimetic and fantastic. *Looking Backward* occupies the fantastic until Dr. Leete explains the historical inevitability of Nationalism to Julian. During this delay the reader experiences what Tzvetan Todorov calls the fantastic dilemma: "The fantastic occupies the duration of this uncertainty. Once we choose one answer or the other, we leave the fantastic for a neighboring genre, the uncanny or the marvelous. The fantastic is that hesitation experienced by a person who knows only the laws of nature, confronting an apparently supernatural event" (Todorov 1973, 25). The sense of the fantastic persists only as long as the uncertainty lasts. In utopian fiction, once the traveler comes to a decision or a recognition as to where he is, in time and space, the fantastic evaporates and we pass into the genre of the "uncanny," which has a natural explanation. Thus, the notion of reality must be present for the fantastic to exist at all. Julian's narrative fades from the fantastic into the uncanny as Dr. Leete and Edith reveal the logic of Boston in the year 2000.

In *Looking Backward* these two narrative modes represent different stages in Julian West's political development. The fantastic passages play with Julian's expectations about industrial capitalism, in order to contradict, subvert, oppose, question, or reverse them, and finally to expose them as false. His bizarre awakening after a century-long nap confronts him with both social and technological information that does not conform to the ground rules of 1887; ultimately it calls into question his, and perforce our, very modes of perception.

Indeed, accurate perception becomes a central metaphor for the text, as Julian realizes that capitalism represents a dangerous world of illusion, which endures through the myopia of class. His first acknowledgment of the power of "disinformation" is his recognition that he has inhabited a mysterious world of money without work, enjoying what he calls the unnatural magic of "warmth without combustion" (Bellamy 1888, 10). Such dislocation of familiar assumptions cannot but stimulate feelings of terror, fear, and uncertainty, along with wonder and curiosity. Not only does his long trance disrupt his identity; the "happy accident" also deprives Julian of the defenses of his inheritance, his wealthy sweetheart, his house, and fellow members of his class, who always provided "abundant sympathy" to his anger at "workers in general and . . . strikers in particular" (p. 27). He asks the utopian Edith, "Has it never occurred to you that my position is so much more utterly alone than any human being ever was before, that a new word is really needed to describe it?" (p. 417).

The traditional psychic alienation of romance is a consequence of Julian's social alienation. His descent into the underground womblike vault initiates a release from the repressive as well as oppressive ties of the nineteenth century, for his marriage to the original Edith was delayed by a strike in the building trades, stopping work on their new house, "which postpon[ed] my wedded bliss." While the vault, the sleeplessness, and the hypnotic trance recall many a tale by Poe and "The Birthmark" by Hawthorne, Bellamy's favorite author, the fact that the walls of the vault were laid in hydraulic cement and the door lined with asbestos hints that this romance will be tinged with the wondrous new technology. Nevertheless, the house over the vault burns down, a portent of conflagration in the world above.

It is autumn, a time of wisdom and maturity, when Julian awakens in the home of a prestigious socialist, Dr. Leete, and his daughter Edith. Julian is tired and ill, a common complaint with travelers to utopia, suggesting a birth pain through the political passage. Although he is still in Boston, the thought of socialism, advanced technology, and a new form of personal relations daunts the capitalist, who begins his quest for right thinking as a familiar figure from romance: a lonely traveler in a strange land.

In the process of Julian's conversion, the optimism embedded in utopian thinking replaces the fear embedded in the fantastic mode. As Julian acknowledges the possibilities of Nationalism, the narrative mode shifts

and the fantastic passes into the uncanny, the world that could be. This
shift returns us to the paradox of the utopian pun. Boston A.D. 2000
derives plausibly from Boston A.D. 1887. The narrative of Julian's conversion from one era to the next ratifies the utopian axiom that the seeds of the
future are immanent in the present. But the fact that this transformation
relies on a literary device returns us to *outopia*, the nonexistent destiny.

Perhaps the most significant way that the mimetic confronts the fantastic, that *outopia* confronts *eutopia* in *Looking Backward*, is in the finitude of
history. Unlike the modern utopia described by Ursula LeGuin in *The
Dispossessed* (1974), which argues for permanent revolution, *Looking Backward* discounts notions of further political evolution. This denial of change,
perforce a denial of history, reflects Bellamy's fear of radical change, a fear
that Julian embodies. Without a concept of historical change, it was impossible for Bellamy to use the narrative structures of the American novel of
the 1870s and 1880s. Henry James's *American* (1877) and William Dean
Howells's *Rise of Silas Lapham* (1885), for example, are predicated on the
moral and, at times, financial growth of characters as they interact with
society. But as Georg Lukács notes in discussing the fictional consequence
of socialist realism, "If . . . the elimination of this antagonistic character
(that is, social contradiction and class struggle) is seen as something immediately realizable, rather than as a process, both the antagonism and contradiction, the motor of all development, will disappear from the reality to be
depicted" (Lukács 1964, 120). Lacking change, *Looking Backward* seems
to mark the end of history.

I would argue that this absence of change generates the implicit and
necessary "estrangement" in reading *Looking Backward*, for it challenges
the nineteenth-century experience of a world in flux. True, nothing much
changes in utopia. Because everything is predetermined in Boston A.D.
2000, we observe no dialectic between character and environment: Dr.
Leete and Edith do not affect the plot nor are they affected by it. Certainly
they assure us as readers that we do not have to worry about Julian in the
new Boston because everything there, by definition, is good. In addition to
this happy tautology, the literary form itself defuses our emotional engagement because Dr. Leete's commentary and political analysis alternate with
the romance, an episodic structure that further weakens our involvement.

According to Bellamy, utopia marks the end of the popular sentimental
romance. After reading a novel from the new Boston entitled *Penthesilia*,
Julian notices the absence of fictional conflict: "The story-writers of my
day would have deemed the making of bricks without straw a light task
compared with the construction of a romance from which should be ex-

cluded all effects drawn from the contrasts of wealth and poverty, education and ignorance, coarseness and refinement, high and low, all motives drawn from social pride and ambition, the desire of being richer or the fear of being poorer, together with sordid anxieties of any sort for one's self or others; a romance in which there should, indeed, be love galore, but love unfretted by artificial barriers created by differences of station or possessions, owning no other law but that of the heart" (Bellamy 1888, 235). Yet Bellamy introduces these very contrasts, shaped as historical or epochal contrasts, to dramatize the romance between Julian and Edith II.

The powerful engagement of *Looking Backward* stems, in my view, from Julian's deep confusion over his historical role. The tension resides not within the utopian present, but between the utopian present and the nonutopian past. As an emigré from capitalism, Julian stands outside the history of social transformation. Overly impressionable as a tourist, rather immature in his loves and loyalties, and vulnerable as a displaced person, he has been unintentionally thrust into utopia. The utopian present, emblemized by Edith Leete, will teach him to transcend the past and help him win the utopian grail, a new political identity. His ritualized love for Edith symbolizes his naturalization as a citizen of utopia. Yet the tension of the genre persists. We never doubt that Julian (a literary descendant of the reformed rake of Restoration drama, the domestic novel, and the dime novel) will be persuaded, for our familiarity with the romance tradition assures us that he will win a transformed consciousness. At the same time, however, our familiarity with the determinants of progress assures us that his real function is only to interrogate the nation's fate, the text of his personal subtext.

Julian's two narrative functions, then, mark his two personalities: when he is with Edith, Julian expresses his isolation and struggles with his aristocratic allegiances, but when he is with her father he becomes a dry and inadequate foil—curious, ingenuous, and easily convinced, happily launching the wise doctor into yet another explanation of the logic of state socialism. In the romantic fable, Julian exposes the frightened individualism of a lost member of the haute bourgeoisie, but in the political manifesto, he is an inadequate spokesman for industrial capitalism. In a series of parables, analogies, and extended metaphors, the visitor learns that economic equality rests on a simple moral claim: to each according to his humanity. Julian, who never worked a day in his life, discovers that the social creation of value undercuts the right of profit, because "Many people work on a product, from its historic conception to its current design, manufacture and distribution" (Bellamy 1888, 197). Edith and her father also show him how equality has eliminated what Thorstein Veblen called the "honorific expenditure" on waste. When Edith takes Julian shopping at a distribution center, instead of garish advertisements he finds only small information cards; merchandise in itself no longer signifies status.

But even if he does not have to pay for them, many gadgets tempt Julian. He falls asleep listening to music over a telephone, wakes up to a clock radio, and dials a sermon. William Morris, often something of a Luddite, attacked *Looking Backward* for its mechanistic materialism and called it a "Cockney's paradise." William Dean Howells, who in 1894 abandoned machinery in his pastoral utopia, confessed that at first he saw Bellamy's gadgets as "sorry patches on the rags of our outworn civilization, or only toys to arouse our greed and vanity," but he later understood that the inventions themselves were "part of Bellamy's democratic imagination." Bellamy, he saw, promised "things for lives hitherto starved of them" (Howells 1898, 254). Science in the new society has liberated its citizens from drudgery and fear. Yet the technology for all of these inventions was available in the late nineteenth century. For example, mass-produced clothing developed for the production of uniforms during the Civil War has, in the year 2000, eliminated the sweat shops and home-finishing trades where in the 1880s entire families sewed buttons or stitched buttonholes all night long. Now machinery has replaced heavy manual labor and pneumatic tubes deliver hot meals to the home. Technology, along with economic equality, is a precondition for morality in Bellamy's utopia, allowing citizens to merge in "transcendental" solidarity.

Through a vision in which prosperity is a foundation for Christian humanism, Bellamy resolved his era's conflict between spiritual and technological growth, thereby dissolving the conflict between the real and the ideal: one simply preceded the other in an elegant view of human progress. Adding technology to a Social Darwinist scheme of the evolving society, Bellamy built a postindustrial model for human perfection. Julian's only task is to acknowledge that the utopia promises spiritual as well as industrial growth. Like the rosebush transplanted from the swamp, "watered with black bog water, breathing miasmic fogs by day, chilled with poison dews at night" (Bellamy 1888, 405), the vermin and mildew would automatically disappear from Julian's soul in the garden of Nationalism.

Yet in Bellamy's cosmos, development is, ultimately, ahistorical. Compare Julian's indoctrination to Georg Lukács's description of growth in the realist novel: "Only in the interaction of character and environment can the concrete potentialities of a particular individual be singled out from the 'bad infinity' of purely abstract potentialities, and emerge as the determining potentiality of just this individual at just this phase of his development" (Lukács 1964, 24). But *Looking Backward* precludes such "interaction" because characters cannot choose to affect their society, which is "utopian," that is to say, which is nonexistent and already perfect. Julian does not need to make decisions that would determine the social growth of his new community; he cannot make decisions that would determine the social growth of his nineteenth-century world. Instead, *Looking Backward* achieves its effect by accumulation, piling up enough details to convince Julian, and by extension the reader, of the perfection of a Nationalist world. We expect Julian to attain self-knowledge and fall in love with Edith because these actions represent stages of his initiation.

While Bellamy posits an impact of environment on character, both Julian and Edith are stuck in the nineteenth-century sentimental romance. Perhaps Bellamy's toughest problem was how to reconcile his promise of political equality for women with his utopian females descended on the material side from women in the gothic and domestic novel who were modest, pious, and compliant. In the creation of women characters, Bellamy affirms that the future ideologically replicates the present. Here utopia fails to transcend the mediations of popular culture and the ideology of the Cult of True Womanhood (Welter 1966). On the one hand, women in Bellamy's utopia benefit from his admiration for Frances Willard, the Women's Congress of 1873, and the suffrage movement. By assigning domestic work to the category of unskilled labor, Bellamy appears aware of the plight of the working woman in the factory, the sweat shop, or domestic service. In his year 2000 all women earn the same income as men; they have their own branch in the industrial army and obey only female judges and generals. The highest governing council reserves one seat for a woman, who may veto any issue relating to her sex. Edith eats meals cooked in centralized kitchens and sends her dirty clothes to the centralized laundry. Most surprising, if she chooses to do her own housework, she is paid. At a time when married women were not allowed to own property in their own names, Bellamy announced that wives should "in no way be dependent on their husbands for economic security" (Bellamy 1888, 256). After Frances Willard read *Looking Backward,* she wrote to Bellamy's publisher, "Some of us think that Edward Bellamy must be Edwardina—i.e., we believe that a big-hearted, big-brained woman wrote this book. Won't you please find out?" (Bowman 1958, 120).

But, on the other hand, in believing that economic factors alone constitute women's inequality, Bellamy perpetuated images of female inferiority and created socialist female characters who conformed to the Cult of

True Womanhood: pure, pious, domestic, and submissive. He restricts women to a few traditional jobs because they are "inferior in strength to men and further disqualified industrially in special ways" (Bellamy 1888, 257). Only women who have been both wives and mothers reach high ranks in the industrial army because "they alone fully represent their sex" (p. 257). Dr. Leete tells Julian that the best function for utopian women is to inspire utopian men; they are men's "incentive to labour" (p. 257). Indeed, men only "permit women to work because it makes them more attractive and fulfilling companions" (p. 256).

Thus, *Looking Backward* opens a narrative space in which historical contradictions play against one another rather than become effaced through conventional literary conclusions. Given the inspirational powers of the ideal woman, it is hardly surprising that Julian finally becomes a socialist not so much because of Dr. Leete's persuasive lectures but because he is loved by a utopian lady. In discussing the work of Louis Marin, Eugene Hill has observed that "within the universe of discourse of a given society at a given moment, the utopian text constructs a schematic or imaginary synthesis of the historical contradictions which beset that society" (Hill 1982, 173). The fact that utopia is "nowhere" requires that the synthesis be imaginary, rather than mimetic. In *Looking Backward*, the synthesis resides in Julian's altered consciousness. Darko Suvin notes that in *Looking Backward*, "The construction of a social system for the reader is also the reconstruction of the hero" (Suvin 1979, 174). I believe, however, that the reconstruction of Julian West has more to do with the recuperative powers of sentiment than with socialism. Julian recovers from his jet lag of 113 years because Edith II looks, acts, and sounds so much like Edith I. And Edith II has little to do with Nationalism. Julian never sees her at work—he never even bothers to ask what she does in the industrial army. Instead, he falls in love with her as he watches her set the table, arrange flowers, tend the garden, and shop, all the while recalling his original love. Edwin Fussell has traced the proximity of Edith to the recurrent phrase "sympathy" throughout the text. Circumscribed by Bellamy's characterization of the nurturing female, Edith mothers Julian into a socialist consciousness (Fussell 1980).

What finally stands between Julian and Nationalism is guilt for his nineteenth-century wealth and his nineteenth-century sensibilities. Bellamy long held that everyone has a dual consciousness with an "impersonal" or altruistic side and a "personal" or egocentric side (Bellamy 1984). An "impersonal" state of mind reflects a healthy balance between self-interest and social commitment, while a "personal" state promotes vanity, paranoia, or guilt, which chain an individual to the past until released by an image of impersonal love.

In Julian West, Bellamy first explored the political implications of an inflated "personal" character, blinded by aristocratic affiliation. Now, wandering in an impersonal society, the traveler faces a terrifying loss of identity: "There are no words for the mental torture I endured during this helpless, eyeless groping for myself in a boundless void. No other experience of the mind gives probably anything like the sense of absolute intellectual arrest from the loss of a mental fulcrum, a starting point of thought, which comes during such a momentary obscuration of one's identity. I trust I may never know what it is again" (Bellamy 1888, 105). Without his "fulcrum" or "starting point of thought"—that is, his class map—Julian has lost his historical identity.

Perhaps Chekhov or Sartre could better finish this scene, for Julian's "intellectual arrest" is a story of historical guilt. His is the atrophied conscience of an "eyeless" class that refused to see what it had created until confronted by its opposite in utopia. Tempted by both realities, he endeavors to perpetuate the utopian paradox of residing in the world and the meta-world at the same time: "The idea that I was two persons, that my identity was double, began to fascinate me with its simple solution of my experience" (p. 105).

Lodged in the world of romance, however, Julian cannot undertake the sorts of activity that would commit him to the world of historical change. No matter how dramatic it appears to be, activity in romance reveals a sequence of events closer to moral "states" than to novelistic action (Jameson 1975, 139). Rather than a historical actor, Julian is a "registering apparatus" who learns to tell the difference between good and evil, static principles that undermine Bellamy's need to account for change. Through the fable of the reincarnation of Edith and Julian, Bellamy resolves the tension between the no place and the good place by dissolving the disjunction between the nineteenth century and the future. The love story promotes an essentialist view of character that neutralizes historical change.

Julian's transformation, then, hinges on the purgation of guilt rather than on the persuasion of socialism. Because guilt arrests the development of a social conscience, it binds Julian to nineteenth-century capitalism. Bellamy's genius—and this also helps explain the popularity of *Looking Backward*—was to absolve Julian as an innocent product of his times. The sentimental heroine, with her traditional literary devotion to social victims (from slaves to prostitutes to drunks) easily redeems Julian through the power of sympathy: "Promise that you will come to us, and let us sympath-

ize with you," she reiterates (Bellamy 1888, 114). Reduced by convention
to this one virtue, Edith "symbolizes the humanity of the race." Neither
Julian nor Edith has traveled far from 1887. Pictured as a utopian woman,
time loses its destructive force and the future heals. And, as so often
happens in romance, the hero returns to a familiar identity.

Looking Backward is a form of historiography that purports to represent
change while it affirms that the future mirrors the present. This conservative subtext in a tale of radical transformation is articulated through the
narrative conventions of the romance. Ultimately, the disjunction between
text and subtext, between political manifesto and romantic fable, ruptures
a sense of closure. There are, in effect, two endings to *Looking Backward*
that thereby repress a conclusion about Nationalism, indeed, about utopianism. An indeterminate ending is endemic in a genre that attempts to
represent the future: "The vision of future history cannot know any punc-
tual ending . . . at the same time that its novelistic expression demands
some such ending" (Jameson 1982, 148).

But what is the function of the ending in utopian fiction? Karl Mannheim, in his seminal work *Ideology and Utopia,* observes that in utopia,
"events which at first glance present themselves as mere chronological
cumulation take on the character of destiny" (Mannheim 1952, 188).
Northrop Frye similarly suggested that utopia records the "end at which
social life aims" (Frye 1965, 25). The ending orders the historical and
romantic acts because utopia is teleological, the culmination of a predetermined passage toward a finite state that marks the end of change.

However, the passage that is supposed to establish the depth of Julian's
conversion calls into question the very project of utopianism. In a dream,
Julian returns to the Boston of 1887. Like the hunter in the romance in
pursuit of a new identity, Julian becomes his own prey, projecting his past
consciousness onto other aristocrats, who reproduce his early assumptions.
Utopian tales often realize such a doubling effect through the contrast of the
utopian with the preutopian world. To complete his initiation, the utopian
traveler often must return to his first world through a fantastic telescope,
drugs, dreams, or simply memory. Generally, the return ratifies and rein-
forces the persuasive values of the particular utopian inversions. For Julian,
however, the return exposes the limits of the transforming function of the
utopian experience.

Restored to the nineteenth century, Julian now notices poverty, reads
headlines announcing the employment of young girls in the coal mines, and
observes advertisements defacing windows and pavements. His sojourn in
Nationalism has penetrated the blinding isolation of his class: "No more

did I look upon the woeful dwellers in this Inferno with a callous curiosity as creatures scarcely human. I saw in them my brothers and sisters, my parents, my children, flesh of my flesh, blood of my blood. The festering mass of human wretchedness about me offended now not my senses merely, but pierced my heart like a knife, so that I could not repress my sighs and groans. I not only saw but felt in my body all that I saw" (Bellamy 1888, 458). Beyond mere vision, his new utopian perception calls forth a transcendent fusion of subject and object.

As a social experiment, however, utopianism fails. Overwhelmed by the sights of waste and loneliness in the city, Julian dines at the home of wealthy friends, where the women dress in satin and the table glitters with silver and china. Motivated by the disparity between the sumptuous meal and his new perception of poverty, Julian lectures his own class on cause and effect, waste and utopia: "With fervency I spoke of that new world, blessed with plenty, purified by justice, and sweetened by brotherly kindness, the world of which I indeed but dreamed, but which might so easily be made real" (p. 466). But rather than enlisting in Julian's cause, the women are disgusted and the men call him "madman," "fanatic," and enemy of society.

Ostensibly the book ends happily: Julian awakes from the dream in his utopian bed. Utopia has defeated the forces of the reality principle. Julian's utopian imagination has, to borrow from Marcuse, achieved "the reconciliation of the individual with the whole, of desire with realization, of happiness with reason" (Marcuse 1955, 134). The utopian images that negate present reality have contributed to the general opposition to dominant relations and values.

But within the text, the experiment has failed. Julian is powerless to use his vision of a just and attractive future to effectuate a significant change in the consciousness of the dominant class of his own time. To what degree is Bellamy acknowledging the limits of his selected form? Certainly, Bellamy has hopscotched history, plunging Julian into what Engels would call the realm of untimely illusion (Engels 1935, 56). We might read Julian's defeat as a form of self-doubt.

Or we might read Julian's defeat as an acknowledgment that humanity cannot really renew itself through a literary device. The romance form itself limits the transforming function of utopianism. In describing Shakespeare's *Tempest*, Frank Kermode observes that in art ideas "can develop as it were of themselves, with ideal clarity, as if to show that a formal and ordered paradigm of these forces is possible when life is purged of accident, and upon the assumption that since we are all willy-nilly Platonists we are perfectly able to understand the relevance of such a paradigm" (Kermode

1962, lvi). A Platonic model, Boston A.D. 2000 exists mainly for our
admiration and contemplation.

But as an "ideological critique of ideology" (Marin 1976, 71), *Looking
Backward* derives its critical power from its capacity to simultaneously
project and subvert contemporary discourse about history, which is a
process rather than a fact. Suvin reminds us that "as of the 19th century,
the only consistent novelty is one that constitutes an open-ended or dynamic system" (Suvin 1982, 7). The text engages us not merely as a recipe
or a blueprint but rather as an evocation of longing. True, Bellamy's
imaginary society secularized images of personal reward. Extracting and
developing tendencies from early industrial capitalism, he fulfilled reform-
ist hopes that property would someday belong to the community as a
whole. And he popularized demands for universal suffrage, humanistic
technology, a clean industrial environment, and universal education. By
focusing on the development of society as a whole and by representing
prosperity as a collective process, Bellamy attacked the ideology of competitive individualism, and represented *eu*topia, the good place.

Julian's frustration appropriately returns us to the utopian pun. The
power of *Looking Backward* resides in its contradiction. Bellamy's Boston
in the year 2000 is purposefully nowhere because Julian's dream is about
itself. It confronts us and leaves us with both the resolution and the rupture
of the utopian vision.

Works Cited

Bellamy, Edward. 1888. *Looking Backward, 2000–1887*. Boston: Ticknor.
———. 1890. "Why I Wrote *Looking Backward.*" *Nationalist* 2 (May).
———. 1894. "How I Came to Write *Looking Backward.*" *Ladies Home Journal* 11
    (April).
———. 1984. *The Religion of Solidarity*. London: Concord Grove Press.
Bloch, Ernst. 1970. *A Philosophy of the Future*. Translated by John Cumming. New
    York: Herder and Herder.
———. 1971. *On Karl Marx* (selections translated from *Das Prinzip Hoffnung*,
    1959). New York: Herder and Herder.
Bowman, Sylvia E. 1958. *The Year 2000: A Critical Biography of Edward Bellamy*.
    New York: Bookman Associates.
Engels, Friedrich. 1935. *Socialism, Utopian and Scientific*. New York: International
    Publishers.
Frye, Northrop. 1965. "Varieties of Literary Utopias." In *Utopias and Utopian
    Thought*, edited by Frank Manuel. Boston: Beacon Press.
Fussell, Edwin. 1980. "The Theme of Sympathy in *Looking Backward.*" Un-
    published, Dept. of English, University of California at San Diego.

Hill, Eugene D. 1982. "The Place of the Future: Louis Marin and his *Utopiques*." *Science Fiction Studies* 9: 167–79.

Howells, William Dean. 1898. "Edward Bellamy." *Atlantic Monthly* 82: 254.

Jameson, Fredric. 1971. *Marxism and Form: Twentieth Century Dialectical Theories of Literature*. Princeton: Princeton University Press.

———. 1982. "Progress versus Utopia; or, Can We Imagine the Future?" *Science Fiction Studies* 9: 147–58.

Kermode, Frank. 1962. "Introduction" to *The Tempest*. Arden Shakespeare. New York: Methuen.

Ketterer, David. 1973. "Utopian Fantasy as Millenial Motive and Science-Fictional Motif." *Studies in the Literary Imagination* 6: 79–103.

Lukács, Georg. 1964. *Realism in Our Time: Literature and Class Struggle*. Translated by John Mander and Necke Mander. New York: Harper and Row.

Mannheim, Karl. 1952. *Ideology and Utopia*. New York: Harcourt Brace.

Marcuse, Herbert. 1955. *Eros and Civilization*. Boston: Beacon Press.

Marin, Louis. 1976. "Theses on Ideology and Utopia." *Minnesota Review* 6: 71–75.

More, Thomas. 1966. *Utopia*. Translated by Ralph Robinson. New York: AMS Press.

Moylan, Tom. 1982. "The Locus of Hope: Utopia vs. Ideology." *Science Fiction Studies* 9:159–66.

Suvin, Darko. 1979. *Metamorphoses of Science Fiction*. New Haven: Yale University Press.

———. 1982. "Narrative Logic, Ideological Domination, and the Range of Science Fiction: A Hypothesis With a Historical Test." *Science Fiction Studies* 9: 1–25.

Todorov, Tzvetan. 1973. *The Fantastic: A Structural Approach to a Literary Genre*. Translated by Richard Howard. Ithaca, N.Y.: Cornell University Press.

Welter, Barbara. 1966. "The Cult of True Womanhood: 1820–1860." *American Quarterly* 18: 151–74.

Gender, Class, and
Race in Utopia

Sylvia Strauss

In 1888, when Edward Bellamy's *Looking Backward* was published, the woman question was seen as the key to whether the progress of the nineteenth century could be sustained in the twentieth. The woman question preoccupied scientists, philosophers, essayists, novelists, and politicians. Women's voices were being heard on a scale heretofore unknown. Social reformers, both male and female, believed for ideological and practical reasons that woman's sphere must be enlarged. Conservatives sought inducements to keep women in their traditional domestic sphere, fervently believing that the preservation of civilization depended on it.

Bellamy acknowledged that the late nineteenth century was a crucible for women. He himself looked forward not to the twentieth but to the twenty-first century for the radical changes in social, political, and economic institutions that he designed for the happiness and well-being of men and women. Bellamy, an avowed socialist seeking allies in a supremely individualistic America, was heartened that women had been discussing social reforms, technological improvements, coeducation, the psychological and moral ramifications of motherhood, fashion reform, and community kitchens and laundries. In his editorials in the Springfield *Union*, Bellamy called the woman question the "Proteus of the age, confronting us in every shape, assuming every form as we wrestle with it" (cited in Bowman 1958, 272).

Strongly influenced by the American feminist philosopher Thomas Wentworth Higginson, Bellamy was among a group of male feminists who supported women's suffrage at a time when the issue was foundering.[1] After the Civil War, feminists, dismayed that their erstwhile Republican allies had refused to insert women's rights into the Fourteenth Amendment, which granted civil rights to black males only, had a falling out over how to respond to what they regarded as a betrayal. Some, including Susan B. Anthony and Elizabeth Cady Stanton, thought the Fourteenth Amendment should be defeated. Others, including Lucy Stone, spokeswoman for a group of feminists who agreed with the Republican rationale that this was "the Negroes' hour," urged women to bide their time. Thus a schism developed in the suffrage movement. The Anthony-Stanton wing united to form the National Woman Suffrage Association (NWSA). They kept up a steady drumbeat for the suffrage but they were also willing to consider radical ideas imported from Europe such as free love. The "wait and see" advocates adopted the name American Woman Suffrage Association (AWSA). They were aghast at free love and looked askance at the NWSA leaders' hopes of coalescing with working-class women. The members of the AWSA were attuned to American ideals and values that Edward Bellamy personified. As their hopes for the suffrage in the immediate future dimmed, many turned to Edward Bellamy, since he offered a vision of a better tomorrow for women.

During the period when the woman suffrage issue was in limbo, there was a proliferation of women's organizations espousing a variety of causes. The one that had the most durable impact was the Women's Christian Temperance Union (WCTU), which carried on crusades for both prohibition and the suffrage. The General Federation of Women's Clubs advocated municipal reforms, child labor laws, and educational and cultural facilities for the working class. The Women's Club Movement bypassed the suffrage issue and managed to get legislation passed for public parks, schools, and cultural opportunities for the working class by stressing women's moral influence as a force for progress. They believed that women's philanthropic instincts had remained largely untapped. The Association for the Advancement of Women (AWA), composed of female college graduates, encouraged women to enter the professions and specialized scientific fields to prove that women's brains were equal to men's. Feminists in the American Social Science Association (ASSA) defended women's right both to earn equal wages with men and to organize their own unions. The American Equal Rights Association maintained that women's dependence on men was based on an exaggeration of sexual differences.[2] While these organizations had different goals, all had in common the fact that the women who joined them were middle class, believed in science and technology as the potential liberators of women, and viewed centralized government as the means of bringing about the reforms they sought.

Since women articulated their demands on a wide range of issues, Bellamy sought their support for his radical reorganization of American society. He was acutely aware of the economic and sociological facts of late nineteenth-century American life and found them disturbing. During the Civil War, when preserving the Union—a laudable purpose to Bellamy—

was the aim, American corporations had been given license to do what needed to be done in supplying the army, expanding the railroads, and exploring new mechanical inventions requiring large initial investments. The profits derived from government contracts and subsidies were so enormous that the number of millionaires in the country increased from three in 1860 to thirty-eight in 1890. The words "rapacious," "avaricious," and "greedy" were consistently employed by Bellamy to characterize these men. Not surprisingly, *Looking Backward* is, first of all, an excoriating indictment of the capitalist system that made such accumulation possible.

As Bellamy saw it, the millions of dollars that capitalists acquired through "ruthless" exploitation of labor enabled them to buy government officials. Political scandal and corruption flourished with the growing economic power of the capitalists. Bellamy's harsh feelings toward the industrialists were, however, tempered by his belief that, coarse though they were, they enabled society to progress technologically, a factor of overriding importance to the futurist visionary in Bellamy. This progress, Bellamy felt, must be continued on an evolutionary basis but linked to a more equitable system of distribution.

If Bellamy's attitude toward capitalists was ambivalent, so was his view of the working class. He sympathized with their plight and empathized with their exasperation, but, in the last analysis, he was nostalgic for the days when Chicopee Falls, his home town in Massachusetts, was a pastoral haven unblemished by unemployed workers living in holes they dug in the riverbeds. The workers' only recourse was the strike, a tactic Bellamy deplored. The immigrant workers' inclination toward Marxism and anarchism gave rise to fears that the country would once again be rent by violence—this time along class rather than regional lines. Labor unions appeared to Bellamy as a new species of vested interest that hindered progress. In *Looking Backward* Bellamy rejected the notion that the working class had any constructive role to play in renewing American society. As for working-class women, they were totally absent from the portrait of labor and the analysis of proletariat-bourgeois conflicts drawn by this self-proclaimed feminist. It seems unlikely that Bellamy would have viewed working women's increasing militancy, and the fact that fifty thousand working-class women were absorbed into the Knights of Labor in 1886, as a sign of progress.

Although Bellamy argued for a socialist society, his socialism, based on a quixotic interpretation of American history, had little connection with any of the European models. While the goals of Marx's international and Bellamy's national socialism were the same—economic equality and abundance for all—in Bellamy's socialist society, the Yankee middle class—professionals, technocrats, and small businessmen—would provide both the ethos and the leadership, much as the Founding Fathers—themselves solidly middle class—had provided the values and stewardship of the American republic.

The descendants of the Founding Fathers with roots planted deep in American history were standing helplessly on the sidelines while capitalists—the few—fought it out with the largely immigrant masses—the many—who were struggling to improve their impoverished lives. Strikes were rampant during the 1870s and 1880s, and the middle class feared that industrial warfare presaged a general revolution during which the immigrants would become their economic and political masters. The immediate inspiration for Bellamy's novel was provided by the 1886 Haymarket incident in Chicago, in which seven policemen and two civilians were killed in the melee that ensued during a demonstration against the McCormick Harvester Company. Although whoever threw the bomb at the police was never identified, the authorities exacted vengeance by hanging four anarchists who were not suspects in the crime but whose death was to serve as a warning to the workers to cease and desist. But the martyrs of the Haymarket riot merely inspired others to vindicate them.

Bellamy was confident that a new social order was an idea whose time had come and that middle-class men and women seeing all their most cherished values subverted would be attentive. Since the feminist movement in Bellamy's time was a native American phenomenon and consisted of literate middle-class women, Bellamy saw them as potential converts. To further attract female readers, who, more than men, were drawn to the novel as a source of entertainment and enlightenment, Bellamy cast his socialist program in the form of a conventional romance. Julian West, the protagonist, goes to sleep in the strife-torn Boston of 1887 and wakes up in the Boston of the year 2000—a city so changed in design, architecture, and economic and political institutions that West suffers an acute case of culture shock that threatens to deteriorate into insanity. Only the ministrations and soothing demeanor of Edith Leete, the daughter of his guide and mentor, Dr. Leete, helps him to accept the startling changes all about him. Not surprisingly, he falls in love with Edith. After learning that she is the great-granddaughter of his nineteenth-century sweetheart, also named Edith, West finds himself once again in the Boston of 1887. Was it all a dream, the reader wonders? Was West, after seeing the future, and finding it ennobling, destined to return to the Boston—corruption-ridden and plagued by strikes—he was now glad he had left behind? Julian West's conversion to the religion of solidarity, the glue that holds Bellamy's utopia together, is so profound that it enables him to span 113 years and return again to the rational and serene world of the year 2000.

West's first view of the Boston of the future is mind-boggling. He had left a city so noisy that he had had to build a soundproof room underneath his house in order to sleep; the air outside was so begrimed and fetid with the odors emanating from the working-class slums that it inhibited breathing. He awakens to a city straight from the drawing boards of nineteenth-century futurists who had the active support of feminists, a city laid out in "miles of broad streets, shaded by trees and lined with fine buildings. They were not in continuous blocks but set in larger and smaller enclosures which stretched in every direction" (Bellamy 1926 [1888], 38). Parks and fountains dot the landscape within the city's perimeters. West learns that in each square there are community kitchens, laundries, and dining halls. Women have been freed from the chains of housekeeping, a goal long sought by, among others, the feminist writers Abby Morton Diaz (1874) and Marie Howland (1874). Their pleas had evidently been heard by Bellamy.

In *The Schoolmaster's Trunk,* which purports to be notes left by a wise schoolmaster, Diaz deplores the fact that women spend an egregious amount of time in the kitchen: "When a woman uses herself up in cooking and as a consequence dies or half-dies, what is that but human sacrifice? It is about time to stop this woman-killing" (pp. 13, 14).

While attending a sewing circle, the schoolmaster hears that women's aspirations go beyond cooking and cleaning; he feels they should be allowed to realize their talents and abilities and indulge their desires to read and travel. Diaz advocates scientific housekeeping. She provides recipes with the time allotted for each item, which would allow women to choose the least time-consuming menus.

The enemy in *Schoolmaster's Trunk* are men "who don't understand," who wish women to be good-natured and to fulfill their wants, their homes cleaned daily, three meals a day provided, their clothes washed and ironed—and "the right to criticize" (p. 53). Diaz urges women to make time for intellectual and cultural activities and admonishes them, "Let women remember to keep the ship in order but steer for some port" (p. 70).

Papa's Own Girl goes much further in providing independence for women than *The Schoolmaster's Trunk.* Marie Howland was a cosmopolite who hobnobbed with radicals on both sides of the Atlantic. Deeply influenced by French Utopian Socialists, her "Social Palace" was based on Charles Fourier's experiment in communal living, the Familistère that he had constructed in Guise, France.

In the novel, Papa's own girl is Clara, daughter of Dr. Delano, an enlightened male feminist. He encourages his daughter "to make herself the champion of women's rights, and women's social and political emancipation." He firmly believes that when women do their full share of the world's work, "there will be forgotten the history of many pygmies that would have swelled to glory under the pens of their own sex" (Howland 1874, 335).

Clara plans to build an industry for women workers who wish to be independent. Her idea is fleshed out when she meets Count Frauenstein, whose very name reveals his feminist credentials. Despite his aristocratic title, Frauenstein is described as a leading member of the "International" (p. 414). Together they conceive the Social Palace, where men and women live and work in surroundings that are the last word in utility and beauty. The Palace is built by recruiting the volunteer service of labor unions. The landscape, manicured lawns, and terraced gardens presage Bellamy's Boston of the twenty-first century. The Social Palace is completely self-sufficient. Food is grown in the orchards and fields surrounding the Palace. There is a central kitchen where food cooked by chefs can be bought at minimal cost. In a central laundry clothes are washed by steam machines. The Palace has a child-care center, library, astronomical observatory, game room for children and adults, and a fully equipped hospital. Sustaining the Palace is a brickworks for men and a silk-producing industry for women, who also cultivate flowers. The profits from the industries are distributed equally.

Clara and Count Frauenstein find love as they see their brainchild come to fruition. The count rejects his title, observing that the aristocracy consists of "Parvenus of 200 years who would drag down the nobler aristocracy of labor, which is as old as civilization itself" (p. 540).

With women's appetite for freedom from household drudgery whetted by Bellamy's precursors, one can readily imagine his female readers scanning the page with bated breath when Julian West asks Mrs. Leete, "Who does your housework?" They were not disappointed when she describes the dimensions of the new freedom gained by women: "There is none to do," she replies. "Our washing is all done in public laundries at excessively cheap rates, and our cooking at public shops. Electricity, of course, takes the place of all fire and lighting. We choose houses no larger than we need and furnish them so as to involve the minimum of trouble to keep them in order. We have no use for domestic servants" (Bellamy 1926 [1888], 118–19).

Influenced by feminists such as Abby Morton Diaz and Marie Howland, and believing they articulated the dreams of all women, Bellamy incorporated their ideas into *Looking Backward*. But Bellamy did not give women much scope for the leisure time they had and which both Diaz and Howland provided for in their respective books. Dr. Leete, Bellamy's surrogate in the novel, does not have a high regard for women's intellect, capacity to govern, or ability to pull their weight equally with men in the labor force. Nor did Bellamy believe that women had the flexibility to abandon conventional religion and adopt the religion of solidarity—the engine that powered his egalitarian society.

Bellamy, born in 1850, was the son of a New England Baptist minister, and both his parents instilled Calvinist values in him during his boyhood. In his early twenties, however, Bellamy suffered a crisis of conscience and abandoned the religious teachings of his parents. He developed a personal religion devoid of a forbidding, punitive deity. Instead, Bellamy described God as the "All-soul" or the "not-self," the "universal," the "centripetal force," and the "infinite" (Bowman 1958, 28). Dr. Leete states the religion's scope and import as succinctly as possible: "If I were to give you in one sentence, a key to what may seem the mysteries of our civilization as compared with that of your age, I should say that the solidarity of the race and the brotherhood of man, which to you were but fine phrases, are, to our thinking and feeling, ties as real and as vital as physical fraternity" (Bellamy 1926 [1888], 134). According to Dr. Leete, a portion of this universal spirit exists in all men, forcing them to merge with each other and abandon their individualism or "self-centeredness." This divine essence—the real self—makes all men half-gods, potential Christs, and forges a bond of fellowship among them.

On closer scrutiny, however, Bellamy's religion of solidarity was one in which the individual was completely subordinated to the state—a civic religion where individuals had no needs or yearnings that were beyond the power of the state to fulfill. The religion of solidarity was a form of distinctively male bonding that excluded women. Bellamy regarded women as the main pillars of the churches of his day. In this capacity, he believed they were enemies of social progress and bulwarks of the status quo. Bellamy viewed women's acceptance of church hierarchy as the cause of their shriveled lives, making them docile, clinging, and superstitious. Given women's religious conservatism, they were potential dissidents from the state religion. The ground was thus prepared for providing women with a lower status than men enjoyed in Bellamy's utopia.

In *The Feminization of American Culture* (1977), Ann Douglas posits that women did indeed bring new strength to the waning religious beliefs of nineteenth-century society. Elizabeth Cady Stanton, however, rejected the stereotype of women as the devout half of the population.[3] During the 1880s, Stanton became convinced that the Bible and the churches were the main obstacles to equality between the sexes. Her analysis of the Bible persuaded her that women were a mere afterthought in creation, forever tarnished as the carriers of evil. Stanton wanted the role of women in revealed religion made an issue in feminist politics. Not to do so she regarded as "cowardice," asking, "How can woman's position be changed from that of a subordinate to an equal without the broadest discussion of all the questions involved in her present degradation?" (Stanton 1972 [1895], 404). *The Woman's Bible*, the first part of which she published in 1895, was greeted with almost universal denunciation. Bellamy, however, saw in Stanton's critique and invitation to a dialogue the possibility of women's progressive disillusionment with religion, and in *Equality* (1897), the sequel to *Looking Backward*, he credits women's mass conversion to the religion of solidarity as a major factor that made possible the evolutionary socialism he espoused.

In the society depicted in *Looking Backward* there are no churches and no clergy. Dr. Leete is a committed member of the religion of solidarity, but Edith Leete and Mrs. Leete, still true to tradition, avail themselves of Sunday sermons based on Christian ethics. These sermons, given by ordinary citizens who feel inspired to speak, are piped into the houses through stereophonic devices.

Patriarchal authority, pervasive in *Looking Backward*, is most blatantly revealed in the industrial army, the novel's most important institution. Bellamy's state, it is essential to note, is a corporate state: all industries and all individuals have been absorbed and subsumed to nationalist goals. Organized along strict military lines, the industrial army is staffed by a hierarchy of officers who enforce discipline and supply earned rewards to their underlings, the foot soldiers consisting of all the men and women in the society. The chief duty of citizenship is maximum contribution to the economic well-being of the community through labor. Men and women between the ages of twenty-one and forty-five serve in the industrial army. They uncomplainingly provide goods and services because each receives the same share of the society's wealth as any other individual, including professionals and political leaders.

To prevent slackers from taking advantage of this economically egalitarian society, the religion of solidarity comes into play, for it induces the selflessness "that is the logical outcome of the operation of human nature under rational conditions" (Bellamy 1926 [1888], 116). Malingering on the part of laborers is further deterred by putting shirkers on short rations: "A man able to do his duty, and persistently refusing, is sentenced to solitary confinement on bread and water till he consents" (p. 128). Such men are also exposed to public ridicule and are rejected by women. Denying misfits the possibility of love and marriage is, of course, a rough form of eugenics, for dissidents would be unable to reproduce themselves and perpetuate their "kind." Like the Social Darwinists of his day, Bellamy viewed character traits as inborn and believed that the morally as well as the physically unfit must be weeded out if human beings were to evolve to a higher state.

The leader of the industrial army is also the ruler of the state or president of the United States, leadership being the reward for distinguished service in the industrial army and compliance with all the rules and regulations mandated by the state. The several steps through which the position of general-in-chief of the industrial army is attained are each given a military rank. The industrial army is itself divided into ten guilds or groups of allied trades, each with a major general in charge. The general-in-chief must have risen through all the ranks from buck private or common laborer on up to major general. The president or general-in-chief is chosen indirectly by members of the honorary guild, elders who have already served time as generals of their guild and have been out of office for some years. Clearly intended as a version of Plato's philosopher king, the president is elected by a process Bellamy called "the suffrage" (p. 188). But he is elected undemocratically, for Bellamy specifically excluded members of the industrial army from the vote (p. 189). Women elect leaders of their own industrial guilds but have no voice whatsoever in the presidency. Politics was to be a male preserve, and Bellamy's version of the suffrage is a travesty of the universal suffrage for which feminists were striving in the nineteenth century. Bellamy's earlier support of woman suffrage fell by the wayside as he elaborated his socialist society with its underpinning of integral nationalism.

Where constructive service and devotion to duty is the key to status, women would seemingly find it easy to achieve equality with men. But, as Dr. Leete puts it, "They are under an entirely different discipline and constitute rather an allied force than an integral part of the army of men" (p. 258). Women are under an exclusively female regimen, led by a woman general-in-chief who cannot, however, attain the presidency of the United

States—a prohibition explained in part by Bellamy's belief that there are immutable differences between the sexes. These differences, considered part of the evolutionary process, are not only to be recognized but also to be cultivated, for they eventuate in the improvement of the species. To the extent that women may wish to transcend these differences, they are subject to harsh criticism. Dr. Leete, Bellamy's alter ego, maintains, "The lack of some such recognition of the distinct individuality of the sexes was one of the innumerable defects of your society" (p. 259). Dr. Leete castigates the feminist reformers of his day—those who believed in equality between the sexes—for seeking to obliterate the differences between the sexes rather than allowing them free play. The passions that attract the sexes to each other, Dr. Leete avers, obscure the profound differences that make members of each sex capable of sympathy only with their own. Dr. Leete is proud of the fact that in the year 2000, "we have given them [women] a world of their own, with its emulations, ambitions, and careers" (p. 259).

Domestic feminists of the early nineteenth century, such as Catharine Beecher, would have found his ideas to their liking. In 1847 Beecher published her *Treatise on Domestic Economy*, stating her belief that women's sensibilities were different from men's, and that women were not cut out to enter the male sphere in the world of either work or politics. She wanted women's domestic sphere to have higher status through a better education and working women to receive special protection because American women suffer from "a delicacy of constitution which renders them early victims of disease and decay" (Beecher 1972 [1847], 177). Certainly Beecher's goals are achieved in Bellamy's utopia, where women get equal pay for comparable work and have shorter working hours and more frequent vacations than men.

Feminists who believed in equality between the sexes articulated their disappointment with Bellamy's feminism. Mary H. Ford insisted that women be treated not as weaker vessels but as human beings capable of fully participating, on an equal basis with men, in the world's work. She was a feminist and a socialist who believed that women in public life could do much to challenge boss rule and machine politics (Ford 1891, 290–94).

Ford's critique was to the point. Bellamy was not proposing sex segregation in the interests of feminine self-identification and sisterhood—the only rationale feminists might find acceptable. His aim was not to provide potential women leaders with the opportunity to practice their untried capacities for exercising power free of male competition. Quite the reverse. To Bellamy, women segregated among their own were no "unnatural"

rivals of men (Bellamy 1926 [1888], 259), thus assuring not only the
survival but also the evolution of the species. Women's aspirations, Bellamy
implies, must give way when the male ego is at stake. According to Bellamy,
keeping women from competing with men would increase their power of
giving happiness to men.

None of Bellamy's female predecessors or contemporaries would have
condoned enforced wifehood and motherhood—but in Bellamy's utopia a
woman is not complete unless she is married and a mother. Both positive
and negative reinforcements are provided to induce women to opt for the
status of wife and mother. To ensure their economic independence from
their husbands (an issue Bellamy recognized as crucial), wives and mothers
receive their credits from the state even if motherhood requires them to
temporarily leave the work force. Added prestige and status are also in the
offing. Positions of leadership in the women's division of the industrial
army are closed to women who have not been wives and mothers, "as they
alone fully represent their sex" (p. 261).

Since only the wealthy had a chance for higher education in 1887, Dr.
Leete and Julian West invariably come around to an examination of the
utopian school system. Dr. Leete boasts that all people have the opportunity for higher education, and education is itself compulsory for everyone
between the ages of six and twenty-one. When West asks the obvious
question as to whether the expense of a college education is not wasted on
those who are not intellectually equipped to benefit from it, Dr. Leete
expounds on the three purposes served by equal education: "first, the right
of every man to the completest education the nation can give him on his
own account, as necessary to his enjoyment of himself; second, the right of
his fellow-citizens to have him educated, as necessary to their enjoyment of
his society; third, the right of the unborn to be guaranteed an intelligent
and refined parentage" (p. 222). The egalitarianism of the educational
system would be more convincing if Dr. Leete did not consistently describe
the recipients as men. Men *and* women are referred to only in the context of
physical education, which is a requirement of the system.

The limited extent to which Bellamy practiced his vaunted feminism in
Looking Backward is also revealed by the women's wardrobes. In the
nineteenth century, dress reform was a major feminist issue as women
realized they could not lead an active life wearing the hoop skirts, bustles,
and corsets that were in vogue. From 1856 to 1863, Lydia Sayer Hasbrouk
edited a feminist paper, *Sybil,* devoted exclusively to suffrage, temperance,
and dress reform. The chief contributor to the paper was Dr. Mary Walker,
who advocated short dresses and also endorsed the Amelia Bloomer tunic

outfit. She advised each woman "to make [herself] better acquainted with her physical organization that she might better be able to preserve her own health." She urged women to "throw aside their embroidery and read mental philosophy, moral science and physiology, and then go to a Smith's and have their dressical and dietitical chains severed that they may be free and sensible women" (Snyder 1962, 24). Disappointed that the short skirt did not catch on, Walker became even more controversial by wearing men's suits, which became the ultimate in avant-garde fashion.

Bellamy paid lip service to dress reform, but when Julian West opens his eyes to see his first example of twenty-first-century fashion, he finds Edith Leete's dress no different from that worn by his nineteenth-century fiancée, Edith Bartlett. Male attire is exactly the same as that worn in the nineteenth century (Bellamy 1926 [1888], 40).

Bellamy wanted his readers to recognize themselves in his utopia so they could identify with the men and women in it. Once the book was published and had attracted a host of feminist fans, he was willing to entertain the ideas of radical feminist fashion reformers like Dr. Walker. In *Equality* (1897), Bellamy goes into much greater detail on the subject of women's fashion. The long dresses, corsets, and hoop skirts of Bellamy's own day are virtually banished, as women's fashions combine utility with beauty. Although the making of women's clothing is still segregated in the women's work force, there is an infinite variety of styles, the only criterion being comfort. Women can choose styles from every age of history, from the loose free-flowing Greek and Roman style that Bellamy himself preferred, through the medieval style, to advanced contemporary styles like the Bloomer and Walker outfits. As she discusses the subject with Julian West, Edith Leete herself wears pants—a drastic departure from the Victorian dress she wore in *Looking Backward*.

In *Looking Backward* Edith Leete not only faithfully follows the fashions of Bellamy's own day, she also demonstrates traditional female nurturing traits. She comforts and supports West as he is initiated into twenty-first-century life. But as soon as the conversation turns to weighty matters like economics and politics, she scurries from the room, unable to participate in "man talk." If she is a productive member of the industrial army, nowhere is this indicated. If she is under twenty-one, why is she not attending college? In fact, she is at the beck and call of West, ever ready to reassure him about his state of mind. Having been freed from housework by the blessings of communal arrangements, Edith Leete is shown to do little work more strenuous than flower arranging (Bellamy 1926 [1888], 176). And far from being a producer of goods or a provider of services to society,

Edith Leete is an avid consumer of both the goods and services that exist in abundance in Bellamy's technocracy.

When West asks about shopping in the twenty-first century, Dr. Leete refers him to his daughter as the qualified expert in this matter. Each ward, Edith Leete explains, has a building somewhat analogous to the contemporary department store. The building contains only samples of the huge store of goods available to all citizens in good standing. After making her selections, Edith Leete calls a clerk who writes down the cost—payable with coupons from the individual credit card that is legal tender in utopia. The clerk then sends the order to a central warehouse via pneumatic tubes, and by the time Edith Leete reaches home all her purchases have been delivered. In this ultimate consumer society where saving is unpatriotic and unnecessary, the privileged women seem intended to find happiness and fulfillment through endless shopping sprees.

Although ostensibly a feminist and socialist, Bellamy was unable to transcend his middle-class and patriarchal attitudes in *Looking Backward*. The industrial army with its stern discipline is apparently meant, as already noted, for the immigrants whose frequent strikes unnerved proper Bostonians in the 1880s. Dr. Leete and his family act like members of a leisured class. The doctor has perfect rapport with Julian West, a wealthy and conservative Bostonian from the 1880s whose character was formed by a supposedly deplorable society. Dr. Leete is retired and thus has abundant leisure time to act as West's mentor. But he admits that professionals like himself are exempt from the industrial army. As a privileged caste in utopia, the professionals have their own governors in a board of regents over which the president and generals of the industrial army have no control. Physicians like Dr. Leete appear to serve primarily as mind manipulators (see the discussion of *Dr. Heidenhoff's Process*, below). Bellamy, the visionary who provided the gadgetry and technological advances that more than anything else delighted at least his female readers, had little faith that scientists could cure the diseases shadowing the lives of humankind—perhaps because he found them so deficient in treating the tuberculosis with which he was afflicted. He finesses the issue by assuring his readers that citizens of the future are a healthier species because they have discarded the oppressive economic conditions and polluted environment of the past (p. 43). Dr. Leete plies West with mysterious potions when he becomes too overwhelmed by his new surroundings. These drugs induce immediate sleep and ensure revitalization upon waking. Dr. Leete is not unlike Dr. Pillsbury, the "quack" calling himself a "Professor of Animal Magentism," who hypnotized Julian West into sleep and forgetfulness in the Boston of old.

When it comes to class and gender in Bellamy's new order, *plus ça change, plus c'est la même chose*. The Boston of the year 2000 would have been familiar to Bellamy's male readers, for women are to be found in their accustomed place. Because the women have been freed from household tasks, they have ample time and means for buying the goods this mechanized society produces in such abundance. Women's supreme accomplishment seems to be making men happy. Bellamy depicts a world through which women move uncomplainingly, with grace and style. But it is a world they had no part in making.

In *Looking Backward*, Bellamy does not deal with controversial issues that might have alienated his middle-class readers. In the decades preceding the publication of Bellamy's novel, the issue of free love created a lively debate among feminists. It was actively promoted by Marie Howland and by Victoria Woodhull and Tennessee Claflin, sisters who published their unorthodox ideas in their paper, *Woodhull and Claflin's Weekly*. An integral part of European socialist ideas, free love stipulated that both men and women enter a relationship purely for the sake of love, unencumbered by legal ties. Each would be free to reject the other when love ceased to be the binding force of their commitment. Elizabeth Cady Stanton and Susan B. Anthony exhibited sympathy for free love in *The Revolution*, the official organ of the NWSA. Marie Howland actively endorsed free love, and in her Social Palace there would be no distinction between legitimate and illegitimate children. But it was anathema to Bellamy's mostly moral minded followers, and so he ignored it.

All factions of the feminist movement advocated a greater frankness and candor between the sexes, and Dr. Leete maintains this ideal as a feature of his version of twenty-first-century America. Criticizing the artificiality that characterized relations between the sexes in West's time, Leete maintains that honesty and unconstraint have made the sexes more equal. Women, he asserts, can breach the proprieties of Julian West's day by avowing their love for a man before he makes known his intentions. "Coquettry would be as much despised in a girl as in a man," he maintains (pp. 255–56). Yet coquettish is an apt description of Edith Leete. She is demure, blushes when West casts inviting glances at her, and waits for West to proclaim his love for her before acknowledging that she has loved him all along. In this respect, too, she is no different from her Victorian ancestors.

Bellamy's treatment of class and gender is biased in favor of his middle-class and patriarchal outlook. His attitude toward race requires a different explanation. Living near Boston, the soul and center of abolitionism before the Civil War, Bellamy came to the conclusion that freeing the black slaves was the first stage toward the just society he foresaw in the twenty-first century. Bellamy was profoundly inspired by Thomas Wentworth Higginson, an ardent abolitionist who enlisted in the Union army and commanded the first all-black brigade in the war (Strauss 1982, 177). Higginson channeled his zeal into the feminist movement in the post–Civil War period, a time when he and Bellamy became close friends.

As opposed to the Irish and Italian immigrants who poured into Boston from the mid-nineteenth century on, blacks were not a threat to the dominance of the old line Bostonians. But Bellamy, a journalist, was acutely aware that racial conflict was a dark cloud hovering over the American landscape. In *Equality,* Julian West points out, "In my day, a peculiar complication of the social problem in America was the existence in the Southern States of many millions of recently freed slaves as yet unequal to the responsibilities of freedom" (Bellamy 1969 [1897], 364). Dr. Leete elaborates Bellamy's solution: blacks were destined for the industrial army, where they would receive the discipline, tempered with paternalistic benevolence, that would enable them to elevate themselves to the level of civilization already achieved by whites.

Bellamy was mindful of the sensibilities of an unexpected group of followers—farmers in the Populist party, who also felt victimized by capitalism. Many of the latter were Southerners, and Bellamy would not deprive them of their prejudices. When reminded of the existence of white racism, Dr. Leete remains unperturbed and insists "there was absolutely nothing in the system to offend that prejudice. . . . Even for industrial purposes the new system involved no more commingling of races than the old had done. It was perfectly consistent with any degree of race separation in industry which the most bigoted local prejudices might demand" (p. 365).

Women, who were second-class citizens in *Looking Backward*, moved up the social ladder in *Equality*. But blacks, completely ignored in *Looking Backward*, were expected to be as servile and submissive as they were under slavery. They had no future in what purported to be an egalitarian state. If Bellamy truly believed in racial inequality, his utopia is fatally flawed. More likely, Bellamy's waffling on women's rights and his outright rejection of racial equality reveal him to be an opportunist who trimmed his sails to the prevailing belief of his audience regarding race, class, and gender.

Bellamy did not have the depth of a futurist like H. G. Wells. He had such supreme faith in the benefits of science that he could never conceive, as Wells did, that scientific wonders could just as easily be used to destroy lives as to improve them. In addition, Bellamy did not consider the international ramifications of his utopia. He might have been an isolationist who adhered to the idea of "socialism in one country." More probably, he believed that the mission of the Founding Fathers had been derailed by alien elements but could be put back on the right track through Nationalism. When liberty and equality were restored in the United States, the rest of the world would realize that peaceful change was more durable than revolution and would follow the American example. In this, Bellamy was the quintessential American nationalist.

In his enthusiasm for efficiency and order, Bellamy could even contemplate turning people into machines. A sinister side to Bellamy's vision can be seen in his novels, short stories, and other writings. In his plan "A Reorganization of Society to Extirpate Sorrow," Bellamy wrote of the grief and unhappiness that accompany intimate relationships such as those between children and parents, between close friends, and between lovers. Since Bellamy believed that parental love was the greatest source of pain, he sought to eliminate it by restricting family ties. To foster impersonal relationships, Bellamy would take children away from their parents to be raised and educated by the state, making it easier to inculcate them with the mass religion of solidarity that transcends all personal relationships.

In *Looking Backward*, impersonal relationships are implicit. Dr. Leete and Mrs. Leete have no given names. The Leetes live as a conventional family but display a curious detachment from one another. No one seems to need any of the others, either for affection or companionship. Dr. Leete expresses more fatherly concern for Julian West than he does for his own daughter. The passion that West initially brings to his relationship with Edith Leete appears to derive from another world and another time, and Edith Leete's love for West is unconvincing, stemming as it does from the fact that he was her great-grandmother's fiancé. West is more like a prized heirloom than a man with whom she wishes to spend her life. There is no mention of consummating their love, and Edith Leete becomes an affable hostess to West as he continues his reeducation in *Equality*.

Another way of dispensing with sorrow, passion, grief, and guilt—the whole range of human emotions that people experience in the course of their lives—is elaborated in Bellamy's 1880 novel *Dr. Heidenhoff's Process*. Here Bellamy argues that memory is at the root of unhappiness and he would literally remove this function from the human brain. Dr. Heidenhoff explains: "Memory is the principle of moral degeneracy. Remembered sin [guilt] is the most utterly diabolical influence in the universe." In this novel, a woman consumed with guilt is offered by her lover for the experimental operation to eliminate the pain of thoughts associated with her past actions. Thought extirpation, Dr. Heidenhoff assures the lover, will bring about a moral revolution. In Dr. Heidenhoff's universe, consciousness would exist only in the present. In an eternal present, with memory removal done on a mass basis, solidarity and brotherhood could finally be achieved (a scenario that ominously foreshadows Zamyatin's famous dystopia *We,* in which acquiescence to a totally regimented and mechanized society is brought about through an operation that resembles a lobotomy). Heidenhoff predicts that a race of supermen would ensue who would exchange bondage to the past for the freedom of utopia (Bellamy 1969 [1880], 119ff.).

Bellamy also toyed with the idea that memory extirpation would enable people to live in a present suffused with brotherhood and solidarity. They would even find it unnecessary to communicate verbally. This theme appears in several of his stories, in which individuals are capable of putting themselves in the place of another, with perfect sympathy and understanding following. Feelings can be taken for granted and need not be expressed, or can be expressed through a kind of telepathy. Bellamy maintained that were this to be achieved, the species would have evolved to its highest stage.

In *Looking Backward,* Bellamy stuck resolutely to the problems of his world and his time. The novel acquired an immense following for Bellamy among middle-class men and women who could identify with the Leetes and imaginatively realize their destiny as the leaders of this utopia. To his disciples, Bellamy's nationalist religion might have seemed like another Evangelical Awakening. Although the Founding Fathers studiously avoided any mention of economic equality, Bellamy claimed that his socialism—equality for all—had its origin in the Declaration of Independence. Bellamy's socialism thus seemed consistent with an American tradition that rooted for the underdog and put great store in fair play and "justice for all." But when one factors in aspects of Bellamy's agenda in large part unacknowledged in *Looking Backward*—the state as deity; individualism denounced; a docile army of immigrant and women workers who have no memory of past injustice and are ruled over by an elite completely impersonal and indifferent in their attitudes to their charges; women who must be childbearers to be accepted into the society and who must further assume the responsibility for a policy of eugenics by rejecting as husbands those men deemed unfit; no durable family ties; officially condoned race and gender discrimination; an absence of conscience to prevent guilt feelings;

no verbal communication (the ultimate in thought control)—all these factors gleaned from Bellamy's writings suggest that his utopia is, in fact, disconcertingly similar to such dystopias as Zamyatin's *We*, George Orwell's *Nineteen Eighty-Four*, and Aldous Huxley's *Brave New World*.[4]

The sales of *Looking Backward* are testimony to its popularity. After a slow start, sales in the United States shot up to almost 214,000 between 1888 and 1890. By 1897, approximately 400,000 copies had been sold. *The Nationalist*, a reform journal inspired by *Looking Backward*, began publication in 1888 and circulated Bellamy's ideas to an ever-widening audience. *Looking Backward* prompted the publication of at least eleven other reform journals, including (after the demise of *The Nationalist* in 1891) *The New Nation*, edited by Bellamy himself (Lipow 1982, 30). Library circulation was phenomenal and millions of copies derived from numerous editions were published around the world.[5] The Bellamy or Nationalist clubs founded soon after *Looking Backward* was published were forums for discussing Bellamy's ideas, and also promoted sales of the book.

The first Nationalist Club was established in Boston in 1888 under the aegis of the staunch male feminist, Thomas Wentworth Higginson. The locale was considered a good omen by Bellamy, because of its association with the Boston Tea Party. The abolitionist movement had also been centered there, so it seemed appropriate that this final movement for the people's liberation should emanate from the same place. The objective of the Boston Bellamy Club was " 'the elevation of man' through the dissemination of the 'view . . . set forth in *Looking Backward*' " (Bowman 1958, 124). In 1891, there were no fewer than 165 Nationalist clubs stretching from coast to coast all spreading the Gospel according to Bellamy.

The female contingent in the Boston (Bellamy) Club included Mary Livermore and Frances Willard—suffragists and leaders of the Women's Christian Temperance Union (WCTU); Lucy Stone, first leader of the AWSA; and Abby Morton Diaz, already discussed as the author of one of the harbingers of *Looking Backward, The Schoolmaster's Trunk*. All were willing to set aside their misgivings about the lack of the suffrage and the gender segregation in utopia. Livermore and Willard were deeply disappointed that Bellamy allowed sipping of wine and smoking in utopia.

What drew them to Bellamy? All of the aforementioned women are identified by Dolores Hayden (1981) as materialist feminists who believed in domestic science and considered women's release from housework a major priority. These women, active in the public sphere, were convinced that their homebound sisters were thirsting for greater intellectual challenges than housework and routinized child care afforded. Abby Morton

Diaz and Marie Howland transmitted their ideas through male characters, evidently thinking that male support was essential to the achievement of their goals. Bellamy appeared to them an "understanding man" who mainstreamed their ideas and made them part of a national crusade.

Frances Willard started corresponding with Bellamy in 1887 regarding a manifesto on Nationalism that she wished to publish. In her presidential address to the WCTU in 1888, Willard urged the members to read *Looking Backward*. She was particularly impressed with the social solidarity in utopia and looked forward to the time when " 'We, us and company' can agree to organize one 'trust' in our own interest, whose dividend will be declared, and whose combinations concentrated for the greatest numbers' greatest good" (Bordin 1986, 146). Bellamy resolved one of Willard's greatest dilemmas—how to rid the country of exploitative capitalists without violence. Bellamy promised a peaceful transition and orderly change.

Mary Livermore was a veritable dynamo who showed her administrative abilities during the Civil War, when she went to work for the United States Sanitary Commission. The work involved fund-raising, inspection tours of military hospitals, and distribution of food and medical supplies to the Union Army. Livermore demonstrated her rhetorical skills after the Civil War by her suffrage speeches and her support for temperance. Livermore and Willard were charismatic leaders who integrated suffrage and temperance into the feminist movement.

Livermore used *The Woman's Journal*, the house organ of the AWSA, to propagate her conviction that cooperative housekeeping was the key to harmony and well-being. Since previous community housekeeping experiments had been done on a small scale, Livermore warmly endorsed Bellamy's evolutionary socialism, where an entire society was based on domestic science. Both Livermore and Willard were inclined toward millenarianism. They looked forward to a future of justice and harmony through the intervention of a highly centralized state, which Bellamy provided. Livermore was extremely compelling when she asserted: "For ages, the world has carried in its heart a dream of a better day for the race and a vision of a divine far-off civilization when peace and love shall displace strife and hate. . . . The future is radiant with its coming glory . . . the whole humanity is slowly but surely moving forward to where it beckons" (Livermore 1897, 609). Bellamy's utopia was such a promised land, and both Livermore and Willard were convinced that citizens who had gained economic security and a bountiful life would cease to crave liquor.

In 1890, Charlotte Perkins Gilman joined one of the Bellamy Clubs and quickly became a featured speaker. Novelist, essayist, editor, short-story writer, and poet, Gilman is generally regarded as the most influential woman thinker of the pre–World War I generation and the most advanced of the materialist feminists, according to Dolores Hayden (1981). Gilman insisted on her own right and the right of all women of all classes to be treated as human beings—not as decorative objects if middle class, virtual slaves if workers. She further claimed for women the right to choose their own work and the right to be producers rather than merely consumers, for productive women were independent women. Gilman maintained that "economic independence for women necessarily involves a change in the home and family relation. But if that change is for the advantage of industry and race, we need not fear it. It does not involve a change in the marriage relation except in withdrawing the element of economic dependence" (Gilman 1972 [1898], 598).

During the two years she was a Bellamyite, and later through travel, Gilman developed the ideas that brought a mass audience to her own book *Women and Economics,* published in 1898. Gilman readily adopted the idea of communal housekeeping and believed, like Bellamy, that women's labor must be paid, not philanthropic. But she rejected Bellamy's conviction that the physical differences between men and women meant they must lead segregated work lives.

As revealed in *Looking Backward,* Bellamy believed that males and females had evolved in different directions and that their distinctive features should be preserved. Gilman believed that the inferior position of women and their association with such characteristics as weakness, passivity, and nurturance, were an evolutionary aberration, the result of women's age-old dependence on men. The fiction that women could only be nurturers and mothers, Gilman maintained, deprived society of valuable talents and did irreparable damage to women who were no more suited to devoting their lives to motherhood than all men were to fatherhood. In the last analysis, she believed that women who were kept in their domestic sphere were hindering human progress, and she encouraged women to become preachers.

While Bellamy maintained conventional family relationships, tentative though they were, Gilman, like Marie Howland, felt that women encumbered with child-caring concerns were neither good workers nor good mothers. According to Gilman, "The mother as a social servant instead of a home servant will not lack in true mother duty. She will love her child as well, perhaps better, when she is not in hourly contact with it, when she goes from its life to her own life and back from her own life to its life, with ever new delight and power. She can keep the deep, thrilling joy of motherhood far fresher in her heart, far more vivid and open in voice and eyes and tender hands, when the hours of individual work give her mind another channel for her own part of the day" (Gilman 1972 [1898], 598).

Although the Bellamy clubs provided a forum for daring ideas such as those put forth by Gilman, they were both exclusive and impeccably middle class, which is the way Bellamy wanted it. His goal, and his explicit aim in writing *Looking Backward*, as he proclaimed in 1888, was to convert the cultured and educated classes (Bowman 1958, 124). Constitutions of the Bellamy clubs stipulated that members be elected, and only individuals who could devote time and money or lend personal prestige to the clubs were accepted. Bellamy clubs sought men who had been successful in the professional or business world and individuals of either sex who were both educated and progressive-minded. The club constitutions specifically excluded the foreign born, the uneducated, and zealots, and automatically rejected debtors.

Bellamy was acutely conscious of the critics who faulted him for the authoritarianism that was pervasive in his utopia and for failing to provide a convincing plan for the peaceful evolution he had promised. He answered his critics in *Equality*. Bellamy characteristically responded to events instead of staking out and rationalizing a philosophical position. In 1890 the NWSA and AWSA reunited to form the National American Woman Suffrage Association (NAWSA) and resumed their efforts for the suffrage. Thus Bellamy gave women the suffrage in *Equality*. He also implied equal intellectual capacities between the sexes by allowing schoolgirls as well as boys to explain the intricacies of the political and economic system to a Julian West still agog and receptive. Realizing that women could be critical of revealed religion, à la Elizabeth Cady Stanton, he gave them the credit for making the transition to utopia a nonviolent one by their conversions to the religion of solidarity (Bellamy 1969 [1897], 143). Bellamy alienated his devoted followers in the WCTU because he rejected their goal of curbing drinking through legislation. It is likely, however, that political motives caused him to distance himself from the WCTU women. His Populist party followers, who were incorporating Bellamy's anticapitalist stance into their party platform, were opposed to temperance.

It is unlikely that either Bellamy's concessions or his contradictions were noted. The Bellamy boom was surprisingly short. In the early 1890s it started to decline and by 1894 had been spent. Bellamy was unable to capitalize on the concessions he made to the Populist farmers, since he died in 1898, a year after *Equality* was published. Bellamy's middle-class followers, both male and female, drifted into the Progressive movement.

Equal rights feminists such as Elizabeth Cady Stanton who were prominent in the NWSE were never impressed with Bellamy, and Stanton herself pointedly refused to join a Bellamy Club. Bellamy attacked the equal rights wing of the feminist movement in *Equality*. He was irked that women put the onus of their oppression on men and explained that it was "the system . . . which was the cause of the whole evil" (p. 133), apparently overlooking the fact that men ran the system.

Although Stanton appreciated the urgency of a radical transformation in the relations of labor and capital (Nies 1977, 91), she distrusted an all-powerful state and would not dismiss working-class and woman suffrage as cavalierly as Bellamy had done in *Looking Backward*. She maintained her faith that through the suffrage all women would be able to forge ahead, just as men had done. Stanton condoned neither the gender segregation and the elitism of *Looking Backward* nor the racism evident in *Equality*.

The Bellamy phenomenon was a fad, a popular response to troubled times. *Looking Backward* gained its enormous success because Bellamy was an expert at the sort of self-promotion that today is called media hype. This explains why Henry George, Bellamy's contemporary, who in *Progress and Poverty* (1880) proposed a redistribution of wealth simply and immediately through the single tax, was virtually ignored.

Nevertheless, Bellamy reflected and expressed an enduring American optimism and faith in science as a panacea to society's ills. Despite the fact that two world wars have revealed in a singular way the destructive capacity of science, despite the acknowledged effects of toxic wastes, acid rain, and other types of pollution on the environment, Americans' abiding faith in the benefits of science and technology, their belief in the malleability of human nature, remain undiminished and have kept Edward Bellamy in the public eye throughout the twentieth century. It is quite likely that in the year 2000, Americans will measure their material progress by the criteria Bellamy established.

Notes

1. For a detailed account of the male feminists, see Sylvia Strauss (1982).
2. William Leach (1980) describes in detail the numerous women's societies, and the diversity of their agendas, that were formed in the latter half of the nineteenth century and makes clear women's interest in moving into the public sphere.
3. For a detailed account of women and religion, see Aileen S. Kraditor (1965).
4. For other discussions of Bellamy's authoritarianism, see John L. Thomas (1983) and Arthur Lipow (1982).
5. For Bellamy's influence in other countries, see Sylvia E. Bowman (1962).

90 SYLVIA STRAUSS

Works Cited

Beecher, Catharine. 1972 [1847]. "On the Peculiar Responsibilities of American Women." In *Roots of Bitterness*, edited by Nancy F. Cott. New York: E. P. Dutton & Co.
Bellamy, Edward. 1926 [1888]. *Looking Backward*. Reprint. Boston: Houghton Mifflin.
———. 1969 [1880]. *Dr. Heidenhoff's Process*. Reprint. New York: AMS Press.
———. 1969 [1897]. *Equality*. Reprint. Westport, Conn.: Greenwood Press.
Bordin, Ruth. 1986. *Frances Willard: A Biography*. Chapel Hill: University of North Carolina Press.
Bowman, Sylvia E. 1958. *The Year 2000: A Critical Biography of Edward Bellamy*. New York: Bookman Associates.
———, et al. 1962. *Edward Bellamy Abroad: An American Prophet's Influence*. New York: Twayne.
Diaz, Abby Morton. 1874. *The Schoolmaster's Trunk*. Boston: James R. Osgood.
Douglas, Ann. 1977. *The Feminization of American Culture*. New York: Knopf.
Ford, Mary H. 1891. *Who Wins? A Story of Social Conditions*. New York: Lee and Shepherd.
George, Henry. 1929 [1880]. *Progress and Poverty*. New York: Robert Schalkenbach Foundation.
Gilman, Charlotte Perkins. 1972 [1898]. "Women and Economics." In *The Feminist Papers*, edited by Alice S. Rossi. New York: Columbia University Press.
Hayden, Dolores. 1981. *The Grand Domestic Revolution: A History of Feminist Designs for American Homes, Neighborhoods, and Cities*. Cambridge: MIT Press.
Howland, Marie. 1874. *Papa's Own Girl*. New York: John P. Jewett.
Kraditor, Aileen S. 1965. *The Ideas of the Woman Suffrage Movement, 1890–1920*. New York: Columbia University Press.
Leach, William. 1980. *True Love and Perfect Union: The Feminist Reform of Sex and Society*. New York: Basic Books.
Lipow, Arthur. 1982. *Authoritarian Socialism in America: Edward Bellamy and the Nationalist Movement*. Berkeley: University of California Press.
Livermore, Mary. 1897. *The Story of My Life*. New York: A. D. Worthington & Co.
Nies, Judith. 1977. *Seven Women: Portraits from the American Radical Tradition*. New York: Viking Press.
Snyder, Charles McCool. 1962. *Dr. Mary Walker: The Little Lady in Pants*. New York: Vintage Press.
Stanton, Elizabeth Cady. 1972 [1895]. "Introduction to the Woman's Bible," part 1. In *The Feminist Papers*, edited by Alice S. Rossi. New York: Columbia University Press.
Strauss, Sylvia. 1982. *"Traitors to the Masculine Cause": The Men's Campaign for Women's Rights*. Westport, Conn.: Greenwood Press.
Thomas, John L. 1983. *Alternative America: Henry George, Edward Bellamy, Henry Demarest Lloyd and the Adversary Tradition*. Cambridge: Harvard University Press/Belknap Press.

Bellamy and Technology: Reconciling Centralization and Decentralization

HOWARD P. SEGAL

Looking Backward is at least as much about technology and its use and abuse as it is about cooperation, corruption, and socialism. Yet this basic fact has frequently been overlooked or minimized. No less important, the role of technology in *Looking Backward,* which this essay will try to illuminate, is complex and subtle and reveals new dimensions of Bellamy's scheme.

Technology is at once a principal cause of and solution to the problems Bellamy identifies throughout the book: inefficiency (overproduction and underproduction, idle capital and labor, excessive competition, and mismanagement); inequality (of opportunity and of income); immorality (greed, monopoly, and exploitation); and urban blight (slums, crowding, disease, poverty, and child labor). The purposeful, positive use of technology—from improved factories and offices to new highways and electric lighting systems to innovative pneumatic tubes, electronic broadcasts, and credit cards—is, in fact, critical to the predicted transformation of the United States from a living hell into a heaven on earth.

More specifically, the United States of the year 2000 is very much a technological utopia: an allegedly ideal society not simply dependent upon tools and machines, or even worshipful of them, but outright modeled after them. In some respects the citizens of Bellamy's paradise seem to be quite willing cogs in the new industrial order, and their carefully regimented lives seem happily to emulate the mechanized processes that have helped to create their world.

Bellamy, however, believed he was describing a society in which greater freedom and creativity (and spirituality) would exist than was possible in his own society—itself an example of "bad" management and moral disorder. As his fictional spokesman Mr. Smith replies to a skeptical "lover of freedom" in a Bellamy essay defending his Nationalist scheme:

I wish to acknowledge the assistance of Professors John Thomas of Brown University and Cecelia Tichi of Vanderbilt University in the preparation of this essay.

Well, aren't we parts of a great industrial machine now. The only difference is that the present machine is a bungling and misconstructed one, which grinds up the bodies and souls of those who work in it, and turns out poverty, prostitution, insanity and suicide as its finished products, while the new machine will be scientifically constructed, with an equal view to the comfort of the workers and the increase of the product. (Bellamy 1969 [1938], 45–46)

Indeed, the continuous "scientific" management of all citizens from birth to death is as critical to utopian society's well-being as are the tools and machines that surround them. Management of people, as epitomized by the industrial army, is as much an integral part of modern technology as the "hardware" itself. That bureaucracies in highly technological societies like our own epitomize *mis*management and *in*efficiency should not obscure their place in Bellamy's day as exemplars of the very opposite trends: as paragons of a new civic and industrial order leading ultimately to utopia.

Technological societies do not, moreover, have to be identical in design, appearance, shape, or size. Instead, it is a hallmark of modern technology to provide choices in these matters. Consequently, alternatives can and, by now, do exist. Principal among such alternatives are those of centralization versus decentralization. Where it has long been assumed that modern technology requires ever greater centralization of both facilities and personnel, recent critics—above all the late E. F. Schumacher and his disciples—have argued otherwise (Schumacher 1973; McRobie 1981). They have demonstrated that modern technology can and ought to be made "appropriate" to different economic, social, cultural, and political contexts. Much of their work has dealt with "underdeveloped" countries, but the general notion of appropriate technology has international applications. It is a relative term with varied meanings.

Moreover, any number of enthusiasts for computers, word processors, electronic mail, video display terminals, and other components of the current "information revolution" have claimed decentralization as their own position. For them, however, the key is not so much the smaller scale of operations, as with Schumacher, as the ability to work in or near one's home and to make decisions far away from the central office. The vision of an "electronic cottage" in Alvin Toffler's work (1980) is nevertheless at least as utopian as any of the schemes in Schumacher's writings. In both cases decentralization is deemed a positive development if not an outright panacea.

Decentralization, then, is a multifaceted term. Any one of its manifestations, however, does not necessarily translate into another: spatial separation, for example, may be large or small in scale and may be democratic or nondemocratic in operation. Hence the recent concern for the welfare of geographically isolated but often closely monitored workers in "electronic cottages"—whether their own homes or small offices or factories—who may be exploited as much as were workers centuries ago in the original cottage industries in England and elsewhere. Likewise, small-scale appropriate technology projects may not be havens of democracy in decision making either. The same instruments that have created the information revolution and that in turn have made decentralization a reality can thus be used to enslave as well as to liberate, just as with so many prior technological devices.

Consequently, the values and practices of decentralization in one sense of the term or in one situation may nowadays conflict with those in another sense or in another situation. Put differently, the current image of pure decentralization may conceal lingering centralization, with some of the ills associated with it.

To be sure, *Looking Backward*'s technology clearly predates contemporary "high-tech" devices. And like most other prophets of technological utopia, Bellamy's imagination in at least this respect was outrun by actual developments long before the date given for utopia's realization. If, however, high tech's parlance can be applied retroactively, Bellamy's pneumatic tubes, electronic broadcasts, electric lighting systems, and credit cards, among other technological marvels, were surely "state-of-the-art" for turn-of-the-century America.

More pertinent here is the presence throughout the book of subtle tensions between technology-based centralization and decentralization akin to those contemporary ones noted above. The situations are not, of course, identical, and the tensions in *Looking Backward* do not produce overt conflict, where those of our time probably will. If anything, in Bellamy's scheme, these tensions are the (almost) inevitable result of his attempt to create, administer, protect, and refine a huge utopian community of national dimensions supposedly catering to the needs and desires of its millions of individual citizens as well as to those of society in general. Indeed, Bellamy was not unaware of the communitarians of the antebellum period and was sympathetic toward their own crusades. As he observed retrospectively in 1892, "In a broad sense of the word the Nationalist movement did arise fifty years ago" in the form of "the Brook Farm Colony and a score of phalansteries for communistic [communal] experiments." But then the overriding concern for ending slavery redirected the energies of "these humane enthusiasts" (Bellamy 1892, 743). Now the time for such small-scale enterprises had, for better or for worse, passed. Although their avowedly decentralized schemes were not wholly outdated, they nonetheless had to take new forms amid the changes that had occurred since their heyday.

On the one hand, then, technology as depicted in *Looking Backward* has led to centralization in the form of the overall administration of society (the industrial army); of society's decision-making processes (the president of the United States and the other top administrators of the industrial army's "ten great departments"); of its production, distribution, and consumption facilities (its department stores and warehouses); of its domestic enterprises (cooking, dining, laundering, and tailoring); and of its large urban apartment complexes. But on the other hand, technology has led to decentralization in the form of widely separated towns and villages; of smaller-scale department stores and warehouses near them; of electronic broadcasting systems (through music from music halls and sermons from churches in each city wired to home telephones); and of dining facilities within individual apartments (for meals other than dinner).

Technology, then, has spurred centralization and decentralization alike. Moreover, several of these developments in themselves mix centralizing and decentralizing tendencies. Whatever tensions might result from such a mixture would for Bellamy be a modest price to pay for the perfection of his overall scheme. And those tensions would be minimized by technology as well. Without the various technological devices and accompanying social arrangements cited above, his scheme would have been far less realistic and, presumably, far less appealing.

Using technology in these and other forms, Bellamy, I believe, also sought a balance—and a minimal tension—between collectivism and individualism, homogeneity and heterogeneity, wholesale equality and equality of opportunity, industrialism and agrarianism, cities and towns/villages, and population concentration and dispersal. As John Thomas has observed about one dimension of Bellamy and his contemporaries Henry George and Henry Demarest Lloyd, "their working model of the good society [w]as a composite of city and country," or a "vision of an urban-rural continuum running from village neighborhoods to gateway cities" (Thomas 1983, 359). In this as in other respects Bellamy's ideals were not unique to him. I have elsewhere identified more than a score of other prophets of technological utopia who published their visions between 1883 and 1933 and who were frequently influenced by *Looking Backward*'s themes and, no less important, by its exceptional popularity. All agreed on the basic values, design, and organization of future society (Segal 1985).

Why should Bellamy have attained fame and influence while his fellow technological utopians remained obscure? One possible explanation is simply that Bellamy, a seasoned writer, wrote better. A second explanation is that he wrote just at the onset of what has been termed the late nineteenth-century crisis of confidence in America, where all but one of the rest of them wrote during or after its peak. A third and complementary explanation is that imitations of *Looking Backward*, or unauthorized sequels to it, as were most of these works, could hardly generate the enthusiasm of the original. A final and deeper explanation, which excludes none of the other three, is that the emphasis of *Looking Backward* on cooperation and community as well as on technological advance offered a more balanced and more appealing vision than the strictly materialist focus of nearly all the other works. That this balance would be socially engineered and technologically based is exactly my point.

More broadly, *Looking Backward* may now be seen as a pioneering attempt to offer an alternative to the increasingly urban, industrialized, and—yes, centralized—America emerging in Bellamy's day. His was not, however, a conventional conservative critique calling for a wholesale return to farms and to agrarian values. But neither was it a conventional radical critique, seeking unadulterated socialism and workers' control. Instead, Bellamy provided a middle ground between these and the other "extremes" noted earlier, and repeatedly used what was then modern (or even futuristic) technology—as, again, both hardware and management—to try to effect it. Insofar as the course of modern technology in America and elsewhere has, with few exceptions, led routinely toward centralization of structure and decision making and toward ever larger scale and size, Bellamy's overall scheme may be more pertinent today than most of his otherwise outdated particulars would suggest.

The design and layout of Bellamy's utopia embodies and illuminates these objectives. The envisioned domestication of both technology and nature will resolve the tension that Leo Marx, among others, has deemed irresolvable: the tension between the industrial and the agrarian orders, between the machine and the garden, a tension that Marx believes lies at the heart of the American experience (Marx 1964; Segal 1977). Bellamy (and the other technological utopians) would resolve the tension by the modernization rather than abandonment of the garden, by transporting it out of the

wilderness and relocating it in the city—a city itself to be transformed from
a lethal chaos into a healthy order. As Julian West describes the Boston of
the year 2000:

> At my feet lay a great city. Miles of broad streets, shaded by trees and lined
> with fine buildings, for the most part not in continuous blocks but set in larger or
> smaller enclosures, stretched in every direction. Every quarter contained large
> open squares filled with trees, along which statues glistened and fountains
> flashed in the late-afternoon sun. Public buildings of a colossal size and architec-
> tural grandeur unparalleled in my day raised their stately piles on every side.
> Surely I had never seen this city nor one comparable to it before. Raising my eyes
> at last toward the horizon, I looked westward. That blue ribbon winding away to
> the sunset—was it not the sinuous Charles? I looked east—Boston harbor
> stretched before me within its headlands, not one of its green islets missing.
> (Bellamy 1982 [1888], 55)

The new "industrialized garden" does not, then, take the form of Leo
Marx's "middle landscape" or of Jefferson's ideal of an agrarian-based yet
technologically proficient yeoman republic. Rather, it takes the form of a
series of what have since been termed megalopolises: massive combinations
of urban and suburban tracts covering vast areas. As West recounts in
Equality (1897), Bellamy's sequel to *Looking Backward:*

> Still we swept on mile after mile, league after league, toward the interior, and
> still the surface below presented the same parklike aspect that had marked the
> immediate environs of the city. Every natural feature appeared to have been
> idealized and all its latent meaning brought out by the loving skill of some
> consummate landscape artist, the works of man blending with the face of Nature
> in perfect harmony. . . . "How far does this park extend?" I demanded at last.
> "There seems no end to it." "It extends to the Pacific Ocean," said the doctor.
> "Do you mean that the whole United States is laid out in this way?" "Not
> precisely in this way by any means, but in a hundred different ways according to
> the natural suggestions of the face of the country and the most effective way of
> co-operating with them." (Bellamy 1897, 296)

The megalopolises are tributes not only to philosophical ingenuity,
which reconciles machine to garden and centralization to decentralization,
but also to the scientific planning of which Bellamy and the other technological utopians are so proud. Here millions of persons live, learn, work,
and play in perfect comfort, contentment, and happiness, ever free of dirt,
noise, chaos, want, and insecurity. As Bellamy wrote in his Postscript to the
second edition of *Looking Backward,* the work, "although in form a fanciful

romance, is intended, in all seriousness, as a forecast, in accordance with the principles of evolution, of the next stage in the industrial and social development of humanity" (Bellamy 1982 [1888], 232).

Such scientific planning is not, of course, limited to the physical environment but also extends to the administration of society and to the rest of the social and cultural environment. As West confesses with envy to Dr. Leete, his guide through utopia, "nowadays everybody is a part of a system with a distinct place and function. I am outside the system, and don't see how I can get in" (p. 137). West's sense of alienation is, of course, temporary, and his visit shortly thereafter to a huge city warehouse confirms the practicality of a society that balances centralization and decentralization, collective and individual needs and desires, in this as in most other areas: "It is like a gigantic mill, into the hopper of which goods are being constantly poured by the trainload and shipload, to issue at the other end in packages of pounds and ounces, yards and inches, pints and gallons, corresponding to the infinitely complex personal needs of half a million people" (p. 139).

I do not wish to ignore Bellamy's repeated emphasis on solidarity, on virtually forced cooperation, and on militarylike discipline. Lines like the following are still chilling to read even when so much else of the book seems overly sentimental and contrived:

> Well now, Mr. West, the organization of the industry of the nation under a single control, so that all its processes interlock, has multiplied the total product over the utmost that could be done under the former system. . . . The effectiveness of the working force of a nation, under the myriad-headed leadership of private capital, even if the leaders were not mutual enemies, as compared with that which it attains under a single head, may be likened to the military efficiency of a mob, or a horde of barbarians with a thousand petty chiefs, as compared with that of a disciplined army under one general—such a fighting machine, for example, as the German army in the time of Von Moltke. (Pp. 176–77)

Yet *Looking Backward* cannot be reduced to an early totalitarian utopia on the order of *Nineteen Eighty-Four* or *We*, notwithstanding Arthur Lipow's recent study (1982). An avowed democratic socialist and severe critic of the bureaucratic stultification of much of modern socialism, Lipow reads *Looking Backward* as a literary blueprint for what he calls authoritarian socialism and the Nationalist movement as its political embodiment. He treats the technocratic hostility toward politics, the envisioned industrial army, the distrust of workers and undisciplined masses, and the obsession with submerging individuality into a mystical whole as antecedents of

twentieth-century communism and fascism alike. Surely such an interpretation at once exaggerates these visionaries' hidden agenda and gives
them considerably greater foresight and influence upon genuine authoritar-
ians than they deserve.

Still, Bellamy and his fellow Nationalists were not simply well-meaning
democratic reformers who blended easily into the Populist and Progressive
crusades—themselves, of course, the subjects of revisionist historical analysis in recent years. Their traditional image as genteel middle-class reformers frightened by contemporary crowding, corruption, strikes, disorder, and other social ills does not account for the particular spatial,
organizational, and cultural dimensions of *Looking Backward* and related
utopian writings of the same period. Nor does it put their crusade into
proper historical perspective.

In the final chapter of his book *Alternative America* (1983), Thomas has
outlined what he aptly terms "the legacy" of Bellamy, George, and Lloyd.
Their individual and collective influence ranged from Scientific Management and Technocracy to regionalism and the Tennessee Valley Authority,
from elitist to grass-roots economic and social planning, and from right-
wing to left-wing political schemes. Nearly all, however, either used or
would have used technology to create a balance between centralization and
decentralization in the manner described earlier. This "adversary tradition," as Thomas calls it, "was not simply an exercise in nostalgia but the
climactic expression of an American 'third way'" (Thomas 1983, 364)
between geographical, economic, political, social, and cultural extremes. It
was also, I suggest, a multifaceted and not always systematic attempt to
accommodate preindustrial values and ways of life to emerging industrial
"modern" society. *Looking Backward* may not have directly inspired all of
these reformers, but, as the following case study will suggest, it certainly
anticipated many of their later efforts.

Among the most interesting and explicit expressions of this phenomenon—and one with which Thomas does not deal—are the "village industry" experiments developed by automaker Henry Ford and his associates
between 1918 and 1944. Ford is commonly associated with many diverse
aspects of twentieth-century American life—from peace crusades to square
dance revivals to eclectic museums—but large-scale, heavily centralized,
and predominantly urban systems of mass production are surely foremost
among them. No American contributed more than Ford to the development of giant factories and assembly lines.

Yet Ford was a complex man whose cultural and social values frequently
conflicted with and even undermined his business practices. The farm boy

whose mechanical skills led him into the manufacture of the very vehicles that threatened the agrarian way of life he cherished never resolved his mixed feelings about modernity, above all the heterogeneity, impersonality, and materialism of twentieth-century America's industrial cities. But rather than renounce outright either large cities or the large industries that helped bring them about, Ford devised various means of coping with these ills: from periodic retreats to the countryside, to the lifelong embrace of farmers (particularly those who had purchased Ford tractors), to the collection of innumerable agricultural as well as industrial artifacts at Dearborn beginning in the 1920s, and, not least, to the establishment of nineteen "village industries" in southern Michigan to manufacture and/or assemble parts for cars.

When lumped together with those other odds and ends of Ford's colorful life, the village industries can easily be characterized as merely antiquarian and nostalgic efforts to "freeze" history, as flights from reality having no relevance to Ford's own time, much less to ours. But this is a gross simplification. Whatever Ford's other motives for their establishment may have been—whether, say, for profits or for public relations—the village industries were intended by him as serious experiments: as small-scale, widely dispersed, frequently pastoral alternatives to the huge urban industrial systems characteristic of modern technological society, the very systems Ford himself had helped devise. More precisely, they represent pioneering experiments in decentralized technology and society going well beyond anything Bellamy conceived but reflecting the values of *Looking Backward*—this despite it being a book Ford almost certainly never read and may not have known about.

Set along the often picturesque Rouge (7 sites), Raisin (5), Huron (4), Saline (2), and Clinton (1) rivers in southeastern Michigan—none of them more than sixty miles from Ford world headquarters in Dearborn—these communities were all either self-contained or adjuncts of nearby small communities (Ford Motor Company 1936). As William Simonds, a Ford publicist, described them in 1927, "Industrialism does not necessarily mean hideous factories of dirty brick, belching smoke stacks and grimy workmen crowded into ramshackle hovels." Instead, "The little Ford plants are placed in leafy bowers and surrounded with flowering shrubs, green bushes and trees. The spots you would select for a picnic Henry Ford has picked for factory sites" (Simonds 1927, 653).

The village industries varied considerably not just in type of automobile part manufactured and/or assembled on the premises but also in building design and in size of work force. Some, like the first two, Northville (which began operations in 1920) and Nankin Mills (1921), were reconstructed nineteenth-century mills, usually abandoned grist mills. Others, however, like the next two, Phoenix (1922) and Plymouth (1923), had completely new, modern buildings, though sometimes on the site of former grist mills. Sharon Hollow (1939) had the smallest work force, ranging between 17 and 19 employees; Ypsilanti (1932) had the largest, between 740 and 1,500. Most of these workers were men, but several locations had at least a few women, and Phoenix's work force was over 90 percent female.

Ford's dream was to employ exclusively farmers, craftsmen, and other rural folk who could either walk or quickly drive (their Fords!) to work. For the most part this aspect of his vision was realized, and few urban dwellers, including city-bred workers in older Ford plants, were ever hired. Instead, the largely rural-bred workers in the nineteen sites were strongly encouraged to retain or acquire a plot of land on which to grow crops for personal consumption in their spare time: that is, before and after working hours and during their days off. These full-time factory workers were, then, also part-time farmers and, Ford claimed, beneficiaries of the very modern technology at work and at home alike that allowed them the leisure to supplement their income.

Despite the clear differences between the village industries and conventional branch automobile plants, the former were nevertheless integral parts of the Ford Motor Company. All were directly linked, in terms of both production and transportation, to the huge Highland Park and Rouge complexes Ford had already created near Detroit. The raw materials and finished products therefore had to be small and light enough to be transported efficiently from Highland Park and Rouge to and from the village industries (and sometimes between the latter). Hence the choice of such items as gauges, horns, valves, regulators, switches, and taps for manufacture and/or assembly.

Ford's village industries did not come about in a vacuum, as the realization of one very rich and powerful man's unique fantasies. Rather, they were part of efforts elsewhere in America between the two World Wars to alter the course of industrial urban life: whether by forsaking large-scale industrialization and large cities together, as with such diverse reformers as Ralph Borsodi, Helen and Scott Nearing, and the Nashville Agrarians of *I'll Take My Stand* fame; or, more akin to Bellamy, by trying to balance modern technology with small-scale rural living and working conditions, as with Arthur Morgan in the early days of the Tennessee Valley Authority, of which he was first chairman of the board of directors. Ford chose the latter course, and there are several parallels between his efforts in the private sector and those of Morgan in the public sector. Indeed, the village industries themselves constituted a system that took on regional dimensions akin to TVA—but a system that Ford, like Morgan at TVA, hoped would inspire changes in the predominantly large-scale urban systems described earlier. The 1930s and 1940s, moreover, were a period of extensive academic and public discussion about regionalism in America and about America as fundamentally a nation of regions.

Just as TVA never resembled the "grass-roots democracy" described by its long-time director David Lilienthal (Lilienthal 1944), so the village industries never resembled the bastions of yeoman purity described by Ford and his publicity agents. Like TVA, they were commercial enterprises as well as social experiments, and like nearly all else in the Ford empire, they were under the constant scrutiny of Ford himself. Yet the village industries did enjoy a measure of freedom. They were not conventional company towns, were not owned by the Ford Motor Company, and were comparatively free from the notorious Ford Sociological Department. The workers appear to have enjoyed their diversity of employment and the proximity of their residences to their workplaces. Not a few workers—and whole towns—were thereby saved from financial ruin during the Depression.

To this extent, the village industries do represent pioneering examples of decentralized technology and society. As Ford argued, it was precisely small-scale, widely dispersed forms of the same modern technology already available in conventional large-scale, heavily urban automobile plants that made these rural enterprises possible—just as with the towns and villages, smaller department stores and warehouses, credit cards, home telephones, and other aspects of Bellamy's utopia. Yet physical location, scale, and size are, as noted, issues separate from decision making and control; and the major decisions regarding the village industries remained under the firm control of Ford and his top subordinates. Moreover, Ford, like Morgan at TVA, resorted to a giant technical organization in order to create (or renew) semiagrarian small communities, much as Bellamy might have done in similar circumstances. Once again, then, decentralization is a complex, multifaceted phenomenon whose particular applications may be neither uniform nor complete.

It would be as easy to condemn Ford as a hypocrite as it would be to dismiss him as an eccentric. But this, too, would be a gross simplification. In his unsystematic, unorthodox way Ford understood a good deal more about the direction of modern technological society than did most of his seemingly more sophisticated contemporaries. Like Bellamy, he sought a limitation on the ever greater size, scale, and impersonality of technological development and a concern for other aspects of the "good life." Yet the limits he would impose were clearly relative, not absolute—unlike, say, the Nashville Agrarians or the Nearings.

Nevertheless, most of these nineteen experiments were eventual failures. The Ford Motor Company sold nearly all of them in the years after Ford's death, though a few are, under different ownership, currently involved in high-tech enterprises. The rest have become county and municipal government offices, community centers, antique shops, and garages. One, at Willow Run (1941), has been abandoned and dismantled.

Still, as noted at the outset, decentralized technology is today more popular—and more practical—than ever before, thanks to computers, word processors, and other devices. Meanwhile the decentralization of society—whether of government, of industry, of schools, or of other institutions—has become public policy in many quarters, and not just in the United States. Consequently, these largely forgotten and unexplored experiments are, like Bellamy's own vision, of more than antiquarian interest. They provide an alternative form of technological development that seeks a necessary balance between the all too common antitechnological and protechnological extremes. Such a new "middle landscape" or "middle way" may even be termed progressive.

Aldous Huxley, I believe, had such a vision in mind when he wrote his foreword to the 1946 reprint of *Brave New World*—a book that, most ironically, uses Ford and Ford's large-scale, heavily centralized assembly lines as the focal point for its brilliant satire of future technological utopia or, more precisely, dystopia. As Huxley conceded about his 1932 work:

> In the meantime, however, it seems worth while at least to mention the most serious defect in the story, which is this. The Savage is offered only two alternatives, an insane life in Utopia, or the life of a primitive in an Indian village, a life more human in some respects, but in others hardly less queer and abnormal. At the time the book was written this idea, that human beings are given free will in order to choose between insanity on the one hand and lunacy on the other, was one that I found amusing and regarded as quite possibly true. . . . If I were now to rewrite the book, I would offer the Savage a third alternative. Between the utopian and the primitive horns of his dilemma would lie the possibility of sanity—a possibility already actualized, to some extent, in a community of exiles and refugees from the Brave New World, living within the borders of the Reservation. In this community economics would be decentralist and Henry-Georgian, politics Kropotkinesque co-operative. Science and technology would

be used as though, like the Sabbath, they had been made for man, not (as at present and still more so in the Brave New World) as though man were to be adapted and enslaved to them. (Huxley 1969 [1946], vii–viii)

Huxley, then, might have approved of the village industries—about which he probably knew little or nothing—even if he condemned the rest of the Ford ethos and empire. And Huxley might likewise have looked with a favorable eye on the decentralized components of Bellamy's utopia even if he surely would have condemned—and perhaps did condemn—its overly centralized ones.

A decade before *Brave New World* initially appreared, Lewis Mumford published *The Story of Utopias*. Mumford is a key figure bridging the Western utopian tradition and the practical (and philosophical) proponents of decentralization ranging from Bellamy and Ford through Schumacher and Toffler. In this his first book Mumford, eventually to become a distinguished critic—and defender—of technology and utopias alike, saw decentralization as a means of balancing stability and change. Long before he had attacked the modern "megamachine," he had here shown that any future utopias, or any genuinely good societies, could use technological advance to preserve and improve local communities and that technological advance need not homogenize the United States or other nations in the name of progress. The focus on local community did not entail isolation or parochialism; modern transportation and communications networks allowed mobility and exchange of persons and ideas, but not at the expense of different local (and national) cultures. As Mumford put it,

> If the inhabitants of our Eutopias [that is, authentic utopias] will conduct their daily affairs in a possibly more limited environment than that of the great metropolitan centers, their mental environment will not be localized or nationalized. For the first time perhaps in the history of the planet our advance in science and invention has made it possible for every age and every community to contribute to the spiritual heritage of the local group. . . . Our eutopians will necessarily draw from this wider environment whatever can be assimilated by the local community; and they will thus add any elements that may be lacking in the natural situation. (Mumford 1962 [1922], 306–7)

The road from *Looking Backward* to *The Story of Utopias* to *Small Is Beautiful* is neither smooth nor straight. And it frequently detours in the direction of *Brave New World* or *The Third Wave* or other questionable schemes—questionable, that is, for those not enamored of shallow technocratic solutions to profound moral and social problems. Yet Bellamy's interesting and complex uses of technology, as toward both centralization and decentralization, make *Looking Backward* a less technocratic and so a more timely work than has long been assumed.

A product of America's peak of faith in technology as the solution to social problems, not just technical ones, *Looking Backward* nevertheless recognizes the need for economic and especially ethical constraints on otherwise unadulterated technological advance and unbounded materialism. No less important, it also provides for flexibility in the design, organization, and administration of an otherwise overly rigid technocratic regime. The particular mix of values and arrangements that Bellamy devised hardly appeals to us now as it did in his day, and his middle-of-the-road stance in this as in so much else—surely a key to the book's popularity—often makes for dull reading today. But Bellamy's anticipation of some basic dilemmas of and solutions to our postindustrial society justifies a careful rereading and renewed appreciation of *Looking Backward* on the hundredth anniversary of its publication.

Works Cited

Bellamy, Edward. 1892. "Progress of Nationalism in the United States." *North American Review* 154: 742–52.

———. 1897. *Equality.* New York: Appleton.

———. 1969 [1938]. *Talks on Nationalism.* Reprint. Freeport, N.Y.: Books for Libraries Press.

———. 1982 [1888]. *Looking Backward, 2000–1887.* Reprint. New York: Penguin.

Ford Motor Company. 1936. "Ford's Little Plants in the Country." *Ford News* 16:127–28, 137.

Huxley, Aldous 1969 [1946]. *Brave New World.* Reprint. New York: Harper and Row.

Lilienthal, David E. 1944. *TVA: Democracy on the March.* New York: Harper.

Lipow, Arthur. 1982. *Authoritarian Socialism in America: Edward Bellamy and the Nationalist Movement.* Berkeley: University of California Press.

Marx, Leo. 1964. *The Machine in the Garden: Technology and the Pastoral Ideal in America.* New York: Oxford University Press.

McRobie, George. 1981. *Small Is Possible.* New York: Harper and Row.

Mumford, Lewis. 1962 [1922]. *The Story of Utopias.* Reprint. New York: Viking Compass.

Schumacher, E. F. 1973. *Small Is Beautiful: Economics as if People Mattered.* New York: Harper and Row.

Segal, Howard. 1977. "Leo Marx's 'Middle Landscape': A Critique, a Revision, and an Appreciation." *Reviews in American History* 5: 137–50.

————. 1985. *Technological Utopianism in American Culture*. Chicago: University of Chicago Press.

Simonds, William A. 1927. "Rural Factories along Little Streams." *Stone and Webster Journal* 41: 649–55.

Thomas, John L. 1983. *Alternative America: Henry George, Edward Bellamy, Henry Demarest Lloyd and the Adversary Tradition*. Cambridge: Harvard University Press.

Toffler, Alvin. 1980. *The Third Wave*. New York: Morrow.

Dreams of Reason: Bellamy, Wells, and the Positive Utopia

W. WARREN WAGAR

Utopia: Romantic and Positive

Arthur Lipow, in his unsparing assault on the liberal-democratic credentials of the author of *Looking Backward*, renders the verdict that utopias take a "necessarily authoritarian viewpoint." They all assume—Bellamy's included—that "a better social order can be created only by the action of an agency outside of society and the operation of its laws" (Lipow 1982, 52). As betrayed by his addition of the phrase "and the operation of its laws," Lipow's own viewpoint is Marxist. It was just this foreclosure of the human future, he notes, that prompted Marx to reject "all utopianism."

Non-Marxist critics of utopia may sniff at "laws of society," but they are no less ready to condemn the illiberal and antidemocratic bias that pervades most, if not all, utopianism. From Karl Popper onward, they have deplored the classic utopian image of the closed society, first articulated by Plato, which substitutes the wisdom of planners for the will of citizens. As Gorman Beauchamp observes, "there are no politics in utopia." Whether the utopographer be Plato or Bacon, Bellamy or Wells, and whatever form of government is prescribed, even anarchy, the denizens of utopia are bloodless pawns, and the utopias themselves "inescapably totalitarian" (Beauchamp 1979, 49, 55). One is reminded of Frazier, the genial Lycurgus of B. F. Skinner's *Walden Two*, who denies that utopia needs a dictator. "Set it up right," he says, "and it will run by itself" (Skinner 1962 [1948], 234).

Set it up right! Just so. Once a perfect or best possible social order has been established, nothing is left, either to the imagination or to the free play of politics. In this sense, Beauchamp's complaint is like criticizing lions for being lions. What good are civil liberty and democracy in a society blessed, from the start, with harmony, happiness, justice, and truth?

Little wonder that even when utopias, like Morris's *News from Nowhere* or Bellamy's "populist" fantasia, *Equality*, depict the masses deciding their own affairs in town meetings or referenda, their doings seem more like a child's street game than serious business. Dr. Leete admits to West that since "all our vital interests are secured beyond disturbance by the very framework of society," there is no need for citizens to trouble themselves with affairs of state. They do so anyway, in this sequel to *Looking Backward*, for the sheer fun of it. "We . . . find the exercise at once as exhilarating as it is in the highest sense educational." But this same Dr. Leete, earlier in the same novel, makes democracy virtually synonymous with equality and decrees that "the only really important" interests of men and women are economic (Bellamy 1897, 275, 26, 7). The point is that utopias, *by definition*, are systems of prearranged harmony, dictatorships of gnosis or science. Utopian texts cannot furnish models of the good political life because politics presumes conflict and uncertainty.

Indeed, the only thing that distinguishes one utopia from another is the source of authority. It can be the proclamation of an archetypal noetic lawgiver, the revelation of a god, or the collective will of the *Volk*. Or it can be the expert knowledge of scientists, engineers, and managers. The first class of utopias, which comprises a broad spectrum of visions from those of Plato, More, and Rousseau to the millenarian hallucinations of Adolf Hitler, are—in the most general sense of the term—romantic, drawing their truth from the many-tiered realms of the suprarational. The second class, the distinctively modern form taken by the utopian imagination, are positive utopias, whose intellectual forebears include Bacon, Condorcet, and Comte, and whose best known literary texts are Edward Bellamy's *Looking Backward* and H. G. Wells's *Modern Utopia.*

In principle, the phrase "positive utopia" is an oxymoron. Knowledge and society enter the "positive" stage, as Auguste Comte insisted, when they exchange the authority of superstition and metaphysics for that of empirical science. Clearly, empirical science, as practiced at its leading edge, is anything but gnostic: self-correcting, never absolute, always on its way to fresh understandings that it would be a lie to call "truth." The problem is simply that whenever social philosophers have expropriated the methods and findings of the natural sciences, these same methods and findings have been called upon repeatedly to fill the void left by the collapse of the traditional suprarational belief systems. "Science" has become the new Bible, the new pope, the new gnosis. The masters of its mysteries have been appointed the ruling class of utopia. Again to quote Frazier, in Skinner's *Walden Two*, "When a science of behavior has once been achieved, there's no alternative to a planned society. . . . We can't leave the control of behavior to the unskilled" (Skinner 1962 [1948], 264, 266).

The two authors of utopian texts who brought the values of the modern positive utopia to the widest reading public are Bellamy and Wells. Many of their contemporaries and successors made their own contributions in other ways, in journalism, scholarship, and partisan tracts, whether influenced by Bellamy and Wells or not: Laurence Gronlund and Lester Ward, the Fabian socialists in Britain, Thorstein Veblen and James Burnham, the architects of the New Deal and the welfare state, and a scattering of European Marxists and anarchosyndicalists.

What holds all these disparate forces together, along with such latter-day utopographers as Skinner and Aldous Huxley (in *Island,* not in his earlier satire of the positive utopia, *Brave New World*), is faith. Specifically, faith in the power of positive knowledge to shape a good society from which politics can be excluded and happiness can be engineered by trained elites. Terms such as meritocracy, technocracy, managerialism spring to mind, but at the heart of the positive utopia is a simple granitic belief in the power of modern science to tell us precisely what we need and how to get it. The positive utopographer, in short, is a prophet of scientocracy: the dominion of science. Never mind that real science fumbles in the dark. As it appears to most writers of positive utopias, science is apodictic, so firm and hard and clear that the multiple options of liberal or even revolutionary politics lose all sense, and humanity has no choice but to take the "One Right Path" that science reveals to its wondering eyes.

It follows that the ruling class in scientocratic utopias consists of the people who have mastered the secrets of the pure and applied sciences, ranging from physics and mathematics to civil engineering and management. The utopographers differ on the question of which elements of this scientocratic elite, if any, belong at the apex of the pyramid. Some emphasize one group, some another. The chief groups, in any case, are only four in number: scientists (natural and social), technologists (inventors, engineers, doctors, and technicians), managers (industrial, commercial, and financial), and public administrators. But in the prophetic imagination of the positive utopographers, it is never really men and women, however wise, who rule. Acting through them, science itself rules, filling the place left by the no longer audible divine Word. Humanists routinely turn away in derision or disgust from such profound innocence, but for anyone who puts his or her faith in the illuminating powers of modern science, the scientocratic vision is well-nigh inescapable. "There is one sole right way," Wells wrote in *The Shape of Things to Come,* "and there are endless wrong ways of doing things. A government is trying to go the right way or it is criminal" (Wells 1933, 256–57).

Edward Bellamy and the Great Society

In the case of Bellamy, the rule of science meant primarily efficient management of human affairs by those skilled in the organization of the world's work. In *Looking Backward*, there are no armies, political parties, politicians, lawyers, juries, or jails, because society is virtually free of conflict and crime; national governments survive, but play little more than a ceremonial role. Wars and taxes are things of the past, and the need for fresh legislation is slight. All real power resides in the industrial army and its allies in the liberal professions. The "officers" of this army receive their commissions by appointment, up to the level of "colonel" (superintendent), above which Bellamy provides for a system of elections by the retired elders in each guild, with the members of the liberal professions also participating in the election of the supreme commander of the industrial army, the president of the United States. A system of inspectors and judges keeps the army on its toes, and all is better than well.

But, again, what really rules in Bellamy's year 2000 is not this or that leader or elite class but the wisdom embodied in its design, a marvel of social engineering. "The fundamental principles on which our society is founded," Dr. Leete remarks, "settle for all time the strifes and misunderstandings which in your day called for legislation. . . . Now society rests on its base, and is in as little need of artificial supports [i.e., laws] as the everlasting hills" (Bellamy 1967 [1888], 230). As Charles and Mary Beard once noted, *Looking Backward* was "the first utopia of applied science" (cited in Lipow 1982, 93). It may not have been the first—if Bacon's claims are ignored, the distinction goes either to Cabet's *Voyage to Icaria* or Comte's *System of Positive Polity*—but the phrase is apt. John L. Thomas adds that "Bellamy's industrial army, in fact, prefigured most of the assumptions and techniques of twentieth-century industrial planners and proponents of scientific management" (Thomas 1983, 251).

Just as politics had no place in Bellamy's vision of the great society, so he saw no need for a political strategy to effect the transition to utopia from the muddle and corruption of present-day life. Proletarian socialists might see advantage in entering the civil wars of democracy. But for Bellamy, at least until his rapprochement with Populism in the 1890s, a socialism of expertise could triumph only through the sheer logic of economics, spurred on by corresponding progress in the formation of a responsible national conscience. "The solution came," we are not surprised to hear, "as the result of a process of industrial evolution which could not have terminated otherwise. All that society had to do was to recognize and cooperate with that evolution, when its tendency had become unmistakable." From independent corporations to trusts to the "Great Trust" of nationalized industry, the process unfolded inexorably, and "the obvious fact was perceived" (Bellamy 1967 [1888], 122, 127). Neither force nor argument could resist so strong a tide. A comparable reliance on "economism" took hold of many socialists in Europe in the generation after Marx—think only of the career of Rudolf Hilferding—with paralyzing effect in the political arena, leading ultimately to the catastrophes of 1914 and 1933.

Lipow and Thomas both interpret Bellamy's Nationalist crusade as a scheme for empowering the nonentrepreneurial middle class as it steered its perilous course at the end of the nineteenth century between the Scylla of big business and the Charybdis of organized labor. So it was, and so are many other scientocratic utopias, including those of H. G. Wells. But Bellamy and most of his followers would not have seen it in this light and with good reason. They did not, in any conscious way, indulge in what they would have considered the easy thrills of class politics. In their own eyes they had taken a higher road, working for the good of the whole nation. If a Bellamyized America would give more power to some individuals than others, such power would be held not for the sake of the individuals or their class, but for the service of the nation, the species, and perhaps even the universe. As Dr. Leete rhapsodizes in *Equality,* "The control and leading of humanity go already largely, and are plainly destined soon to go wholly, to those who have the largest souls—that is to say, to those who partake most of the Spirit of the Greater Self" (Bellamy 1897, 153).

References to the "Greater Self," which Dr. Leete explains "is one of our names for the soul and for God" (p. 153), may seem out of place in a positive utopia. In a sense, they are, since most nineteenth-century positivists were atheists. But most also followed the example of Comte in feeling a need to match their vision of the unity, integrity, and impersonality of science with the quasi-Hegelian vision of a racial being or mind transcending and incorporating all individual minds. Comte called it "The Great Being of Humanity." For those like Bellamy who retained significant elements of Christian faith in their world view, God (who, after all, had furnished Comte with his model for "The Great Being"!) made a perfectly serviceable substitute. In either case, the notion of an all-encompassing higher reality lent authority to the science of the scientocrats and the collectivism of scientocracy. What need for ballot boxes or partisan politics when subjects and rulers alike were mirrors, bright or dull as the case might be, of the World Mind?

There is no reason to doubt Bellamy's sincerity. He came from a family of clergymen and spent much of his life wrestling with religious questions. One of his first essays, "The Religion of Solidarity," written when he was still in his early twenties, foreshadows the moral cosmos of *Looking Backward* with astonishing fidelity, as Bellamy himself acknowledged in a note appended to the still unpublished manuscript in 1887 (Bellamy 1955, 26). "The Religion of Solidarity" viewed the individual person as a "mere temporary affection of the universal," "of so little importance, of such trifling scope, that it should matter little to us what renunciations of its things we make." The "cardinal motive of human life" is to be absorbed in the common life of the race, and "the greatest of all loves . . . is that of an individual for his remnant, the universe" (pp. 13, 17, 18).

In a minor profusion of short stories and novels written over the next fifteen years, Bellamy elaborated on the ideas broached in "The Religion of Solidarity." What emerges from a reading of these works of a utopographer's apprenticeship is the picture of a tormented soul, shy and insecure, who sought relief from his anxieties in fantasies of transformation and self-denial. William Dean Howells, a friend and admirer, wrote in the year of Bellamy's death that "in Edward Bellamy we were rich in a romantic imagination surpassed only by that of Hawthorne" (Howells, "Biographical Sketch," in Bellamy 1898, xiii). Howells exaggerated. But some of Bellamy's stories have a curiously disquieting appeal, as if they had been written in the One State of Zamyatin's *We*—with the imprimatur of the Well-Doer.

One of these, the novel *Dr. Heidenhoff's Process* (1880), offers a scientific answer to the problem of unassuageable guilt. When one is racked with memories of bad deeds, the recollections that give pain, Bellamy speculates, can be removed galvanically by a doctor's apparatus. The patient starts over again with a clean slate, like the subjects of the One State liberated by lobotomy from the burden of their imaginations in *We*. Even more chilling, perhaps, are Dr. Heidenhoff's thoughts on the future progress of "thought extirpation." He tells the hero of the tale that in twenty years, he can guarantee "the complete extirpation of any class of inconvenient recollections . . . whether they were morbid or healthy . . . as readily as a dentist pulls a tooth." The world might be a better place, indeed, if people had no memories at all, since they afflict us with a sense of continuity with our past selves that is—like individuality itself?—an illusion. "Memory," the doctor continues, "is the principle of moral degeneration" (Bellamy 1880, 100–101, 120).[1]

Two later short stories mounted further attacks on memory and individuality. "The Blindman's World" (1886) is a tale of earth, seen from the point of view of Mars. Like every other intelligent species in the universe except for terrestrials, the Martians possess the faculty of foresight. Knowing their futures, they are spared all anxiety; but their powers of recollection are weakly developed, which shields them from the misery of painful memories and the ache of nostalgia. They live only for present and expected joys, pitying the "blind" folk of earth.

When the narrator asks his alien informant if it ever occurred to Martians to wish to alter the future, the Martian replies that no one but an earthling would ask such a question. "To foresee events was to foresee their logical necessity so clearly that to desire them different was as impossible as seriously to wish that two and two made five instead of four." Since all things great and small are woven together, "to draw out the smallest thread would unravel creation through all eternity." The narrator ends his story with the hope that some day mankind may also learn to live with its face to the future, no longer "doomed to walk backward, beholding only what has gone by, assured only of what is past and dead" (Bellamy 1898, 25–26, 29). As in *Dr. Heidenhoff's Process*, individuality—which in real earthlings is preserved by memory and expectation alike—comes under attack, and Bellamy's blissful amnesiacs win release from the struggle for existence by submitting to a destiny they are excused from even wishing to change.

Having disposed of memory, in "To Whom This May Come" (1889) Bellamy went on to abolish privacy. Shipwrecked in the Indian Ocean, the narrator encounters a race of mind readers. These joyful telepaths know nothing of injustice or deception, or even the anxieties of courtship. Dispensing with names and titles, they are all one family. The narrator anticipates a great good time when the "mutual vision of minds" will be available to all peoples. In no way, he adds, will it "so enhance the blessedness of mankind as by rending the veil of self, and leaving no spot of darkness in the mind for lies to hide in. Then shall the soul no longer be a coal smoking among ashes, but a star in a crystal sphere" (Bellamy 1898, 405).[2]

One readily agrees with Sylvia E. Bowman that Bellamy's early essays and stories prepared him well for the writing of *Looking Backward* and *Equality* and for his mission as an evangelist of "Nationalism" in the 1890s (Bowman 1958, 110–11). He was widely, although not deeply, read in the utopographers, sociologists, economists, and exponents of socialism of his century. He tempered his positivism with a dash of mysticism and Christian piety, but what stands out most in his social philosophy is its typically late nineteenth-century rejection of liberal and democratic values in favor of collective action marshalled by men of experience and expertise. Its *telos* was not a society of free individuals resolving public issues among themselves and otherwise pursuing their several destinies, but a hive of happily humming bees. In the context of the times, in the context of robber baron capitalism and Tammany Hall democracy, the appeal of Bellamy's scientocracy is not hard to fathom. But what he had to offer was scientocracy, not socialism.

H. G. Wells and the Modern Utopia

Bellamy's English counterpart—almost his heir—was H. G. Wells. Sixteen years Bellamy's junior, more gifted as a man of letters, more learned in the mysteries of modern science, he won the battle with tuberculosis that cost Bellamy his life at a relatively early age and lived almost to the middle of that miraculous twentieth century foretold and celebrated in *Looking Backward*. His own million-volume best seller was not a utopia at all but a work of literal retrospection, *The Outline of History* (1920). As a utopographer, he enjoyed less public success than Bellamy, although not from lack of effort. He published six utopias, together with two of the first authentic dystopias.[3]

Wells began his career as a professional writer in the early 1890s, at just the time when *Looking Backward* was all the rage. Its phenomenal popularity in England (well documented by Peter Marshall)[4] no doubt played a part in Wells's decision to explore the future in a long series of utopias, scientific romances, and sociological tracts, of which the first major installment was *The Time Machine* in 1895. But *Looking Backward* directly inspired only one of Wells's books: his dystopian novel *When the Sleeper Wakes*, serialized in 1898–1899, published as a clothbound book in 1899, and issued in a revised edition, with one of its two references to Bellamy deleted, as *The Sleeper Awakes* in 1910.

When the Sleeper Wakes belongs to that rather large category of fictions that "reply" to Bellamy by challenging his assumptions. The most outstanding of these, clearly, was William Morris's *News from Nowhere*, written in 1889 after Morris had reviewed Bellamy's utopia unfavorably for *The Commonweal*. Marshall provides evidence from Morris's friend Andreas Scheu that Morris had vowed to "write something as a counterblast to this," and so he did (Bowman 1962, 90). But *When the Sleeper Wakes* was an entirely different response to Bellamy than *News from Nowhere*. Morris had answered with a romantic blend of Marxism and anarchism that saw no escape from class struggle but also no need for scientocracy—little enough need even for science. For his part, Wells used *When the Sleeper Wakes*, somewhat as he had used *The Time Machine* earlier, to question the premise that capitalism was doomed to defeat. What if the socialists were right in their goals but wrong in their forecasts? What if relentless warfare between the classes were to issue not in the scientocratic synthesis of Bellamy's Nationalism, and not in a classless utopia à la Marx or Morris, but in the ultimate triumph of plutocracy and, beyond that, demagogic tyranny?

In *When the Sleeper Wakes*, history takes the latter course, and all is worse than bad. As Mark Hillegas has shown (Hillegas 1967), Wells's novel was the model for most of the dystopias that have followed it, which makes it one of the most original and influential books of its time. But for readers in the late 1890s, it was little more than a mildly clever inversion of *Looking Backward*, which called into question only Bellamy's optimism, not his values. The parallels with *Looking Backward* and *Equality* are obvious: an insomniac hero who wakes up after a trance and finds himself in the future (two centuries hence, rather than one), in a world glittering with high technology and ruled by centralized capital (although in private hands). Dr. Leete's speculation in *Equality*, published in England before Wells wrote his novel, that it was theoretically possible in the bad old days for one family or even one man to become owner of the whole earth is now a reality, for the Sleeper himself, our innocent hero, finds that the accumulation of his wealth by trustees during the long years of his trance has made him the absentee owner and master of the world. Power is held in his name by a council of evil capitalist oligarchs who decide to kill him, and the story carries on from there. A protofascist dictator usurps the authority of the oligarchs. Having survived the assassination plot, our hero leads a popular uprising and crashes in his "aeropile" just as victory seems at hand.

When Wells started writing utopias of his own, early in the new century, they bore a more than faint resemblance to Bellamy's visions of the year 2000. Gorman Beauchamp is not far off the mark when he notes that *A Modern Utopia*, Wells's first and most elaborate experiment in utopography, "rehearses the techno-bureaucratic ideal of *Looking Backward*" (Beauchamp 1979, 50). But he misses his target altogether when he goes on to suggest that Wells's second major utopia, *Men Like Gods*, echoed *News from Nowhere*. Although similarities with *News from Nowhere* abound, *A Modern Utopia* and *Men Like Gods* both belong to the scientocratic tradition. The difference is that *Men Like Gods* represents a later stage in the evolution of Wells's ideal society, when human engineering has eliminated the need for a separate governing class. In that later stage, everyone is an expert. Wells explained in prefatory remarks that he was "no longer disposed to admit the necessary survival of inferior types" (Wells 1924–1927, 9:28). But the central ideal of scientocracy remains intact in the far future world of *Men Like Gods*. Decisions still need to be made, and in each instance they are made "by the people who [know] most about that matter" (Wells 1923, 62). *Plus ça change, plus c'est la même chose.*

In *The Shape of Things to Come*, an even later utopia, Wells clarified the relationship between the two stages by incorporating both in a single work of imaginary future history, tracing the chief events from 1929 to the year 2106. In the first stage, mankind is ruled by an austere elite of scientists, technicians, and business managers inspired by the work of a Wellsian social scientist named De Windt. "It is no good asking people what they want," De Windt proclaims. "That is the error of democracy." Elites must determine what people "ought to want," tell them what it is, and see that they get it. Elites must also make short work of the parliamentary dogma that every government needs a party in opposition. "About most affairs there can be no two respectable and antagonistic opinions" (Wells 1933, 254, 256).

After several generations of planetary social hygiene, the work of the elite is complete, and its world council is abolished. In the second, higher stage of utopia, coercion and discipline are replaced by education. Qualified specialists plan the best uses of the earth's resources, and people are free to do as they please, although one group of experts remains, the "Behaviour Control," who police the shrinking number of criminals in the society and are also responsible for medicine and schooling. A similar scheme appears in *Men Like Gods*, where government has long since been replaced by education designed to instill altruism, scientific curiosity, and common civility in childhood. If anyone still engages in antisocial behavior, inquiries are made "into his mental and moral health" by psychologists (Wells 1923, 63). One can almost see Bellamy's Dr. Leete nodding his head in grave approval. As he told Julian West, "We have no jails nowadays. All cases of atavism are treated in the hospitals" (Bellamy 1967 [1888], 224).

In the nearer future, however, Wells insisted on coercion and discipline of a less subtle sort. In *A Modern Utopia* a self-selected "Order of Samurai" wields all governmental power, ensuring that the World State runs smoothly and efficiently. The Order draws its members from the ranks of college graduates with demonstrated proficiency in a profession, such as medicine, education, or engineering. It selects all officials and alone votes for delegates to the legislative assembly of the World State. Under its benevolent despotism, the general welfare is assured, but citizens are subject to a variety of legal restraints, from the limitation of parentage to certified couples and a universal program of identification by thumbprint to a system of criminal justice that requires the banishment of habitual offenders to penal colonies. In a realistic modern utopia, "you must resort," wrote Wells, "to a kind of social surgery" (Wells 1905, 142).

Yet even in *A Modern Utopia*, he foresaw that eventually the Order of Samurai would increase until it "may indeed at last assimilate almost the whole population of the earth" (p. 299). His program was the rule of science and expertise, not the rule of an entrenched elite per se. As one of his heroes in another utopia, *The World Set Free*, cries out, "Science is the new king of the world." Sovereignty in the dawning order resides not in the people but in "that common, impersonal will and sense of necessity of which Science is the best understood and most typical aspect. It is the mind of the race" (Wells 1914, 178). Still elsewhere, in a tract with the revealing title of *After Democracy*, Wells entrusted the rule of the earth to "a dictatorship—not of this man or that man, nor of the proletariat, but of informed and educated common-sense." He saw no point in letting politicians and lawyers argue about what should be done. "Why make a dispute of world welfare?" Simply deprive governments of their power to do mischief and turn over the management of world peace, economics, and education to "competent overriding bodies" (Wells 1932, 203).

Mention of "the mind of the race" in *The World Set Free* introduces one additional component of Wells's scientocracy that is almost identical to Bellamy's: the idea of human mental and spiritual solidarity. In works that caught the imagination even of Pierre Teilhard de Chardin, Wells insisted that science sprang from an evolving world mind, which "gathered the results of individual mental effort into a single fund of racial wisdom and grew gradually toward organic consciousness of itself" (Wagar 1961, 100). Individuals could escape their finitude and insignificance only by consecrating their lives to the service of this emergent higher consciousness. As Wells wrote in *First and Last Things* (1908), "I believe in the great and growing Being of the Species from which I rise, to which I return, and which, it may be, will ultimately even transcend the limitation of the Species and grow into the conscious Being, the eternally conscious Being of all things" (Wells 1908, 111). It was Comte's "Great Being of Humanity" all over again, to which Wells added a page from the book of evolution.

In all sorts of ways, then, Wells and Bellamy clearly anticipated the same future for mankind.[5] The emphases may have differed, but not the essence. There is the same plea for the rule of expertise (with Wells placing more stress on science and scientists), the same hope for a disciplined and dispassionate elite of professional managers, the same scorn for capitalism, the same critique of democratic politics, the same half-mystical religion of

human solidarity, the same rejection of proletarian or revolutionary socialism, the same admiration of technology, the same insistence on a planetary
utopia (stronger in Wells, but present in Bellamy's "international council"
and his forecast of eventual world unification), and the same dismissal of
the possibility of alternatives to the advancing utopian society. Reason,
common sense, and history made the scientocratic utopia inevitable. One
might as well quarrel with the stars in their courses.

   This is not to say that Wells borrowed extensively from the writings of
Edward Bellamy. The evidence of direct influence, apart from the plot of
When the Sleeper Wakes, is sparse. Bellamy is not mentioned in Wells's
autobiography, which deals at length with his early years and reading. In a
discussion of utopian texts in *A Modern Utopia*, Bellamy is hailed as the
"American equivalent" of Cabet, who in turn wrote the first rough approx-
imation of a truly modern utopia by insisting on "the escape of man from
irksome labours through the use of machinery" (Wells 1905, 100). Bellamy
is noted briefly on two other occasions, and it is hard to believe, when the
narrator is suddenly returned at the end of the book to present-day London
with its noise, filth, and screaming newspaper headlines, that Wells was not
thinking of Julian West's nightmare of old Boston in the last chapter of
Looking Backward. But that is all. The ideas presented in *A Modern Utopia*
and in the later Wellsian utopias owe far more to Plato, various British
socialists (Fabian or otherwise), and the great French utopographers of the
nineteenth century, than to anything Wells may have gleaned from Bellamy.

   But what matters most is not Bellamy, or even Bellamy and Wells
together, but the extent to which the works of both writers illustrate what
may well be the modern utopia par excellence. For scientocracy—the
vision of a technologically advanced society governed by the masters of
science and applied science—is not the vision of a few isolated cranks.
Although often disguised by lip service to older and grander utopian ideals,
scientocracy is in fact the dominant ideology of the governing classes of
most twentieth-century societies, who take inspiration from the explicit
theoretical and polemical writings of scores of modern social thinkers.
Bellamy and Wells are two such thinkers, but to make clearer their place in
the larger scheme of things, we should look briefly at several others.

From Gronlund to Skinner: Scientocrats on Parade

   When Edward Bellamy began sketching outlines of perfect societies run
by wise managers in the 1870s, scientocracy was already well ensconced in
the Western mind, as we noted earlier. Saint-Simon, Comte, and Cabet had

each advanced schemes for utopias run by experts.[6] Each had left behind an array of ardent followers in France, Britain, and the Americas who carried their gospels forward into the second half of the nineteenth century and in some instances penetrated the higher echelons of government. Comte's successors, both in and out of the international Positivist movement, were especially successful in this regard. Scientocracy also found a foothold in the utilitarianism of Jeremy Bentham and his many disciples in Victorian Britain.

In America, two contemporaries whose thought moved along lines parallel to Bellamy's were Laurence Gronlund and Lester F. Ward. Gronlund the former Marxist and Ward the federal bureaucrat and neo-Comtean sociologist had practically nothing in common except a passion for the rule of technical expertise. Gronlund became deeply involved in the Nationalist movement led by Bellamy in the early 1890s and was also influenced by Ward's writings; Ward moved in other circles. Nevertheless, as Arthur Lipow comments, they "marched to similar tunes" (Lipow 1982, 114).

Gronlund's nonfictional utopia and only serious claim to a place in American intellectual history, *The Cooperative Commonwealth*, was published in 1884. Bellamy declared that he had not read it before writing *Looking Backward*, and probably did not (Morgan 1944, 372), but the resemblances between the two plans for a managerial society are astonishing. In Gronlund's new socialist commonwealth, there is no representative assembly, no presidents or governors, in fact no government at all. The people, explained Gronlund, do not even want such a thing. All they demand is good administration of public affairs by "competent and qualified functionaries" (Gronlund 1965 [1884], 149–50).

In Gronlund's version of the industrial army, unlike in Bellamy's, the workers choose their foremen, the foremen their chiefs, and so on up the ladder, but officials can be removed only by their superiors. The framing of laws is left "to the wisest and most competent." A system of public education by qualified specialists from infancy to adulthood ensures social solidarity, ending "the anarchy of opinion" that characterizes the abnormal, transitory age in which we now have the misfortune to live. In the cooperative commonwealth, it will be "just as natural for healthy men to think and believe alike, as it is for healthy men to see alike" (Gronlund 1965 [1884], 157, 208). Stow Persons understandably finds it difficult to reconcile Gronlund's schemes for a central regulative system "with the idea of democratic participation in decision making" (Persons in Gronlund 1965 [1884], xix). He need not have bothered to try.

The variation on the scientocratic theme played by Ward, who was no writer of utopias or political activist, involved less upset of established institutions than Gronlund's, but came in the end to the same thing. Ward had the deepest respect for government, in whose labyrinths he made his living for decades. Nor did he advocate the replacement of representative democracy by industrial armies. But as a sociologist and a professed follower of Auguste Comte, he took as the proper goal of social advance the transformation of democracy with its puerile games of party politics into something higher and more scientific, a form of government that he repeatedly termed "sociocracy."

Literally, the word meant the rule of society, as opposed to the rule of individuals, on the assumption that the whole was, or must become, greater than the mere sum of its parts. In practice, what Ward understood by sociocracy was the rule of social science. A new science of politics was needed, he wrote, to train the people's elected representatives. Lawmakers and civil servants would become practitioners of social physics, guided in their work by professional scholars. The open sessions of legislative bodies would "doubtless need to be maintained," he wrote in *Applied Sociology* (1906), but would become more and more "a merely formal way of putting the final sanction of society on decisions that have been carefully worked out in what may be called the sociological laboratory" (Ward 1967, 368). As Henry Steele Commager correctly observes, Ward was the "philosophical architect of the welfare state" (Commager in Ward 1967, xxxviii), a figure of great and often forgotten influence. Yet the influence that he exerted was, just like Bellamy's, on behalf of a welfare imposed from the top down by experts rather than by the people thinking for themselves.[7]

On Wells's side of the Atlantic, the obvious and often noted counterpart of Bellamy and his Nationalism was the Fabian Society led by Beatrice and Sidney Webb, Bernard Shaw, and Graham Wallas. Wells also belonged to the Society, from 1903 to 1908, but resigned after a futile attempt to wrest control from the "Old Guard" eloquently defended by Shaw. He had grandiose plans for his comrades, which the Old Guard mulishly resisted, but it was a quarrel over tactics, not premises.

In brief, the Fabians saw their task as the permeation of the established order in Britain. By municipalizing public utilities, by infiltrating the ranks of the governing class, and by showing working people how to collaborate with managers and experts in renovating the economy, they expected to convert the nation to socialism by degrees, without revolution and without violence. Wells decided they were no more permeating British society than the mouse permeates the cat, which may have been true. Yet the Fabian model for the future has worked in its painfully modest way, and Bellamy supplied both moral and intellectual support in the Society's crucial early years from 1888 to the turn of the century. *Looking Backward* was a favorite of several prominent Fabians, including Annie Besant. As Peter Marshall remarks, Bernard Shaw may have taken some of his passion for equality of incomes from Bellamy (Bowman 1962, 105). And when the time came for a U.S. edition of the famous *Fabian Essays* of 1889, the man chosen to write the introduction was none other than Edward Bellamy. The prophet of Chicopee Falls took the occasion to praise the *Essays* as the easiest way to acquire "a general knowledge of the argument for socialism" (Bellamy 1937, 235). But he could not resist the temptation to follow up his praise with the plea to consider a still higher path: the "nationalist" path to equality charted in *Looking Backward*. Again, the quarrel was intramural. The Fabians, too, were scientocrats down to their bones.

As the twentieth century wore on, utopography fell out of fashion, but not the kernel of scientocratic faith. It lived on vigorously in the "efficiency craze" sparked by the writings on scientific management of Frederick Winslow Taylor, which in turn played a considerable role in the thought of Herbert Croly, Walter Lippmann, and other prominent intellectuals of the Progressive era (Haber 1964). It thrived in what John L. Thomas dubs the "technocratic antipolitics" of the economist Thorstein Veblen (Thomas 1983, 259), who called for a general strike by production engineers and a "soviet of technicians" joined by consulting economists in *The Engineers and the Price Revolution* (1921). Joseph Dorfman has documented Veblen's debt in his early years to the influence of Bellamy (Dorfman 1934, 68, passim; cf. Tilman 1985, 885–86, 893), but of course Veblen took his ideas from a rich variety of sources, not least the generic nineteenth-century faith in science, explained in his classic essay, "The Place of Science in Modern Civilisation" (1906, reprinted in Veblen 1919).

Still later came Howard Scott, Harold Loeb, and the Technocracy movement of the early 1930s, much influenced by Veblen and more remotely by Bellamy.[8] Of the Technocrats, only Loeb produced a rounded utopian vision, as Howard Segal points out (Segal 1985, 121–23), but Scott and his engineers also belonged to the scientocratic tradition. Wells commented with favor on their appearance in the news in 1933 (Wells 1933, 263). Next year, completing the circle, Scott wrote to Bellamy's widow that of all the utopias ever published, "I think there can be no shadow of a doubt that Bellamy's is the best of all" (cited in Thomas 1983, 355).

Technocracy faded almost as soon as it burst on the scene, but only the movement, not the ideas it sought to represent. Roosevelt's New Deal was staffed by heirs of Bellamy, Ward, and Veblen, including two prominent

fans of Bellamy, the Brain Truster Adolf A. Berle, Jr., and Bellamy's
biographer, Arthur E. Morgan. Berle, in turn, proved a major influence on
the thinking of James Burnham, author of *The Managerial Revolution*,
another key text in the history of scientocracy. Burnham also borrowed
ideas from the work of Veblen and Hilferding; and Bellamy left his mark,
along with Veblen, on the scientocratic utopia of B. F. Skinner, *Walden
Two*.

In more recent years few scientocratic utopias have reached the best
seller lists. But science fiction and the literature of "future studies" generate apolitical forecasts of the triumphs of science and technology in nearly
unlimited quantities, works such as Herman Kahn's *Next 200 Years* (1976),
Gerard K. O'Neill's *2081* (1981), and Brian Stableford and David Langford's *Third Millennium* (1985). Of equal significance is the plethora of
dystopian novels fiercely assailing the premises of scientocracy, books that
writers would not bother to write nor readers to read if no one found
scientocracy still alluring.

Three of the earliest and best known dystopias are the work of men who
were themselves attracted to the world view of science: Yevgeny Zamyatin,
a politically active Russian engineer and author of *We* (1924); Aldous
Huxley, whose *Island* (1962) is a classic utopia of behavioral engineering
laced with mysticism, but whose dystopian *Brave New World* (1932) is just
the opposite; and George Orwell, apparent apostle of the freedom of science in its struggle with tyranny in *Nineteen Eighty-Four* (1949). Such
dystopias, needless to say, owe their success in good measure to their
skillful exploitation of the fear that applied science in the hands of technocrats threatens to dehumanize man. *We* is an explicit satire both of
Wells's modern utopias and of Taylorism, *Brave New World* of eugenics and
Fordism, *Nineteen Eighty-Four* of the managerial society forecast by Burnham. *We* and *Nineteen Eighty-Four* are also frontal attacks on the Soviet
Russia of Lenin and of Stalin, respectively, but Zamyatin and Orwell were
more alarmed by the faceless technocrats behind the throne, and their
abuse of the powers of science, than by dictators as such. Other examples of
antiscientocratic dystopias, more openly romantic, are C. S. Lewis's *That
Hideous Strength* (1946; in which Wells appears in person as a scientocratic
dupe of Satan), Kurt Vonnegut's *Player Piano* (1952), Walter M. Miller's *A
Canticle for Leibowitz* (1959), Anthony Burgess's *Clockwork Orange* (1962),
and Russell Hoban's *Riddley Walker* (1980). By what we most fear, we
disclose what we most crave.

Nor are the cravings of present-day humanity for the rule of technical,
managerial, and scientific expertise confined to books of fiction. The fiction

is only emblematic of entrenched realities. As I have argued elsewhere and will not take the space to repeat here (Wagar 1979; 1980), our world of welfarism, Gaullism, Eurocracy, Galbraith's "new industrial state," Trilateralism, Pentagonism, centrally planned economies, and multinational corporations is in many respects (the worst ones) a Bellamy or a Wells world already. Scientocracy is here, and it is doing just fine. What in Karl Mannheim's use of the terms was once a utopia is now the covert ideology of a rapidly proliferating worldwide ruling class. From the prophets who brought us the "credit card" (Bellamy 1967 [1888], 147–48) and the "atomic bomb" (Wells 1914, 114–17) came much of the inspiration for this global Disneyland we have all inherited in the second half of the twentieth century. Bringing it under democratic control and saving it from eventual nuclear oblivion will take a lot of doing. Perhaps a lot more doing than can be done.

All we can say in justification of Bellamy and Wells is that scientocracy—with the imaginary exception of "Ingsoc" in Orwell's Oceania—has never been a cynical philosophy designed to justify the depredations of power-mad tyrants or self-serving elites. Scientocracy is incomprehensible save as an earnest belief in the veracity of modern science, its methods, and its applications in industry and government.

As Veblen once wrote, "modern common-sense holds that the scientist's answer is the only ultimately true one." Because he was a philosopher as well as an economist, Veblen lost no time adding, "This latterday faith in matter-of-fact knowledge may be well grounded or it may not" (Veblen 1919, 4). It might even be updated idolatry. But faith in science was itself a fact. Modern men and women trusted it implicitly. Science had showered us with the resources to cope with our problems and live well. "It remains for us," as one Veblen scholar sums up the master's thoughts, "to plan to use these resources intelligently, to solve these problems scientifically, equitably, and economically" (Daugert 1950, 103).

The formula is rational, perhaps even humane. Yet in the absence of one more adverb, "democratically," all is lost. Modern scientists, technicians, engineers, and bureaucrats may wield godlike powers. But they are not gods, and their Logos is not a god's Word. Only people—you and I, he and she, all of us—have the right to decide what shall be done in our names in this curious world of relativity and flux.

Notes

1. Sidney Webb, writing to his future wife, Beatrice, in 1890, thought *Dr. Heidenhoff's Process* "the best thing I ever read of Bellamy's" (Webb and Webb

1978, 1:209). Webb lacked the enthusiasm of his Fabian colleagues for *Looking Backward*, as this comment makes quite clear.

2. Sylvia E. Bowman, in *The Year 2000*, discusses plans for various utopian stories that Bellamy considered writing in the 1870s and 1880s, before he turned to *Looking Backward*. Most sound like dry runs for *We*, *Brave New World*, and *Nineteen Eighty-Four:* a tale of human "stock-breeding" by a wise future state, another in which the highest officials are chosen by lot from a list of meritocrats, a third in which sorrow is banished by having all children reared by the state in order to loosen family ties and promote universal sympathy (Bowman 1958, 108–10).

3. In order of publication, the utopias are *A Modern Utopia* (1905), *In the Days of the Comet* (1906), *The World Set Free* (1914), *Men Like Gods* (1923), *The Shape of Things to Come* (1933), and *The Holy Terror* (1939). The dystopias are *The Time Machine* (1895) and *When the Sleeper Wakes* (1899). Glimpses of utopia or dystopia may be found in dozens of other works, and Wells also published several manifestos of world revolution, including *The Open Conspiracy* (1928) and *Phoenix* (1942), which present his thoughts on how to get from "here" to "there."

4. See Marshall, "A British Sensation," in Bowman (1962, 86–118).

5. For a fuller discussion of Wells's views, see W. Warren Wagar (1961). I divide my exposition into four parts: the philosopher, the educationist, the strategist of world revolution, and the utopian.

6. Etienne Cabet provided in his *Voyage to Icaria* for an elaborate scheme of representative democracy, but in practice everything is decided by committees of experts, whose recommendations are routinely ratified by the people's delegates. Lewis Mumford draws the same conclusions in his chapter on Cabet in *The Story of Utopias*, and closes the chapter with an account of *Looking Backward*. Both visions, he writes, give us "a hint of what machinery might bring us to if the industrial organization were nationalized" (Mumford 1962 [1922], 149).

7. On the subject of Bellamy and the welfare state one should not forget that most quotable line from *Looking Backward:* "The nation guarantees the nurture, education, and comfortable maintenance of every citizen from the cradle to the grave" (Bellamy 1967 [1888], 149).

8. A comparable movement of politically conscious engineers formed a so-called Industrial Party in the Soviet Union in the late 1920s. Stalin crushed the party and gave its leaders show trials in 1930 (Bailes 1974).

Works Cited

Bailes, Kendall E. 1974. "The Politics of Technology: Stalin and Technocratic Thinking among Soviet Engineers." *American Historical Review* 79:2, 445–69.
Beauchamp, Gorman. 1979. "The Anti-Politics of Utopia." *Alternative Futures: The Journal of Utopian Studies* 2, no. 1: 49–59.
Bellamy, Edward. 1880. *Dr. Heidenhoff's Process.* New York: Appleton.
———. 1897. *Equality.* New York: Appleton.
———. 1898. *The Blindman's World and Other Stories.* Boston: Houghton Mifflin.
———. 1937. *Edward Bellamy Speaks Again!* Kansas City: Peerage Press.
———. 1955. *Selected Writings on Religion and Society.* Edited by Joseph Schiffman. New York: Liberal Arts Press.

———. 1967 [1888]. *Looking Backward*. Reprint. Edited by John L. Thomas. Cambridge: Belknap Press of Harvard University Press.

Bowman, Sylvia E. 1958. *The Year 2000: A Critical Biography of Edward Bellamy*. New York: Bookman Associates.

———, et al. 1962. *Edward Bellamy Abroad: An American Prophet's Influence*. New York: Twayne.

Burgess, Anthony. 1962. *A Clockwork Orange*. London: Heinemann.

Burnham, James. 1941. *The Managerial Revolution*. New York: John Day.

Cabet, Etienne. 1842 [1840]. *Voyage en Icarie*. Reprint. Paris: Mallet.

Daugert, Stanley Matthew. 1950. *The Philosophy of Thorstein Veblen*. New York: King's Crown Press, Columbia University.

Dorfman, Joseph. 1934. *Thorstein Veblen and His America*. New York: Viking.

Gronlund, Laurence. 1965 [1884]. *The Cooperative Commonwealth*. Reprint. Edited by Stow Persons. Cambridge: Belknap Press of Harvard University Press.

Haber, Samuel. 1964. *Efficiency and Uplift: Scientific Management in the Progressive Era, 1890–1920*. Chicago: University of Chicago Press.

Hillegas, Mark R. 1967. *H. G. Wells and the Anti-Utopians*. New York: Oxford University Press.

Hoban, Russell. 1980. *Riddley Walker*. New York: Summit.

Huxley, Aldous. 1932. *Brave New World*. New York: Doubleday.

———. 1962. *Island*. New York: Harper.

Kahn, Herman, et al. 1976. *The Next 200 Years*. New York: Morrow.

Lewis, C. S. 1946. *That Hideous Strength*. New York: Macmillan.

Lipow, Arthur. 1982. *Authoritarian Socialism in America: Edward Bellamy and the Nationalist Movement*. Berkeley: University of California Press.

Miller, Walter M., Jr. 1959. *A Canticle for Leibowitz*. Philadelphia: Lippincott.

Morgan, Arthur E. 1944. *Edward Bellamy*. New York: Columbia University Press.

Morris, William. 1890. *News from Nowhere*. London: Roberts.

Mumford, Lewis. 1962 [1922]. *The Story of Utopias*. Reprint. New York: Viking.

O'Neill, Gerard K. 1981. *2081: A Hopeful View of the Human Future*. New York: Simon and Schuster.

Orwell, George. 1949. *Nineteen Eighty-Four*. New York: Harcourt, Brace.

Segal, Howard P. 1985. *Technological Utopianism in American Culture*. Chicago: University of Chicago Press.

Skinner, B. F. 1962 [1948]. *Walden Two*. Reprint. New York: Macmillan.

Stableford, Brian, and David Langford. 1985. *The Third Millennium: A History of the World: AD 2000–3000*. New York: Knopf.

Thomas, John L. 1982. *Alternative America: Henry George, Edward Bellamy, Henry Demarest Lloyd and the Adversary Tradition*. Cambridge: Belknap Press of Harvard University Press.

Tilman, Rick. 1985. "The Utopian Vision of Edward Bellamy and Thorstein Veblen." *Journal of Economic Issues* 19, no. 4: 879–98.

Veblen, Thorstein. 1919. *The Place of Science in Modern Civilisation*. New York: B. W. Huebsch.

———. 1921. *The Engineers and the Price System*. New York: B. W. Huebsch.

Vonnegut, Kurt, Jr. 1952. *Player Piano*. New York: Scribner's.

Wagar, W. Warren. 1961. *H. G. Wells and the World State.* New Haven: Yale University Press.

———. 1979. "The Steel-Gray Saviour: Technocracy as Utopia and Ideology." *Alternative Futures: The Journal of Utopian Studies* 2, no. 2: 38–54.

———. 1980. "Technocracy as the Highest Stage of Capitalism." In *Through the '80s,* edited by Frank Feather, 210–15. Washington: World Future Society.

Ward, Lester F. 1906. *Applied Sociology.* Boston: Ginn.

———. 1967. *Lester Ward and the Welfare State.* Edited by Henry Steele Commager. Indianapolis: Bobbs-Merrill.

Webb, Sidney, and Beatrice Webb. 1978. *The Letters of Sidney and Beatrice Webb.* Edited by Norman MacKenzie. 3 vols. Cambridge: Cambridge University Press.

Wells, H. G. 1895. *The Time Machine.* London: Heinemann.

———. 1899. *When the Sleeper Wakes.* London: Harper.

———. 1905. *A Modern Utopia.* London: Chapman and Hall.

———. 1908. *First and Last Things.* New York: Putnam.

———. 1914. *The World Set Free.* New York: Dutton.

———. 1923. *Men Like Gods.* New York: Macmillan.

———. 1924–1927. *The Works of H. G. Wells: Atlantic Edition.* 28 vols. London: Unwin, and New York: Scribner's.

———. 1932. *After Democracy.* London: Watts.

———. 1933. *The Shape of Things to Come.* New York: Macmillan.

Zamyatin, Yevgeny [Zamiatin, Eugene]. 1924. *We.* Translated by Gregory Zilboorg. New York: Dutton.

Getting "Nowhere" beyond Stasis: A Critique, a Method, and a Case

KENNETH M. ROEMER

Stasis is the perpetual whipping boy of critics of utopia. From their viewpoint contemporary feminist utopists would banish us to an androgynous treadmill, Skinner would turn us all into unchangeable salivating machines, Wells would technocraticize us eternally, Morris would fossilize us in a medieval village guild, Bellamy would unceasingly march us over the hierarchical steps of an industrial army, More would lock us up in a monastery, and Plato would test our mettle and forever mold us into one of several fixed alloys.

Admittedly, I'm overstating my case. Not all critics of utopias are muckrakers ("stuckrakers" might be a more appropriate term) preoccupied with exposing elements in literary utopias that tend toward changeless states. But many of them are, and they, as well as many proponents of the value of utopian literature, base their evaluations of the static or dynamic qualities of a utopia on the assumption that the truly important element in a literary utopia is an accessible, describable, and fixed model of a better culture that utopographers should extrapolate and analyze. The focus on the stasis exposé and the acceptance of the basic assumption about fixed models, as I acknowledge at the beginning of this essay, are still very useful to the study of utopian literature. They sensitize us to many of the contradictions in utopian narratives between their revolutionary or at least evolutionary claims and their sometimes dull portraits of stagnant societies. They also help us to define, organize, and communicate descriptions of specific works, as well as theories about the nature of utopian literature in general. Still, this preoccupation and this method of perceiving utopian literature may obscure as much as it reveals. I discuss this problem at the conclusion of the first section of the essay and suggest an alternative method: in order to begin to understand the complexities of how readers perceive stasis and dynamism in a utopia, it is necessary to complement extrapolations of model societies from texts (1) with analyses of elements of that text that may not explicitly relate to socioeconomic models but nevertheless potentially affect how readers respond to the models, and (2) with examinations of how actual readers have responded to the texts. My case in point, presented in the second part of the essay, is Edward Bellamy's *Looking Backward*. My analysis begins with a conventional socioeconomic content analysis that defines certain static and dynamic elements of Dr. Leete's model society, proceeds with a textual analysis that delineates an implied or ideal reader, and concludes with an examination of the responses of one reader, Edward Bellamy.

This method of examining *Looking Backward* certainly does not come close to exhausting the possibilities for interpreting the relative static and dynamic qualities of the text. But it should demonstrate that before we rush to label Bellamy's utopia as a "rigid" or "static" utopia (a common critical stance)—indeed, before we judge any utopia to be static or dynamic—we must complement socioeconomic content analyses and notions of fixed texts with textual analysis and biographical or historical studies that illuminate potential and actual responses to utopian reading experiences.

Perceiving Stasis and Dynamism

In response to the new types of ambiguous utopias written during the 1970s and 1980s and to a renewed awareness of the complexities of many classical utopias, students of utopia during the last decade have tended to move away from definitions of utopia that stress stasis (i.e., using terms such as "ideal" or "perfect") and have begun to see the limitations of content analyses and the relevance of reader-response theory.[1] Nevertheless, the interest in stasis and a reliance on content analysis and fixed models have in the past been useful and can still help us to understand the nature of utopian literature.

One of the most constructive contributions of the focus on explicit or implicit evidence of stasis in literary utopias is that it sensitizes us to inconsistencies ranging from minor contradictions to the obvious contradictions of grand boasts of dynamic progressivism dramatized in dull portraits of less-than-stirring stagnancy. For example, late nineteenth-century American utopias are rife with such contradictions. In Bellamy's *Looking Backward* Dr. Leete expounds about infinite progress, and in Albert Adams Merrill's *Great Awakening* (1899) the narrator pontificates that "a state of evolution beyond which no progress can be made . . . [is] absurd" (p. 280). And yet, in response to specific questions from visitors to utopias, the spokesmen (and occasionally spokeswomen) of these imaginary worlds find it rather easy to describe absurd states of smug stasis.

Leete modestly proclaims that the "fundamental principles on which our society is founded settle for all time the strifes and misunderstandings which in your day called for legislation" (Bellamy 1967 [1888], 230); William Simpson's narrator in *The Man From Mars* (1891) proudly calls the utopian Martian economy "the stationary state" (p. 134); in *A Traveler from Altruria* (1894) W. D. Howells's Mr. Homos describes Altrurian "civic ideas" as "perfect" (p. 310); and the "Government of Settled Forms" rules Chauncey Thomas's supposedly progressive society (*The Crystal Button*, 1891, 254–55). Late nineteenth-century American utopias may provide the most glaring examples of the dynamic promise/static delivery syndrome, but it is relatively easy to pick out similar examples in utopian texts from any era and from any country.

Another valuable contribution of the preoccupation with exposing stasis relates to the previously mentioned assumption that stasis is usually defined in terms of content analyses that offer portraits of fixed cultural models extracted from the texts. Analyses of these portraits, especially comparative analyses, help scholars to define, organize, evaluate, and thus communicate their ideas about the bewildering bulk and diversity of utopian literature. This method, combined with an appropriate focus on economic, political, social, psychological, or some other combination of perspectives that defines a better culture, enables scholars to organize their extrapolated models into studies as unstructured as annotated bibliographies or as highly structured as stasis/dynamism spectrums bounded by terms such as no freedom/excessive freedom, retrogressive/progressive, and conservative/radical. In terms of opportunities for personal development, a typical spectrum might begin (on the static side) with works such as Plato's *Republic* and Thomas More's *Utopia,* continue with nineteenth- and twentieth-century works such as Bellamy's *Looking Backward* and B. F. Skinner's *Walden Two,* and conclude with twentieth-century works that stressed dynamism: H. G. Wells's *Modern Utopia,* Ursula Le Guin's *Dispossessed* and *Always Coming Home,* Doris Lessing's *Marriages Between Zones Three, Four, and Five,* and Samuel Delany's *Triton.*

Considering the usefulness of stasis exposés grounded in content model definitions and arrangements, it is not surprising that many of the studies of utopian literature, even during the last decade (and including my own studies), have formulated claims about static and dynamic qualities based, to some degree, on constructions of extrapolated models of better cultures (e.g., Pfaelzer 1984; Rooney 1985; and especially Bowman 1986). There are, however, serious flaws inherent in stasis hunts grounded in content analyses. A preoccupation with "stuckraking" can reduce all utopian speculation to suspect covert statements of static, even totalitarian intents. This simplistic reduction not only obscures dynamic elements in utopias, it also leads us away from studies of the many powerful literary and historical forces that incline authors toward contradictory stances. For instance, in an essay or treatise, it may be relatively easy to write *about* states of infinite progress, but in a work of fiction—which conventionally depends upon reduction, particularization, dramatization, and narrative closure—expressing open-ended states of progress may be more difficult to achieve. In the literary utopia, which combines elements of nonfictional and fictional genres, it may be particularly difficult to carry out the dynamic promises of the expository discourse in the dramatic narrative sections of the text. In many, if not all, eras in which utopias have been popular—and especially during the late nineteenth century in America—one of the primary assumptions of the authors has been that they and their readers perceived reality not only in need of moral and sociopolitical improvements, but also as too changeable, even chaotically insecure. To answer this authorial and reader fear with visions of ever-changing utopias would constitute an act of answering chaos with more chaos—perhaps a better chaos, but chaos nevertheless (Roemer 1976, 28–29, 33).

At the risk of creating unfair stereotypes about students of utopia (again including myself), I might also add that one reason they often expose stasis and sometimes underestimate the complex literary and historical forces that incline a utopian author toward contradictory dynamic/static stances is that, because of either their own literary training, their relative economic stability, or their self-perceptions as innovative thinkers, they tend to perceive spontaneity and diversity as more interesting and important than stability.

The reductive tendencies of content analyses become especially obvious when we examine the type of contemporary literary utopia Fredric Jameson has described as the "auto-referential" utopia—a form of discourse that perpetually interrogates its own capacity to exist, i.e., to narrate utopian possibilities (1982, 156). Imagine reducing the interactions between Lessing's Zones Three and Four or the implications of Le Guin's "Ones Who Walk Away from Omelas" to lists of economic and political "content" denoting stasis or dynamism. Of course, similar reservations could be expressed about much older works: imagine reducing the ambiguities and ambivalence of More's *Utopia* to such lists. It seems natural, therefore, that some of the most interesting studies of modern utopias deemphasize reductive content analyses (e.g., Jameson 1982; Khanna 1983) and that several students of utopia have moved toward a type of reader-response criticism that calls into question the usefulness of extrapolating fixed socioeconomic content models from utopian texts produced in any era (e.g., Ruppert 1986).

Still, it would be foolish, in my opinion, to move so far away from content analyses that the study of stasis and dynamism in utopian literature is limited to implied-reader textual analyses of "noncontent" material such as conventions, style, and structure, or to studies of the documented responses of actual readers. Because of the didactic, often prescriptive, nature of and the strong nonfictional elements in much utopian literature, it is evident that the responses of both implied and actual readers are strongly influenced by their own extrapolations of the content that to them is most relevant to the construction of a model of a better culture. Studies of the responses of actual readers certainly demonstrate this (e.g., Bowman 1962; Roemer, "104 + 1 Readers," 1984). Furthermore, implied reader and actual reader studies also involve types of content analyses and extrapolated models, though the definitions of "content" and "model" may be very different from their equivalents in conventional content analyses. We would not be making much dynamic scholarly progress if we simply replaced reductive socioeconomic models of stasis with reductive stylistic and biographical/historical models.

A more appropriate response to the obvious drawbacks of stasis/dynamism studies based on traditional content analyses would be a method that utilizes content analyses, implied reader textual analyses, and examinations of the documented responses of actual readers. Each of these angles of perception articulates significant and different ways of defining stasis and dynamism in utopian literature. The first stresses the importance of certain types of content traditionally associated with utopian models of better cultures (e.g., statements or implications about alternative political, economic, social, religious, cultural, and psychological models). The second deemphasizes these types of content and emphasizes the possibilities suggested by reading conventions, styles, and structures that can invite readers to imagine degrees of stasis and dynamism. The third examines evidence indicating how and why actual readers have accepted or rejected the socioeconomic and stylistic invitations of utopian texts. The results of this three-dimensional method will not be as easy to categorize as conclusions based on conventional content models, nor as compellingly unified as theoretical reader-response analyses, nor as consistently grounded in extratextual documentation as biographical or historical studies of actual readers. But, as I attempt to demonstrate in the following examination of *Looking Backward*, the method may help us to move beyond overly reductive studies and toward an appreciation of the complexity of grasping the meanings of stasis and dynamism in utopian literature.

Three Readings of Stasis and Dynamism in Looking Backward

CONTENT ANALYSIS MODEL CONSTRUCTION   The nature of the cultural model readers extract from a content analysis will, of course, depend upon how they define content. If they are primarily interested in economic systems, they will be prone to "see" economic principles and proposals and to construct a model that emphasizes economics. If their interests focus on gender relationships, gender issues will dominate their model. Since the focus of this essay is stasis/dynamism, the inclination I bring to *Looking Backward* might best be defined by two related questions: Is there potential and/or desire for change in the society described by Dr. Leete and witnessed by Julian West? Is there potential for individual development/freedom within the described and witnessed society?

Both Julian West and Dr. Leete state that there is much room for changing the society of A.D. 2000. In the Preface, a historian reveals that both the readers and writers at the beginning of the twenty-first century are progress oriented. He characterizes the readers as being accustomed "to improvements in their conditions" (Bellamy 1967 [1888], 93). (We later discover that this is most probably the voice of Julian West, who has become a history teacher.) The writers are so fascinated with the possibilities of "progress that shall be made, ever onward and upward" that he feels compelled to balance this bias toward future change with historical comparisons that emphasize the progress made during the past century (p. 94). At several points during the narrative, Leete's celebrations of progress confirm West's characterization of the readers and writers. For instance, in Chapter 1, he specifically associates the restricted horizon of nineteenth-century thought with the belief in a cyclical theory of history instead of the current "idea of indefinite progress in a right line" (p. 102). He returns to this theme in Chapter 15, when he links his culture's astounding renaissance in engineering, science, and the arts to the realization that the "race" had risen to "a new plane of existence with an illimitable vista of progress" (p. 199). In the second edition of *Looking Backward*, the one that began the book's rise to popularity, Bellamy's own voice supports West and Leete when he bases his claims for the possibility of rapid change in the nineteenth century on "principles of evolution" that make believable the "next stage" of society's development (p. 312).

As indicated previously, however, most of Leete's and West's observations delineate a stable, even static, model of social organization. From the first sentence of the Preface, in which West associates the utopian culture with "completeness" (p. 93), to the Postscript, in which Bellamy associates his model with the "ideal society" and "an ultimate realization of a form of society" (pp. 311, 313), the impression given is that Leete's society is a finished product, not a part of an evolutionary process. Many of the key descriptions of this utopian stasis are presented in the form of negations, that is, indications of what is *not* in utopia. This means of defining utopia should have been quite familiar to Bellamy's readers. As Terence Martin has noted, the "national habit" of defining "paradise by negation" was well established by the mid-nineteenth century (1985, 2–3). Leete's statements of negation leading to stasis culminate at the conclusion of Chapter 19 in response to West's questions about the lack of state legislatures, the infrequent meeting of Congress, indeed the disinterest in legislation of any kind:

> "We have no legislation," replied Dr. Leete, "that is, next to none. It is rarely that Congress, even when it meets, considers any new laws of consequence, and then it only has powers to commend them to the following Congress, lest anything be done hastily. If you will consider for a moment, Mr. West, you will see that we have nothing to make laws about. The fundamental principles upon which our society is founded settle for all time the strifes and misunderstandings which in your day called for legislation." (Bellamy 1967 [1888], 230)

If Leete's descriptions of social organization offer little support for his claims about limitless change, perhaps his comments about opportunities for individual development suggest dynamic possibilities on a personal level. Indeed *within* the systems of family structure, free educational institutions, and the industrial army (with its provision of substantial and equal support for all), there are possibilities for personal growth. These systems provide the basic physiological, safety, belongingness, esteem, and self-actualization "needs" (to borrow Abraham Maslow's terminology) that enable individual development. Primarily in Chapters 7 and 9 Leete reveals that parents watch for and encourage budding interests and talents in their children. Teachers reinforce this attention with excellent classes and frequent field trips that allow children to see adults using their talents on the job. After the three years of mandatory menial service in the industrial army (ages twenty-one to twenty-four), the members of this organization can select jobs requiring no specialized training or opt for up to six more years of specialized education/training. Leete admits that all professions are not equally popular and that all workers do not initially get their first choice of work assignment. But he claims that the sliding scale of work hours (fewer for distasteful jobs, more for popular ones) and other mechanisms adjust the job market. Furthermore, provisions are made for individuals who, for personal reasons, want to change professions.

This bright picture of opportunities for personal development is tarnished (especially for twentieth-century readers) when Leete reveals that the choice of jobs for women is restricted, that in the female branch of the industrial army only wives and mothers can attain the highest ranks, and that anyone who is able to serve in the industrial army and who rejects this "absolutely natural and reasonable" requirement of service "is sentenced to solitary imprisonment on bread and water till he consents" to serve (p. 175). In his or her position outside the static concept of social organization, such a person practically ceases to exist. As Leete explains: " 'Our entire social order is so wholly based upon and deduced from [service in the industrial army] that if it were conceivable that a man could escape it, he would be left with no possible way to provide for his existence. He would have excluded himself from the world, cut himself off from his kind, in a word, committed suicide' " (p. 132).

We should recall, however, that for those willing to serve in the industrial army, there are opportunities for personal development *outside* of its organization. During pregnancy and child-rearing years, women are excused from service and still receive their full credit allotment. Hence, most women serve five to fifteen years instead of twenty-four. For women and men there are also other options. Creative individuals, especially writers and artists, can use part of their credit allotment to produce their works. If these are good enough to convince enough people to buy them (popularity is the key criterion), they can live on their creative efforts. (Leete claims that the highly educated citizenry will only support works of excellence.) Another option is early retirement—as early as thirty-three years of age. If, for personal reasons, an individual wishes to retire early, he or she may do so and obtain an honorary discharge and a lifetime credit of 50 percent of the usual annual allotment.

As David Bleich has argued in "Eros and Bellamy" (1964), the regular retirement age (forty-five, with rare emergency callbacks to fifty-five) indicates clearly that Bellamy's concept of personal development went far beyond the context of the industrial army. For half their lives, Leete's fellow citizens can devote themselves to "personal idiosyncrasies and special tastes" and experience the "full enjoyment of our birthright" (Bellamy 1967 [1888], 222). To Leete this means a period when he can pursue

intellectual and spiritual "enjoyments" which "alone mean life" (p. 221).
Bleich observes that this attitude is much closer to Herbert Marcuse's
concept of dynamic personal development than it is to a static view of
development based on the Protestant work ethic (Bleich 1964, 447–49).

How useful is the foregoing model of Bellamy's utopia? My interest in
stasis/dynamism inclined me to a definition of "content" that highlighted
Leete's and West's comments about progress, social organization, and
personal development. From these selected statements, I constructed a
mixed model comparable to models extracted from other utopian texts. On
a general socioeconomic level, Bellamy's utopia seems as static as Plato's or
More's. On the level of personal development, however, there is room for
dynamic development both within and outside the industrial army—not to
the degree we find in works such as Lessing's *Marriages* or Delany's *Triton*,
but certainly to a larger degree than in many classic and nineteenth-century
utopias. The model can also serve as a corrective to interpretations of
Looking Backward that stress the static and authoritarian elements (e.g.,
Lipow 1982) or the dynamic characteristics of the book (e.g., Bleich 1964).
Most significantly, the model can become a touchstone for the type of
studies, so brilliantly done by John L. Thomas (1967; 1983), that speculate
about the relationships between utopian authors' ambivalence about change
and the forces that shaped their personal lives and historical eras. My mixed
model could, therefore, serve as an initial step toward an analysis of how
Bellamy attempted to incorporate dynamism into his utopia without unset-
tling his readers (and himself) with visions so changeable that they offered
little reassurance during an era of bewildering change.

TEXTUAL ANALYSIS/IMPLIED READER CONSTRUCTION   As use-
ful as "content" models can be, they are, as previously noted, based upon a
very limited concept of a utopian text (i.e., the only important elements are
the proposals and models) and upon a false assumption about the act of
reading (i.e., "content" can be extracted from the text, shaped into a fixed
model, and then used as a valid representation of the whole text). Reader-
response theory offers a broader perspective of the text, one that includes
elements not directly related to explicit or implicit statements about proposals and model cultures. (I have been particularly influenced by Wolfgang Iser [1974; 1978] and several other critics [Culler 1980, DeMaria
1978, and Fish 1980].) This critical orientation is particularly useful to the
study of stasis and dynamism because it can help us to understand how the
text can invite readers to perceive dynamic elements in supposedly static or
closed texts and vice versa. In *Reader in a Strange Land: The Activity of*

Reading Literary Utopias (1986), Peter Ruppert advocates the particular usefulness of implied or ideal reader constructs to illuminate how closed utopias can be opened:

> we must look beyond the apparently "closed" form of literary utopias; we must go beyond their reductive solutions and try to disclose meanings that are not objective properties of the text, but which are nevertheless an important part of their critical impact on readers. Such disclosure will allow us to identify what it is about utopian works that enables them to say more than they apparently say, to have an effect that transcends their formulaic solutions and dogmatic assertions. (P. 57)

Thus, instead of perceiving *Looking Backward* as a text whose valid representation is a static social structure that allows some degree of dynamic personal development, we can perceive the text in terms of networks of invitations (some disruptive, some reassuring) that imply a reader who can interpret (or decode) invitations to see dynamic possibilities for increased evil and increased good in his or her own culture.

Directly or indirectly, Robert J. Cornet (1974), Lee Cullen Khanna (1981), Peter Ruppert (1986), and I (1983, "Contexts and Texts," and "Utopian Audiences"; 1988) have examined various aspects of the reader implied by the text of *Looking Backward*. I will limit my discussion to networks of invitations related to the two interrelated roles of Julian West: West as the historian/author who can stand back from his awakening experience and compose a book addressed to twenty-first-century readers; and West as a surrogate reader, an estranged visitor immersed in his responses to and questions about an unexpected and bewildering visit to utopia. The historian/author is most obvious in direct addresses to readers; the estranged visitor is especially evident in question-and-answer sessions and during moments of solitary crisis or liberation that challenge his nineteenth-century concepts of the potential for change.[2]

As the author of a historical romance, Julian West is fond of using direct addresses to his twenty-first-century readers that invite both nineteenth- and twentieth-century readers to question conventional, static notions about their cultures. Given the fictive circumstances of West's position, "Dear Reader" addresses seem natural. West arrived in utopia on September 10, 2000, and, according to the dated Preface, completed his book approximately three months later. Though he is to some degree removed from the traumas of his first week in utopia (which he describes in his romance), he is still very new in town and very self-conscious. This dynamic, in-between stance may well be an invitation to read West's entire narrative as a therapeutic act. The writing of a narrative that celebrates the wonderful fruits of the transition to utopia becomes a way of appeasing his guilt about enjoying, undeservedly, the utopia he did not help to build.

After the Preface, West begins his direct addresses by apologizing for the implausibility of his existence in the year 2000 and for the strangeness of the era of his birth. This pose reverses the conventional returned visitor/reader relationship of utopian literature. Sir Thomas More's Hythloday tries to convince his audience that utopia exists. West tries to convince utopians that the nineteenth century existed. This reversal implies two types of invitations. First, West's initial comments about the nineteenth century would invite readers (especially implied nineteenth-century readers) to feel superior to West's twenty-first-century readers who seem so ignorant about the nineteenth century. But just as the implied readers are beginning to relax in their confidence about their knowledge, West begins asking disturbing rhetorical questions about living off the work of others and the selfishness of his era. Next, the coach analogy further estranges readers by using a familiar image to present an unfamiliar picture of the nineteenth century. Suddenly these readers have lost their sense of superiority. Like the once privileged coach riders, they enjoyed a brief period of security before tumbling into the muck of insecurity. This is, however, a constructive insecurity. Before the ideal readers of Bellamy's text can reconstruct new ideas about the future, they must deconstruct their notions of the past and present.

This implied process of necessary deconstruction is more powerfully expressed in episodes that capture the estranged visitor West in moments of crisis. West's anxiety about his double identity, his dual perception of Edith Leete, and his nightmare return to 1887 offer fascinating examples of this type of episode and have received scholarly attention.[3] Three other episodes, placed strategically at the beginning, middle, and end of *Looking Backward*, also constitute significant invitations to empathize with West, to feel his confusion and guilt, and to want to resolve that guilt in the world West left behind.

In Chapter 3, the paragraph describing West's (and the reader's) initial view of the new Boston offers a paradigm for the way these episodes superimpose images of the past and future to jar static perceptions of both (p. 115). The first five sentences present a bird's-eye view of the "great city," which is practically unbelievable to West. Then comes a transitional sentence as his eyes drift toward the horizon. In the last two sentences he sees the Charles River and Boston Harbor. These familiar sights enable West to believe that he has journeyed to A.D. 2000. The overlay of the new city on the old landscape also instantaneously transforms West's view of the nineteenth and twentieth centuries by demonstrating what his present (Leete's past) could become.

Again in Leete's library (chap. 13), familiar landmarks—Tennyson and especially Dickens—transform static images of past and future.[4] West provides vague hints about the new literary landscape represented by the author Berrian. By contrast he offers an intimate account of his own response to Dickens, an account that invited nineteenth-century readers to see Dickens's portraits of the poor in a new way from the perspective of an estranged twenty-first-century reader. In part this invitation is effective because it is expressed in terms that would be familiar to nineteenth-century readers. West's portrayal of his reading experience evokes two familiar elements of a religious conversion: Jonathan Edward's emphasis on new perceptions and Edward Taylor's stress on Grace as being absolutely undeserved. Because he now understands more about the poverty of the past and the potential of the future, it is as if West, and by implication the reader, were reading Dickens for the first time and using him to understand the future, not the present or past. "Every paragraph, every phrase, brought up some new aspect of the world-transformation. . . . I gradually obtained a more clear and coherent idea of the prodigious spectacle." He knows, however, that he does not deserve such illumination. He is awed by "a deepening wonder" that someone "who so little deserved it" had been suddenly graced with this "new world" (p. 190).

If West's initial view of Boston hints at the possibility of changed perceptions, and his response to Dickens demonstrates progress toward that goal, then the nightmare (chap. 28) represents a complete conversion. During his dream, West's new perceptions of the past and his sense of guilt are so deeply felt that his viewpoint is incomprehensible to the wealthy Bartletts and their friends who know only one very static way to view their world. The obvious invitation of the text is that readers should not be like the Bartletts. They should have the courage to change their perceptions. While critics have commented on the power of the dream sequence (Lewis 1973, 199), few of them have stressed that the nightmare's invitation is reemphasized, even augmented, *after* West awakes. At first he feels relief. But almost immediately he is "pierced" by "shame, remorse, and wondering self-reproach" (Bellamy 1967 [1888], 310). He is tormented by a voice: "'Better for you, better for you,' a voice within me rang, 'had this evil dream been the reality, and this fair reality the dream: better your part pleading for crucified humanity with a scoffing generation, than here drinking of wells you dug not . . .'" (pp. 310–11). True, West has Edith to console him. But their reunion does not represent the attainment of stasis. West is still an anguished, estranged visitor. The clear implication is that this narrative has no resolution within the text. It must be resolved by readers competent enough to discover the networks of invitations, to transform their views of the present and future, and then to alter the static views of their contemporaries so that progress toward a new type of society can begin.

DOCUMENTED READINGS: THE SENDER AS RECEIVER, AS RE- SENDER, AS RERECEIVER   Textual analyses that enable us to speculate about implied readings certainly broaden our concepts of stasis and dynamism. Bellamy's text is no longer limited to being a static social model that incorporates opportunities for some degree of personal development. It can be perceived as a network of possible interactions between text and reader that bars narrative stasis and compels feelings, thoughts, and even actions outside the text. Nevertheless, if we want to consider stasis and dynamism from the perspective of specific, documented reactions as opposed to implied possibilities, we need to examine how actual readers responded to *Looking Backward*. Admittedly this process still involves speculation and reconstruction. We often have to depend upon fragmentary documentation (e.g., letters and diary entries) and potentially misleading evidence (e.g., reviews). These sources do, nevertheless, suggest how actual readers respond to the text's invitations. This has already been demonstrated by studies of reviews and the responses of Bellamy/Nationalist Club members (e.g., MacNair 1957; Bowman 1958; Thomas 1967; 1983; Lipow 1982), by surveys of criticism (Bowman 1967; Roemer 1975; Griffith 1986), by examinations of international responses (Bowman 1962), and by reader-response writing experiments with more than one hundred college students (Roemer, 1984, "104 + 1 Readers").

Another possibility is to perceive Bellamy as an important reader, and rereader, who sends and receives, reinterprets, and resends his text. We can use standard biographies (Morgan 1944; Bowman 1958; Lipow 1982; Thomas 1983) and Bellamy's essays about composing *Looking Backward*, his revisions of the first edition, his articles in *The Nationalist* and *The New Nation*, and his final work, *Equality* (1897) to indicate some of his major responses to *Looking Backward*. These responses suggest an intriguing process of opening and closing the text that was not fully revealed in the content model or implied-reader analyses.

The first written, public evidence of this process appeared in the revisions for the Houghton Mifflin edition of *Looking Backward*, but many crucial responses to the text occurred earlier, as Bellamy indicates in his first essay about composing the book ("How I Came to Write *Looking Backward*"). This essay portrays an author who had no "affiliations" with "industrial or social reformers." He was intent upon writing an open-ended "literary fantasy, a fairy tale of social felicity" (1981 [1889], 22). Suddenly while writing, this author responded strongly to one element of the fantasy, the industrial army, as a realistic rather than a fantastic notion. This new perception transformed a "merely" "rhetorical analogy" into a "prototype" for industrial and social organization (p. 23) and simultaneously began the opening of the text to applications to the "real" world and a closing of the text to fantasies that might divert attention away from the new reading: "A great deal of merely fanciful matter concerning the manners, customs, social and political institutions, mechanical contrivances, and so forth of the people of the thirtieth century . . . was cut out for fear of diverting the attention of readers from the main theme" (p. 24). For similar reasons Bellamy changed the setting from North Carolina in A.D. 3000 to Boston in A.D. 2000.

This process of closing and opening the text continued before *Looking Backward* became popular as Bellamy responded to the first edition with numerous revisions. (These are noted in Thomas's excellent edition, 1967.) Even minor revisions reflect Bellamy's attempt to make his text seem closer to reality. For example, he changed the date of the Preface from December 28, 2000, to December 26, 2000. The twenty-sixth was the birthday of Julian West and of Bellamy's son, Paul. The change signaled a closer bond between author and narrator, and framed the text with the implication that his fiction would be reality for his children: the book opens with his son's birthday and the postscript closes with the promise that "Our children" will "see" the world West visited (Bellamy 1967 [1888], 313).

Major changes in the Houghton edition suggest that Bellamy hoped to create a text that would be more accessible than the first edition to middle-class readers and more open to direct comparisons and applications to reality. For example, in the crucial chapter (12) in which Leete finally reveals the workings of the industrial army, Bellamy made several extensive revisions (pp. 171–73). Some of the changes indicate Bellamy's desire to facilitate reader engagement by cleaning up such awkward lines as, "usually the coarser kinds to this all recruits during their first three years belong" (p. 173n). Other changes indicate a desire to eliminate suggestions of the types of class divisions that might confuse, anger, or threaten middle-class American readers. Bellamy made it clear that "all recruits," not just the "coarser kinds," belonged to the unclassified grade of common laborers during their first three years of service in the industrial army (pp. 171, 173 n). In these same pages, in an obvious attempt to convince educated readers that he had considered the practical aspects of work motivation, Bellamy added numerous details about the industrial army's grading system, incentives, and emblems, whose iron, silver, and gilt composition echoed Plato's divisions of humanity.

The Postscript (pp. 311–13) added to the Houghton edition clearly directs readers not only toward possibilities for practical applications, but also toward perceiving Bellamy's futuristic fiction as *nonfictional* history. In response to another reader (a reviewer for the *Boston Transcript*), Bellamy specifically defined *Looking Backward* as a "forecast" of "industrial and social development" in a real place, America, at a real time, approximately fifty years in the future (p. 312). To support this interpretation, he refers to radical transformations that had already occurred in short periods of time in America, Italy, and Germany. In other words, Bellamy was saying that his type of "history" text was just as practical and real as descriptions of past events. He just happened to be looking the other (future) way. Of course, this opening up of practical and historical readings of his model society also tended to close off readings that perceived Bellamy's fictional world of A.D. 2000 as a "thought experiment" or as an invitation to indulge in fantasies.

During the decade following the revising of *Looking Backward*, Bellamy continued to make public rereadings, and these continued the trend away from contemplative and imaginative invitations and toward historical comparisons and practical applications. Bellamy's second essay about composing *Looking Backward* ("Why I Wrote *Looking Backward*") was written in 1894, after the popularity of his revised text had transformed his life. He was no longer a retiring author of local journalism and psychological fantasies. He had become actively involved in reform politics. This change is reflected in his altered reconstruction of the composition process. Instead of emphasizing his lack of contact with social reform and the surprising transformations of the text, he stressed his long-standing interest in social and economic problems and his intent to solve these problems. He thus gave the impression that even before he sat down at his writing desk, he planned to offer a believable parallel history and practical solutions to real problems. One prescriptive implication of this rereading is that Bellamy now imagined his ideal readers as approaching their reading desks with heightened sensitivities to literal and practical applications and diminished sensitivities to fantastic readings.

As Bellamy biographers from Arthur Morgan (1944) to John L. Thomas

(1983) have indicated, Bellamy's essays in *The Nationalist*, *The New Nation*, and other magazines during the late 1880s and the 1890s further emphasized the practical possibilities of *Looking Backward*. These later writings also involve a reading/interpreting process similar to the one described by David Bleich in *Subjective Criticism* (1978). After a solitary reading, a person may discuss his or her reading with others. During this exchange, each reader may modify his or her interpretations and either achieve a new individual perception or concur with the group's consensus reading. Similarly, Bellamy entered into interpretive "negotiations" (Bleich's term) as he changed from being a rather solitary writer and editor to becoming a very public writer, editor, speaker, and reform leader. These negotiations changed his perceptions of certain aspects of his text. Most significantly, he began to see certain static and negative connotations to the military overtones of the industrial army. He, therefore, deemphasized the necessity of a literal reading of the military aspects of the central analogy that had, during the composition process, altered his view of the entire text. His emphasis on equality and on opening the text to literal applications did not decline, however. If anything, his break with the theory-oriented *Nationalist* and founding of the more activist *New Nation* signaled an increased emphasis on application and a transformation of his definition of what a "text" was. When he began composing *Looking Backward*, utopia was an open-ended book formed in fantasy and crafted with literary tools. As he wrote and spoke during the 1890s, Bellamy conceived of himself as having moved beyond literary nowheres. Now the world was his text, and reading it meant dynamic interaction with municipal and state governments and the creation of political parties.

The culmination (in written form) of Bellamy's openings and closings of *Looking Backward* was *Equality* (1897). *Equality* was written with a sense of urgency sparked by Bellamy's suspicion that this sequel to *Looking Backward* might represent his last opportunity to present a rereading to the public. (He was dying of tuberculosis as he wrote the book.) Certainly there are fundamental elements of this final rereading that demonstrate the strong consistencies in Bellamy's re-creations of his initial ideas about the utopia he envisioned in *Looking Backward:* the very strong emphasis on economic equality, the religious appeals, the celebration of human solidarity, and the use of the fictional settings and characters from *Looking Backward*, to name just a few.

Nevertheless, in *Equality* Bellamy modified many of his earlier views and in the process limited the potential interpretations and audiences of his text. The modified views include his image of the ideal woman, Edith

Leete. In *Looking Backward* she could be read as a model of the frank "new woman" of the future and as a rather predictable (even static) romantic heroine. In *Equality* she is an agricultural worker on a high-tech farm. We see much less of her sentimental side and more of her "new" career woman role. It is clear that this Edith is a product of "negotiated" readings, that is, the criticism Bellamy received about the original Edith and his increased sensitivity to the "woman question." Bellamy also revised his notion of the importance of the details of historical process by including more information about the political, educational, religious, and labor movement activities that led to utopia. These elements were becoming blueprints for action rather than allegories that invited thought and feeling experiments. His rhetoric, especially the increase in his use of such words as "revolutionary," also changed the historical perspective and tone of his utopia.

Most of the changes imply that opening up the imaginative possibilities of utopia (for both writer and reader) was not as important to Bellamy as opening the utopia originally presented in *Looking Backward* to specific and dynamic interactions between West's fictional world and the readers' "real" world. The changes further suggest that engaging middle-class readers—those competent to interpret romantic and utopian literary conventions and willing to engage in speculation but fearful of disruptive changes—was not as important as engaging an audience willing to take many practical, including political, actions to insure that their altered perceptions, originating in a utopian reading experience, would be translated into experiential acts designed to transform the world into a utopian text.

Of course, even before the publication of *Looking Backward*, Bellamy's utopian text invited practical and activist readings. We have documented proof of that. One reader, Edward Bellamy, read the draft of the "mere literary fantasy"—the "cloud-palace for an ideal humanity" (Bellamy, 1981 [1889], 22)—and discovered potential applications to his world. The point is that as Bellamy mused about, composed, read, revised, reinterpreted, and negotiated his utopia, he gradually closed off some readings and opened up others. In terms of multiple literary and speculative possibilities, he made his text much more static. This process began in an unpublished manuscript with changing the setting and eliminating numerous speculations about utopian culture and ended with a form of writing that minimized the differences between fiction and nonfiction, speculation and application. By contrast, from Bellamy's viewpoint, the process represented an exciting, almost frighteningly dynamic experience that began with the surprising discovery of a "new" meaning for an analogy in his manuscript, an experience which, one could argue, he dramatized in West's surprising rediscovery of Dickens. This process of discovery continued with each revision, reinterpretation, and negotiation until it completely revolutionized Bellamy's concept of literature and text: literature became a pretext for action, the text became the world.

To SAY THE LEAST, it would be fascinating if we could invite Bellamy back (forward?) from different stages of his life and ask him to respond to a reading of this essay. No doubt, during his final years, he would prefer the content analysis/model construction method, though he would probably recommend implementing rather than contemplating extracted models, and he would be appalled at my emphasis on the static qualities of Leete's society. To him this model had become a dynamic force that reshaped his life, inspired hundreds of thousands of readers to feel, think, and act, and had influenced the development of several cities, state legislatures, and political parties. "Static" does not describe those experiences. On the other hand, if he responded to this essay early in the 1880s, when he was first musing about his literary fantasy, he might have been sympathetic to the concept of stasis and dynamism indicated by textual analyses that defined implied readers who were as intrigued by Julian West's emotions and psyche as they were by invitations to contemplate the workings of the industrial army. If, however, Bellamy could return with simultaneous and full recall of all his responses to his utopia experienced during the 1880s and 1890s, he would probably say that despite their usefulness and internal consistency, neither the content extrapolation nor the implied-reader methods could adequately account for the many responses and concepts of stasis and dynamics evidenced by the documented reactions of one reader, Edward Bellamy. He might then argue (and I would agree) that the best way to avoid reductive notions of stasis and dynamism in *Looking Backward*, or any other literary utopia, would be to use at least all three perspectives in an attempt to illuminate various characteristics and effects of utopian literature. "That's not too much of a utopian request," he would conclude.

Notes

1. For example, see Khanna (1981), Roemer (1983, "Utopian Audiences"; 1984, "Utopian Studies"); Ruppert (1986); Somay (1984); Suvin (1979, 1986).
2. Parts of the six paragraphs that follow first appeared in my essay "Contexts and Texts" (1983). Permission to use this material in a revised form has been granted by the editor.

3. For example, see Dupont (1941), Lewis (1973), Quissell (1973), Thomas (1983), and Towers (1975).

4. For similar discussions of the Dickens episode, see Roemer (1983, "Contexts and Texts," 220–21) and Ruppert (1986, 64–65, 72).

Works Cited

Bellamy, Edward. 1897. *Equality.* New York: Appleton.

———. 1967 [1888]. *Looking Backward, 2000–1887.* Reprint. Edited by John L. Thomas. Cambridge: Belknap Press of Harvard University Press.

———. 1981 [1889]. "How I Came to Write *Looking Backward.*" Reprint. In *America as Utopia,* edited by Kenneth M. Roemer, 22–24. New York: Burt Franklin.

———. 1981 [1894]. "Why I Wrote *Looking Backward.*" Reprint. In *America as Utopia,* edited by Kenneth M. Roemer, 24–27. New York: Burt Franklin.

Bleich, David. 1964. "Eros and Bellamy." *American Quarterly* 16: 445–59.

———. 1978. *Subjective Criticism.* Baltimore: Johns Hopkins University Press.

Bowman, Sylvia E. 1958. *The Year 2000: A Critical Biography of Edward Bellamy.* New York: Bookman.

———. 1967. "Edward Bellamy." *American Literary Realism* 1: 7–12.

———. 1986. *Edward Bellamy.* Boston: Twayne.

———, et al. 1962. *Edward Bellamy Abroad: An American Prophet's Influence.* New York: Twayne.

Cornet, Robert J. 1974. "Rhetorical Strategies in *Looking Backward.*" *Markham Review* 4:53–58.

Culler, Jonathan. 1980. "Literary Competence." In *Reader-Response Criticism: From Formalism to Post-Structuralism,* edited by Jane P. Tompkins, 101–17. Baltimore: Johns Hopkins University Press.

DeMaria, Robert, Jr. 1978. "The Ideal Reader: A Critical Fiction." *PMLA* 93: 468.

Dupont, V. 1941. *L'Utopie et le Roman Utopique dans la Littérature Anglaise.* Cahors: Coueslant.

Fish, Stanley. 1980. *Is There a Text in This Class? The Authority of Interpretive Communities.* Cambridge: Harvard University Press.

Griffith, Nancy Snell. 1986. *Edward Bellamy: A Bibliography.* Metuchen: Scarecrow Press.

Howells, William Dean. 1894. *A Traveler from Altruria.* New York: Harper.

Iser, Wolfgang. 1974. *The Implied Reader: Patterns of Communication in Prose Fiction from Bunyan to Beckett.* Baltimore: Johns Hopkins University Press.

———. 1978. *The Act of Reading: A Theory of Aesthetic Response.* Baltimore: Johns Hopkins University Press.

Jameson, Fredric. 1982. "Progress Versus Utopia; or, Can We Imagine the Future?" *Science-Fiction Studies* 9, no. 2: 147–58.

Khanna, Lee Cullen. 1981. "The Reader and *Looking Backward.*" *Journal of General Education* 33: 69–79.

———. 1983. "Truth and Art in Women's Worlds: Doris Lessing's *Marriages Between Zones Three, Four, and Five.*" In *Women and Utopia: Critical Interpretations*, edited by Marleen Barr and Nicholas Smith, 121–34. New York: University Press of America.

Lewis, Arthur O., Jr. 1973. "The Utopian Dream." In *Directions in Literary Criticism*, edited by Stanley Weintraub and Philip Young, 192–200. University Park: Pennsylvania State University Press.

Lipow, Arthur. 1982. *Authoritarian Socialism in America: Edward Bellamy and the Nationalist Movement.* Berkeley: University of California Press.

MacNair, Everett. 1957. *Edward Bellamy and the Nationalist Movement 1889–1894.* Milwaukee: Fitzgerald.

Martin, Terence. 1985. "The Negative Structures of American Literature." *American Literature* 57: 1–22.

Merrill, Albert Adams. 1899. *The Great Awakening.* Boston: George Book.

Morgan, Arthur E. 1944. *Edward Bellamy.* New York: Columbia University Press.

Pfaelzer, Jean. 1984. *The Utopian Novel in America 1886–1896: The Politics of Form.* Pittsburgh: University of Pittsburgh Press.

Quissell, Barbara. 1973. "The Sentimental and Utopian Novels of Nineteenth-Century America." Ph.D. diss., University of Utah.

Roemer, Kenneth M. 1975. "Edward Bellamy." *American Literary Realism* 8:191–98.

———. 1976. *The Obsolete Necessity: America in Utopian Writings, 1888–1900.* Kent: Kent State University Press.

———. 1983. "Contexts and Texts: The Influence of *Looking Backward.*" *Centennial Review* 27:204–23.

———. 1983. "Utopian Audiences: How Readers Locate Nowhere." Paper presented at the Society for Utopian Studies Conference, Indiana, Penn., October.

———. 1984. "104 + 1 Readers Reading Utopia." Paper presented at the Society for Utopian Studies Conference, St. Louis, October.

———. 1984. "Utopian Studies: A Fiction with Notes Appended." *Extrapolation* 24: 318–34.

———. 1988. "Perceptual Origins: Preparing American Readers to See Utopian Fiction." In *Utopian Thought in American Literature*, edited by Arno Heller et al. Tübingen, Germany: Gunter-Narr. In press.

Rooney, Charles J. 1985. *Dreams and Visions: A Study of American Utopias, 1865–1917.* Westport, Conn.: Greenwood.

Ruppert, Peter. 1986. *Reader in a Strange Land: The Activity of Reading Literary Utopias.* Athens: University of Georgia Press.

Simpson, William. 1891. *The Man From Mars.* San Francisco: Bacon.

Somay, Bulent. 1984. "Towards an Open-Ended Utopia." *Science-Fiction Studies* 11, no. 1: 25–38.

Suvin, Darko. 1979. *Metamorphoses of Science Fiction: On the Poetics and History of a Literary Genre.* New Haven: Yale University Press.

———. 1986. "The Concept of Possible Worlds (Locus, Horizon, and Orientation) as a Key to Utopian Studies." Paper presented at the Teorie e Prassi Utopiche Nell'eta Moderna e Postmoderna Conference, Rome-Reggio Calabria, May.

Thomas, Chauncey. 1891. *The Crystal Button*. Edited by George Houghton. Boston: Houghton Mifflin.

Thomas, John L. 1967. "Introduction" to *Looking Backward, 2000–1887*, by Edward Bellamy. Cambridge: Belknap Press of Harvard University Press.

———. 1983. *Alternative America: Henry George, Edward Bellamy, Henry Demarest Lloyd and the Adversary Tradition*. Cambridge: Belknap Press of Harvard University Press.

Towers, Tom H. 1975. "The Insomnia of Julian West." *American Literature* 47: 52–63.

Bellamy's Radicalism Reclaimed

FRANKLIN ROSEMONT

"Thinking along lines entirely new":
Bellamy and the Revolutionary Imagination

Few American novels have provoked as many and as varied political and literary responses as *Looking Backward*. The best seller of its time, it exerted a profound and enduring influence on vast numbers of working men and women as well as on intellectuals, not only in the United States but throughout the world. It is a landmark of American literature, of American revolutionary thought, of the American socialist movement. It prompted scores of imitations and hundreds, probably thousands, of rebuttals. It is hardly surprising, therefore, that criticism of Edward Bellamy has focused on this most popular of his books.

However inevitable, this one-sided concentration has had unfortunate consequences. The prevalent view of Bellamy as a "one-book author" has resulted in distortion and trivialization of his ideas. Indeed, the "conventional wisdom" on Bellamy consists largely of the most unfounded judgments of his most ill-informed critics. One especially influential and oft-cited essay goes as far as to pretend that, in Bellamy's utopia, "criticism of the administration . . . would be treason; admiration for the practices of another country would be disloyalty; and advocacy of a change in the method of industry would be sedition" (Mumford 1969, 164). Now it so happens that there is nothing, not a single line, in *Looking Backward* to justify such a statement. Lewis Mumford's hasty and superficial attack is, however, all too typical of Bellamy criticism over the years.[1] Bellamy is notorious for things he never said or did, while his real contributions are all but lost from sight in a bewildering maze of contradictory commentaries. Among this country's outstanding thinkers, Edward Bellamy is a great unknown.

Not only is there more to Bellamy than *Looking Backward*, there is more to *Looking Backward* than even the most scrupulous scrutiny of that book can reveal to a reader ignorant of its author's other writings. Many of Julian West's experiences in the year 2000 can be properly understood only in the light of Bellamy's earlier and later efforts. Of course, *Looking Backward* is his greatest achievement and must remain central to any assessment of his work. When viewed in isolation, however, it simply is not the same book that it is when seen in the context of his work as a whole.

The confused and timorous state of Bellamy studies today warrants a fresh look at the full range of his ideas. Such an inquiry should help us understand the extraordinary impact of these ideas on an entire generation of American radicals. Hopefully it will also help us appreciate the specific and unique contributions of America's greatest utopian socialist and his importance for our own time.

Bellamy did not think of himself primarily as a utopian, much less as a political theorist, economist, or philosopher. He was above all an imaginative writer—a "romancer," in his own more modest expression—and it could be argued that his work has greater affinities with the dreams of poets than with the lubrications of a Robert Owen or an Etienne Cabet. Bellamy's writings abound in dazzling flashes of inspiration, challenging analogies, penetrating insights into unperceived relationships, disquieting reversals of common sense assumptions, and unsparing criticism of things as they are. Like his early science fiction and fantasy tales, *Looking Backward* is first and last a work of the imagination. Unlike most other utopians, he never pretended to have elaborated a finished system, a complete blueprint of the new society. "Revolutions," he wrote, "do not follow prearranged plans" (Bliss 1910, 811). What became known as "Bellamyism" was never a meticulously articulated political theory but rather a spontaneous ferment of ideas and agitation.

This does not mean that Bellamy's work lacks consistency and coherence. On the contrary, the continuity between his youthful jottings and his mature utopia is striking. In 1890 he remarked that *Looking Backward* had begun as "a fairy tale of social felicity" with "no idea of attempting a serious contribution to the movement of social reform" (Bellamy 1937, 199). But four years later, after rereading a lecture he had written when just out of his teens, he wondered why he had not written his utopia twenty years earlier. In this 1871–72 lecture to the Chicopee Falls Village Lyceum, Bellamy argued that

> the great reforms of the world have hitherto been political rather than social. In their progress classes privileged by title have been swept away, but classes privileged by wealth remain. A nominal aristocracy is ceasing to exist, but the

actual aristocracy of wealth, the world over, is every day becoming more and more powerful. . . . What is the name of an institution by which men control the labor of other men, and out of the abundance created by that labor . . . reserve the vast surplus for the support of a life of ease and splendor? This, gentlemen, is slavery. . . . I ask . . . that none labor beyond measure that others may be idle, that there be no more masters and no more slaves among men. Is this too much? Does any fearful soul exclaim, impossible, that this hope has been the dream of men in all ages, a shadowy and utopian reverie? . . . Are the aspirations after liberty, equality and happiness implanted in the very core of our hearts for nothing? Not so, for nothing that is unjust can be eternal and nothing that is just can be impossible. (Pp. 218–21)

Many other early writings confirm that inequality, exploitation, and the possibilities of radical change are subjects Bellamy brooded over for years before writing *Looking Backward*.[2]

Social radicalism is not, however, the only component of his utopianism prefigured in his earlier work. Far more plentiful are the expressions of his moral and psychological radicalism—his provocative observations on dreams, erotic passion, precognition, hypnosis, spiritualism, hysteria, hallucinations, exalted moods, and extreme situations. The author whose utopia "started millions thinking along lines entirely new to them" (J. A. Wayland, quoted in Quint 1964, 73) spent his life trying to think along entirely new lines himself. Inspired by the experience of poetry, he adopted the poets' favorite means of research: "Let others count gold. . . . For me, I prize more the vague and wavering images that visit my soul in hours of revery than any other excitations of the mind" (Morgan 1944, 176). Few Americans of his time cared to ask, "When will man learn to interrogate the dream soul of the marvels it sees in its wanderings?" (Bellamy 1898, 11). A relentless explorer of his own mind, he advanced to the threshold of psychoanalysis and even of surrealism. His aspiration to write "a transcript of the mind itself undominated by single motives and marked with the almost infinite variety of the mind's own operations" (Morgan 1944, 179) reads like a paraphrase of André Breton's definition in the first *Surrealist Manifesto* of 1924: "Surrealism, n. m.—Pure psychic automatism, by which it is intended to express . . . the real functioning of thought. The dictation of thought, in the absence of all control exercised by reason, and outside all esthetic or moral preoccupations" (Breton 1978, 23). Indeed, Bellamy essayed the surrealists' point of departure, automatic writing:

Is not the succession of ideas that in an hour passes the focus of our mental vision . . . a more heterogeneous, and fantastic, procession than ever graced a day of carnival? Solemn, mirthful, gay, and sentimental, grotesque, mournful, sarcastic, earnest, reckless, ascetic, sensual, prudish, prurient, thus they troop along arm in arm, intertwined, hanging to each other, a most ill-assorted, inextricable company. . . . No wonder books are dull. They present thoughts in most unnatural distorted arrangement. . . . Heterogeneity is the law of the mind. . . . For my part I am going for once to follow the law of the mind in making a book. (Morgan 1944, 179–80)

These scattered speculations are important for an understanding of Bellamy's utopia and of the passionate response that utopia inspired. Playfully elaborated in his early fiction and notebooks, Bellamy's psychology was radically opposed to all systems of thought accommodative to repression, Judeo-Christian morality as well as bourgeois rationalism. Its aim was to overcome what he later called the "Jekyll-Hyde existence" (Bellamy 1969 [1938], 98–99) of modern life by creating a situation guaranteeing "free play to every instinct" (Bellamy 1926 [1888], 169). Defense of "the instinctive morality of love" (Bellamy 1897, 142) against all convention became a cornerstone of his utopia. *Looking Backward* is, among other things, a love story, telling of a love that conquers, symbolically at least, not only time but death itself. This marvelous erotic triumph exemplifies another essential feature of Bellamy's revolutionary project: the supersession of time. In "The Religion of Solidarity" (1874) he grappled with the question in transcendentalist terms, protesting "the barrier of time," affirming his lust "not for more life, but for all the life that is," and thus declaring himself for the poets' dream of Eternity (Bellamy 1955, 5, passim). In the story "With the Eyes Shut," the clock is the embodiment of ideological reification. We enter a display room featuring phonographically equipped clocks that mark the time by reciting excerpts from literary, religious, and philosophical works:

There were religious and sectarian clocks, moral clocks, philosophical clocks, free-thinking and infidel clocks, literary and poetical clocks, educational clocks, frivolous and bacchanalian clocks. In the religious clock department were to be found Catholic, Presbyterian, Methodist, Episcopal, and Baptist timepieces, which . . . repeated some tenet of the sect with a proof text. . . . In startling proximity to the religious department I was shown the skeptical clocks. So near were they, indeed, that when [they] announced the hour of ten, the war of opinions that followed was calculated to unsettle the firmest convictions. . . . The effect of an actual wrangle was the greater from the fact that all these individual clocks were surmounted by effigies of the authors of the sentiments they repeated. (Bellamy 1898, 347–48)

A partisan of Blake's "Eternal Delight," Bellamy did not doubt that the "free play" of "every instinct" required the conquest of time by passion. His aversion to capitalism's mechanical measurement of misery is a corollary of his critique of memory and the death-oriented morality based on it. For Bellamy, memory was a "disease" (p. 18) and "the principle of moral degeneration" (Bellamy 1969 [1880], 120). Because of memory, "remorse and shame and wan regret have wielded their cruel sceptres over human lives from the beginning" (p. 105). In *Doctor Heidenhoff's Process* we meet a woman who was happy until "memory laid its icy finger on her heart and stilled its bounding pulse" (p. 86). "Remembered sin," Bellamy argued, much like Baudelaire, "is the most utterly diabolical influence in the universe" (p. 105). He disdained the "ministers and moralists [who] teach us that it is our duty to perpetuate our past sins and shames" in memory's "multiplying mirror" (p. 126), the hypocrites who "preach forgiveness and absolution on repentance," for "the perennial fountain of the penitents' tears testifies how empty and vain such assurances are" (p. 105).

"Fond of speculating what sort of world, morally speaking, we should have if there were no memory" (p. 119), Bellamy took up this problem in "The Blindman's World." On Mars, we learn, precognition is highly developed, but memory is as little-used a faculty on Mars as precognition is on earth. "You have a saying," the Martian explains to a visitor from our planet, "'Tomorrow belongs to God,' but here tomorrow belongs to us, even as today" (Bellamy 1898, 15). "The joys of anticipation and possession are the only food of love with us, and therefore Love always wears a smiling face." On earth, however, "Love feeds on dead joys, past happiness" (p. 19). In a passage especially resonant with implications for Bellamy's utopia, we are told that "heart-burnings and hatreds, engendered on Earth by the strife of man with man, are unknown on Mars" (p. 24). Small wonder that his trip to Mars made our earthling "dream of a world where love always wears a smile . . . and death is king no more" (p. 29).

Bellamy's unremitting hostility to the tyranny of memory underlies his impassioned preference for the future over the past. The Martian dislikes earth's literature, "written in the past tense and relating exclusively to things that are ended" (p. 29), and points out that on the red planet "we write of the past when it is still the future, and of course in the future tense" (p. 24). "Ghosts of the future are the only sort worth heeding," says a character in another story. "Apparitions of things past are a very unpractical sort of demonology . . . compared with apparitions of things to come" (p. 61).

Remarkably, while he was denouncing memory in *Doctor Heidenhoff's*

Process, Bellamy was simultaneously writing a historical novel, *The Duke of Stockbridge: A Romance of Shays' Rebellion* (1879). In preparing this admirable tale of the 1786 Massachusetts revolt of debtor farmers and poor mechanics, he conducted original research in the field, poring through old family records and small-town archives, and interviewing descendants of participants in the struggle. Before Bellamy, historians had followed George Richards Minot's vituperative *History of the Insurrection in Massachusetts* (1788) in portraying Revolutionary War captain Daniel Shays and his comrades in the most unflattering terms. The first to uncover the social and economic causes of the great uprising, Bellamy made no secret of his sympathy with the Shaysites. Later historians have tended to agree with Samuel Eliot Morison that *The Duke of Stockbridge* gives "a more accurate account of the causes and events of Shays' Rebellion than any of the formal historians do" (Bellamy 1962 [1900], xiii).

In *The Duke of Stockbridge*, Bellamy, the enemy of repressive memory, looks backward at a real historic event and at the same time forward to his egalitarian utopia. His romance of the year 1786 shows that his antipathy to memory was no mere intellectual idiosyncrasy but rather the critical lever of a far-reaching dialectic. What he opposed was not memory in the abstract, but the concrete ways it is used as the instrument of guilt and remorse, allowing the dead to dominate the living.

Against immobilizing memory and the tyranny of official history, Bellamy affirmed the unfettered imagination as the key to a fundamental reintegration of the personality, the necessary accompaniment of the social reintegration described in his utopia. Solidarity, one of Bellamy's central concepts, has a psychological as well as a social dimension. The abolition of wage slavery and of class divisions in society would mean the end of the individual's "Jekyll-Hyde existence." The mind would automatically undergo a major readjustment in the new conditions of freedom. This "shifting of the sense of identity," transcending "the false ego of the apparent self" (Bellamy 1898, 410, 411)—expressions from one of his tales that accurately describes the psychological transformation recounted in his utopia—would release all restrictions on the imagination and promote "an evolution of higher faculties" (Bellamy 1926 [1888], 292), a development that Bellamy's tales suggest might place at the disposal of each and all the added gifts of precognition and telepathy. "Instead of the mind-paralyzing worship of the past," we are told in *Equality* (1897), in the new utopia there will be "no limit" to what humankind can know of its "nature and destiny, and no limit to that destiny" (p. 265). The supersession of capitalism's infamous "divided self" goes hand in hand with the resolution of the contradiction between individual and society, clearing the way for what Lautréamont called "poetry made by all."

Those who share this new and higher consciousness find the thought processes that prevailed in the gloomy days of capitalism incomprehensible. "My experiences since I waked up in the year 2000," Julian West tells us in *Equality*, "might be said to have consisted of a succession of instantaneous mental readjustments of a revolutionary character, in which what had formerly seemed evil to me had become good, and what had seemed wisdom had become foolishness" (p. 211). Bellamy's emancipated utopians find it as hard to understand the constricted and degraded reasoning that justified wage slavery as his Martian found it hard to grasp the subservience to memory that prevailed on earth, the planet that, "because of the benighted condition of its inhabitants," the Martians called "The Blindman's World" (Bellamy 1898, 26). Bellamy seems to have perceived this analogy, for in *Equality* he tells of an "odd book" that appeared shortly after the overthrow of capitalism: a compilation of arguments against economic equality, brought together under one cover by a compiler who foresaw that "the time would come . . . as it has come, when it would seem incredible to posterity that rational men and, above all, learned men, should have opposed in the name of reason a measure which, like economic equality, obviously meant nothing more nor less than the general diffusion of happiness" (pp. 382–83). The name of this compilation is *The Book of the Blind*.

For many years Bellamy's critique of the mind's war with itself paralleled his critique of society's war with itself. In *Looking Backward* the two converge into an all-encompassing revolutionary critique of the human condition that is distinctively his own. This double critique, and the utopian vision it inspired, constitute Bellamy's real originality and the essence of his thought. Critics who know only *Looking Backward* have overlooked this originality, and generally have reduced Bellamy's ideas to a ragbag of notions borrowed from others. Nationalization, for example, was not even new in 1848, when Marx and Engels included it in their list of demands in the *Communist Manifesto*. The industrial army, also advocated in the *Communist Manifesto*, was long before that an important feature in the utopia of Charles Fourier. Bellamy's confidence that technology could be safely harnessed was shared by other utopians as well as by Marx and most anarchists. Equality, of course, had been a principle of English-language radicalism at least since the Wat Tyler revolt of 1381.

Bellamy's discovery that the moral and psychological problems posed in his early tales could be solved only by solving the social and economic problems that also troubled him—that these seemingly very different sets of problems were in fact inseparable—became the foundation of his utopia and of the social movement based on it. What he earlier had regarded as little more than puzzles—"attempts to trace the logical consequences of certain assumed conditions" (Bellamy 1937, 224)—became elements of a revolutionary critical theory. It should not surprise us that, having pursued surrealist methods, he reached surrealist conclusions. It was to be expected, too, that distinctive elements of his utopia should turn out to be "logical consequences" of what he found to be the only possible answers to questions raised in his earlier writings. What is truly impressive, however, is the extent to which his answers have been substantiated by subsequent revolutionary theorists following entirely different avenues of inquiry.

A major feature of Bellamy's utopia, for example, is the great diminution of work (most of it is done by automated machinery) and of working time. In a period when the eight-hour day was still more dream than reality, Bellamy's utopia went much further: Many people in the year 2000 work four hours or less and everyone gets half of every year off. No one works before the age of twenty-one, and everyone retires at forty-five or earlier. Bearing in mind that working life in the 1880s often extended to sixty years, at ten hours a day and six days a week, we find by simple arithmetic that Bellamy's utopia reduced the individual's hours of labor by five-sixths or more. In the year 2000, moreover, "the vaccuum left in the minds of men and women by the absence of care for one's livelihood" has been taken up by love (Bellamy 1926 [1888], 261).

Now consider this passage from Herbert Marcuse's *Eros and Civilization* (1962): "Since the length of the working day is itself one of the principal repressive factors imposed upon the pleasure principle by the reality principle, the reduction of the working day to a point where the mere quantum of labor time no longer arrests human development is the first prerequisite for freedom" (p. 138). This would lead, Marcuse continues, to a situation in which "the antagonistic relation between pleasure principle and reality principle would be altered in favor of the former. Eros, the life instincts, would be released to an unprecedented degree" (p. 139).

Marcuse's remarks could pass for an exegesis of Bellamy. They are, however, part of a "philosophical inquiry into Freud" in which Bellamy is not even cited.

The public's enthusiastic response to *Looking Backward* doubtless owed much to this libertarian, antiwork, eros-affirmative undercurrent in Bellamy's utopia. Indeed, given the primacy of unconscious over conscious thought, this factor may well have been decisive, and would help explain how so many people readily overlooked the fact that this undercurrent was contradicted by certain structural and other details in the narrative. That readers by and large responded to the story's emancipatory impulse, and did not take each and every detail too literally, is in keeping with the fact that *Looking Backward* was not a didactic treatise but a work of the imagination. It is not accidental that Bellamy's ringing indictment of class society and his portrayal of the good life were presented not in the academic verbiage of the economist or in the monotonous jargon of a political sectarian, but in the lyrical language of the poet and storyteller. *Looking Backward* is a kind of dream-tale, in which the socialist dream is actually the reality, and what we later mistake for the return to reality turns out to be only a capitalist nightmare. After roaming freely in the new society for nearly three hundred pages, many nineteenth-century readers must have shared Julian West's horror at the thought of returning to the "worldwide bloodshed, greed and tyranny" of capitalism (p. 310).

Bellamy is often credited with having made socialism "respectable," but he did much more than that. He made it enticing, captivating, and desirable. This was his genius, and the results were obvious. Earlier American socialists had reached hundreds and maybe thousands; Bellamy reached millions.

"The bleakness of the future":
The Condition of the Working Class in the United States in 1887

Looking Backward was written during the nation's first Red Scare. Two months before it was published, four workingmen—union organizers and anarchists—were hanged in Chicago after a trial universally regarded today as "a disgrace to American justice" (Altgeld 1986, 6). Even in 1887 clear-sighted observers saw this "judicial murder" of the Haymarket martyrs as an act of terrorism on the part of employers and their government against the organized labor movement (Avrich 1984, 301–11; Roediger and Rosemont 1986, 112–13, 118–24, passim).

The economic and political background of the Haymarket tragedy, a crucial turning point in American labor history, is also the background of *Looking Backward*. To appreciate the popularity and influence of Bellamy's utopia it helps to understand the condition of the American working class in the last years of the nineteenth century.[3]

The 1880s and 1890s were hard times for the United States working population. Even aside from the "Panic of '93," a devastation that lasted several years, the daily lives of wage earners amounted to misery and drudgery. The sixty-hour work week, ten hours a day, six days a week, was the norm, and if some worked fewer hours, many worked more (Bowen and Stewart 1929). Union men made a "living wage," and sometimes a little better. But unionists were a minority, and those who had to endure non-union conditions often earned too little to support their families. With few exceptions, even the better paid women made less than nonunion men. The million-plus children employed in nonunionized industries of course made least of all.

It was a period of rapid technological change and immense industrial growth. Standard Oil served as the model for numerous trusts that followed. Billionaires became an important factor in American politics. Working conditions, however, left everything to be desired. Most workplaces were poorly lit and poorly ventilated, too hot in the summer and too cold in the winter. Sweatshops were common. Even highly skilled and unionized jobs were hazardous and had high disease rates. Few states had laws providing compensation for industrial accidents.

Workers' housing tended to be even worse than their workplaces. Large numbers of urban factory workers lived in makeshift shacks. The constantly expanding tenements—dirty, noisy, vermin-infested—were hardly an improvement. Workers maimed on the job, or those too sick to work, joined the already large "army of the unemployed." Many became "tramps" and wandered across the continent in search of work, food, and shelter.

Employers spared no dirty tricks to keep workers nonunionized. Massive immigration was manipulated to increase competition for jobs and thus to reduce wages. The blacklist and the lockout were widely used devices to keep unionists out of work. The American tradition of "government by injunction" started in 1888 in Bellamy's own state of Massachusetts, where the court forbade striking millworkers' "displaying banners . . . to prevent persons from entering or continuing in the employment of the plaintiffs" (Adamic 1935, 101). Police brutality against strikers and union organizers was common. For tasks too illegal for the police, there were always Pinkerton's hoodlums for hire. State militias and the U.S. army were called in to break strikes. In the early 1890s, one historian has noted, labor-related "disturbances caused the most extensive troop movements since the Civil War, and Major-General Schofield, in command of the army, reported that before they were over the resources of the army were strained to the uttermost to maintain order" (McMurry 1929, 4–5).

Political democracy was widely regarded as a sham. Both sides of the two-party system were intimately allied with the great trusts. Vote frauds were common. Most women and most immigrants couldn't vote at all.

These conditions, in such sharp contrast to Fourth of July ballyhoo about "liberty and justice for all," drove many working people to the depths of despair. Alcoholism, madness, and suicide were rife. Many others, however, funneled their disillusionment into resistance and rebellion. More and more people were talking about socialism, a "cooperative commonwealth," industrial democracy, a truly free society. It was not only the deprivation of the present that stimulated working-class revolt, as Ray Ginger explained, but above all "the bleakness of the future" (Ginger 1965, 34).

Looking Backward portrayed a future that countless working men and women found anything but bleak. Bellamy's society of the year 2000, founded on the abolition of private ownership of the means of production, has done away with social classes, exploitation, poverty, starvation, sex slavery, war, slums, crime, jails, buying, selling, money, banks, censorship, charity, corruption, taxes, custom duties, advertising, housework, air pollution, politicians, merchants, servants, lawyers, the militia, the army, the navy, and the State Department. Government itself scarcely exists, its functions having been reduced to the coordination of industrial production and distribution. Coercion, we are told, is a thing of the past, everything having become "entirely voluntary, the logical outcome of the operation of human nature under rational conditions" (p. 116). Starting at twenty-one, everyone works; at forty-five or earlier, everyone retires. Working hours are short. Work itself has been greatly simplified and, as far as possible, rendered attractive. Workplace health and safety are fully assured; the new society "does not maim and slaughter its workmen by thousands, as did the private capitalists and corporations" back in the 1880s (p. 68). Vacations are long. Insanity has almost disappeared. Emigration is unrestricted. "Liberty is as dear as equality or fraternity" (p. 184).

All this has in turn transformed, or rather liberated, the human personality: "The conditions of life have changed, and with them the motives of human action" (pp. 60–61). In Bellamy's utopia there is no more selfishness, greed, malice, hypocrisy, lying, or apathy; no more "struggle for existence"; no more hunger for power; and no more anxiety or fear as to basic human needs. "The highest possible physical, as well as mental, development for everyone" (p. 222) is the aim of the new education. Everyone is happier, healthier, brighter, and friendlier; more active, more adventurous, and more creative.

If working people were disturbed by *Looking Backward*'s industrial army, with its "officers" and "privates" and "discipline," or by its peculiar retirees-only system of electing public officials, there is little sign of it. Long deprived of real participation in American politics, their lives thoroughly regimented by poverty, unemployment, hunger, and fear, working-class readers seem to have appreciated the book's portrayal of a noncompetitive, happy, healthy, carefree life, as well as its stirring indictment of capitalist injustice, and to have ignored what may seem to us to be less pleasant details. After all, it was only a novel! Interestingly, workers in Petrograd during the Russian Revolution of 1905—workers, that is, who were actively involved in creating a radical new form of democracy, the workers' council—also enjoyed Bellamy's book.[4]

We have no breakdown of sales figures indicating the social class of the purchasers of *Looking Backward*, and no way of knowing how many proletarians may have borrowed it from libraries. But there can be no doubt that a great many workers read this book that was "debated by all down to the boot-blacks on the curbstones" (Lloyd 1894, 528) and that many also urged others to read it. Every significant current of labor radicalism in the late nineteenth and early twentieth centuries—trade unionist, Knights of Labor, Populist, socialist, feminist, anarchist, and IWW—was strongly affected by Bellamy's dream of the year 2000.

"Fighting the common battle of us all": Bellamy and the Trade Unions

Unlike such earlier utopians as Owen, Saint-Simon, and Fourier, who had no use for trade unions, Bellamy was a passionate if critical supporter of the organized labor movement. His criticism was based on his conviction that the workers' struggle required the abolition of wage slavery. An editorial in Bellamy's weekly, *The New Nation*, explained that "until he becomes a nationalist, the trade-unionist will continue to fight a hopeless battle" (*NN* 1 Oct. 1892). Another editorial, however, made it clear that, hopeless or not, Bellamy's solidarity with labor was unquestionable: "From the point of view of nationalism the program of the labor unions is indeed in many respects narrow and short-sighted . . . but on the whole they seem to us to be fighting the common battle of us all against the advancing plutocracy, to which our learned and literary classes are too largely subservient" (*NN* 28 Jan. 1893).

Bellamy did not have that contempt for working people so characteristic of middle-class intellectuals then as now. A *New Nation* editorial urged that "the average college professor who should join a labor union or a farmers' alliance, and pay close attention to the debates, would be in a way to learn a good deal more than he could teach" (*NN* 19 Mar. 1892).

He had not always been so militantly prounion. Although as far back as the early 1870s he had lectured against wage slavery, protested the lack of democracy in industry, and editorialized against child labor, his early writings—and even *Looking Backward*—are ambiguous on the subject of trade unionism. It was the eruption of a new mass movement, in large part inspired by his utopia, that focused his attention on the day-to-day aspects of the labor movement. Significantly, as Bellamy's support for the cause of labor grew more pronounced, most of the middle-class intellectuals who had appointed themselves leaders of the Nationalist movement drifted away. "Nationalism can no longer be twitted as a 'kid-glove' movement," Bellamy declared in the early 1890s. "The workingmen are swelling its ranks very rapidly" (Bellamy 1969 [1938], 90). A new stage of the movement began, with Bellamy himself playing a much more active role.

The New Nation, which began publication in January 1891, with Bellamy as editor, was the central organ of this new, increasingly labor-oriented phase of the Bellamyist movement. Unlike the earlier journal, *The Nationalist*, which was strait-laced and purely "educational," *The New Nation* favored agitation and action. Strike news was regularly and prominently featured, under such headings as "Notes from the Front" and "Guerrilla Warfare Between Capital and Labor."[5] One of the paper's maxims was: "Every strike that occurs is an argument for nationalism" (*NN* 9 Apr. 1892). When it was reported that 28,800 railroad workers had been killed or wounded in 1892, Bellamy's editorial was titled "Twenty-Eight Thousand Eight Hundred Arguments for Nationalizing the Railroads" (*NN* 28 Jan. 1893).

Misled by the platitude that Bellamyism was an exclusively middle-class movement, historians and critics have ignored the impact of Bellamy's ideas on the proletariat, and vice versa. Yet this intense interaction between an imaginative writer and the working class is a drama of no small interest, and those who persist in overlooking it will continue to miss something vital in the development of American radicalism in the 1890s.

The first Nationalist Club of Boston, founded in December 1888, had at least one labor-connected founder, Cyrus Field Willard, secretary of the Boston Central Labor Council, and he was soon joined by Michael Lynch, a plasterer and author of *A Workingman's View of Nationalism* (Morgan 1944, 261, 251). In 1889 an effort was made to unite the Union Labor and socialist parties of Milwaukee on the basis of Bellamy's "great economic truths"

(Gavett 1965, 76). As *Looking Backward* continued to provoke widespread interest and controversy, and as labor unionists noticed that the editors of the big daily papers who "endeavored to smother the book with scorn and ridicule" (Morgan 1944, 292) tended to be the same editors who scorned and ridiculed the cause of union labor, one prominent labor movement personality after another declared himself for Bellamyism. These included Peter J. Maguire, general-secretary of the American Federation of Labor and secretary of the Carpenters' Union, the AFL's largest affiliate; Terence V. Powderly, Grand Master Workman of the Knights of Labor; and Burnette G. Haskell, a cofounder of the Seamen's Union of the Pacific and a one-time leader of the International Workmen's Association (Quint 1964, 85–86; Ginger 1949, 86). J. Mahlon Barnes, a top official of the Cigar-Makers Union (and later of the Socialist party), helped found and served as secretary of the Philadelphia Nationalist Club (*N* 2:7, 282). Eugene V. Debs, not yet a socialist, wrote an enthusiastic review of *Looking Backward* for *The Locomotive Firemen's Journal* (Ginger 1949, 86). Frank K. Foster, a well-known leader of the Typographical Union and of the eight-hour agitation, may also have had ties to the Bellamy movement, for in Frederick Upham Adams's Bellamy-influenced novel, *President John Smith*, the real-life Foster was selected as the vice-presidential running mate of the fictional Nationalist, Judge Smith (Adams 1897, 165).

Samuel Gompers, head of the American Federation of Labor, also indicated a friendly attitude toward the new movement, without, however, actually taking part in it. In his autobiography, he noted that America's first Labor Press Association "was initiated by a group . . . organized to promote the idea set forth by Edward Bellamy in *Looking Backward*" (Gompers 1948, 1:442). Among the founders were J. P. McDonnell, a prominent Typographical Unionist whom Gompers called "the Nestor of labor editors" and who, in earlier years, had been nominated for the General Council of the First International by Karl Marx himself; E. F. McSweeney of the Lasters; John B. Lennon of the Tailors; J. F. Busche of the *Workingmen's Advocate*; A. W. Wright of the *Journal of United Labor*; and Josiah Dyer of the *Granite Cutters' Journal* (pp. 442–43).

Throughout the 1890s, interest in Bellamy and his utopia continued to percolate all through the labor movement and its press. The shorter workday question doubtless helped sustain this interest, for the fact that this utopia *took for granted* a great reduction in the workday (not to mention long vacations) could not have failed to attract workers' interest during this decade when the struggle for the eight-hour day was labor's topmost concern. A recurring topic in *The New Nation*, the shorter workday struggle had Bellamy's total support. When the coal miners went out for the eight-hour day on May Day 1891, *The New Nation* hailed the "great strike" as "a conflict between the most abused set of laborers and the most conscienceless set of employers in the United States. We heartily wish the miners success in their desperate venture" (*NN* 2 May 1891). Another editorial in the same issue saluted "Labor's May Day" in characteristically Bellamyist terms as "the most significant and important anniversary of the year. The sentiment of the other anniversaries is retrospective and concerns the past; the significance of labor's May Day is prospective and portends the future."

Bellamy's important tract, *Why Every Workingman Should Be a Nationalist,* appeared in a labor publication, the *Building Trades Council Souvenir,* in April 1893. Six months later *The New Nation* noted the activity of "nationalist coal-miners in Cherokee County, Kansas" (*NN* 7 Oct. 1893). Labor papers covered even minor incidents of Bellamyist agitation. Bellamy himself opposed the formation of utopian colonies (he regarded them as escapist), but a proposal to establish "a community on the plan of *Looking Backward*" near San Jose, California, was given front-page treatment in the New York *Union Printer* (6 Dec. 1890). Meanwhile, unions all over the country were taking action along the lines that Bellamy proposed. In *The New Nation* for September 23, 1893, for example, we learn that the International Typographical Union appointed a committee to urge government ownership and conduct of railways and the telegraph. Although the extent to which such actions were directly inspired by Bellamy is not clear, their number increased significantly throughout the period when *Looking Backward* was selling thousands of copies a month. The large commercial press, for its part, had no difficulty discerning the specter of Bellamy behind such measures. When the Illinois State Federation of Labor called on the U.S. government to reopen large factories "now idle," in order to make work for the unemployed, the Springfield *Republican* denounced this as "rank nationalism" (*NN* 9 Dec. 1893).

Unemployment was a major problem for the labor movement of the 1890s, especially in the wake of the Panic of '93. The old craft structure of most unions left them increasingly defenseless in this period of swift mechanization of industry, and the hobo "jungle" was the only home for many a highly skilled worker laid off in the name of progress. In view of the AFL's inability to confront the tragedy of jobless millions, Bellamy's proposed remedy, with its strong flavor of direct action and mutual aid, very likely interested many a labor radical seeking a way out of the craft union stalemate.

"Let Our Unemployed Organize Demonstrations," *The New Nation* proclaimed early in 1893 (*NN* 21 Jan. 1893). Such protests, however, were meant only as symbolic gestures to focus public attention on the magnitude of the problem. In his article, "How to Employ the Unemployed," Bellamy outlined his solution:

> Let us say there are 1000 or 10,000 unemployed able-bodied persons . . . who desire work. Out of this number a certain proportion can make shoes, others can spin or weave, others can make garments, others can build houses and do blacksmithing, and others can farm . . . while many more without trades are capable of common labor of any sort. Now, these men and women do not need any one to provide for them; they do not need charity from the state or anyone else. All they need, in order to be fed, clothed and sheltered, is to be set to work to support one another. (Bellamy 1937, 213)

Because Bellamy has often been misrepresented as a proponent of "New-Deal"-type government public works, it is worth noting that his call for "the co-operative employment of the unemployed in mutual maintenance" included his specific disavowal of such programs: "The way to solve the unemployed problem is not to set them at work for the State, but to set them at work for one another. . . . Public works are no more a solution for the unemployed problem than are free souplines" (*NN* 16 Dec. 1893).

"Mr. Bellamy proposes revolution": Bellamy and American Socialism

The foregoing evidence suggests that Bellamy's impact on the mainstream labor movement was probably greater than has been generally recognized. His influence on the emerging socialist movement, however, was all-pervasive and immense. No other American has inspired so many people to become socialists.

Shortly after the turn of the century, Eugene V. Debs summarized this impact. *Looking Backward*, he wrote,

> had a most wonderful effect upon the people. [Bellamy's book] struck a responsive popular chord and his name was upon every tongue. The editions ran into the hundreds of thousands and the people were profoundly stirred by what was called the vision of a poetic dreamer. . . . *Looking Backward*, with its sequel, *Equality*, were valuable and timely contributions to the literature of Socialism and not only aroused the people but started many on the road to the revolution-

ary movement. . . . Thousands were moved to study the question by the books of Bellamy and thus became Socialists and found their way into the Socialist movement. (Debs 1908, 111)

Debs himself, of course, was one of those thousands. In Debs's essay, "How I Became a Socialist," Bellamy is the first of the authors he thanks for helping him "out of darkness into light" (p. 83). Reviewing *Looking Backward* for his union's publication in 1890, he avowed his excitement about the "possibility, or rather many possibilities" outlined in the book (Ginger 1949, 86). Showing his high esteem for "the author of *Looking Backward* and *Equality*," Debs kept a scrapbook devoted to his activities, visited the ailing utopian shortly before his death, and sent a telegram to the memorial services for Bellamy, saluting him for having "filled a despairing world with hope" (Debs 1903, 35; Brommel 1978, 52, 237). The following year, at the founding convention of the Social Democratic party of America, the hero of the Pullman strike helped draft a tribute "to the memory of Edward Bellamy, first to popularize the ideas of Socialism among his countrymen and last to be forgotten by them" (Ginger 1949, 218).

Perhaps as many as half of Debs's fellow delegates had been active in the Nationalist movement earlier in the decade. Indeed, two years later, in 1900, when the vastly larger and more influential Socialist party was formed after a split in the SDP, Bellamyism still provided the movement's major theoretical framework. As the leading historian of the Socialist party has explained, only a few of its founders "had more than the haziest intellectual acquaintance with theoretical Marxism. Certainly the anti-capitalism of many of the delegates derived more from Edward Bellamy's *Looking Backward* than from *Das Kapital*" (Shannon 1967, 3).

In fact, in the late 1880s and 1890s, Marxism scarcely existed in the English-speaking United States (Herreshoff 1967, 104). Few of the major works of Marx and Engels had appeared in translation. The immigrant Germans who monopolized the mantle of Marxism, and who were organized in the small Socialist Labor party, exerted an almost negligible influence on the American labor movement and did not even enjoy the approbation of the very men in Europe whose disciples they vociferously proclaimed themselves to be. A year before *Looking Backward* rolled off the press, Frederick Engels referred to the SLP's executive committee as "idiots" (Kapp 1976, 178). Four years later he ridiculed, as a "comical phenomenon," the fact that in the United States and England "the people who claim to be the orthodox Marxists, who have transformed our concept of movement into a rigid dogma to be learned by heart" were nothing but "a *pure sect*"—that is, socially isolated and politically irrelevant (Marx and Engels 1953, 234). The would-be Marxists' "rigid orthodoxy" that Engels so deplored, together with the arrogance and conceit inseparable from such an outlook, helped give Marxian socialism a bad name among American workers. This was emphasized by Florence Kelley—one of the few American Marxists of that period who actually had studied the works of Marx and Engels, some of which she also translated, and who was, significantly, a cofounder of the New York Nationalist Club—in a letter to Engels dated May 27, 1892: "In the workingmen's meetings Socialists are regarded as bores, nuisances and professional sowers of discord, not only between workingmen and capitalists, but especially among workingmen. And certainly the local [Chicago] Socialist agitators, [Thomas J.] Morgan and the Germans, faithfully earn the dislike with which they are regarded" (Blumberg 1964, 132).

Heightening Engels's disgust with his self-proclaimed followers in the United States was the irony of the situation: The so-called Marxists had reduced themselves to an insignificant sect at the very time when American social conditions seemed ripe for the advent of a Marxian socialist mass movement. In his Preface to the U.S. edition of *The Condition of the Working Class in England in 1844*, Engels wrote that

> In February 1885, American public opinion was almost unanimous on this one point: that there was no working class, in the European sense of the word, in America; that consequently, no class struggle between workmen and capitalists, such as tore European society to pieces, was possible in the American Republic; and that, therefore, Socialism was a thing of foreign importation which could never take root on American soil. . . . No one could then foresee that in such a short time the movement would burst out with such irresistible force, would spread with the rapidity of a prairie-fire, would shake American society to its very foundations. (Engels 1887, i)

In Europe, Engels continued, it had taken the working class "years and years" to come to the realization that they constituted a distinct and, under capitalism, a permanent social class. In the United States, however, this "revolution," as he called it, occurred "within ten months" (p. ii).

This indigenous American movement toward socialism continued to gather momentum—not, however, under the banner of Marxism but of Bellamyism, as some contrasting figures on the two currents' public activity testify eloquently. The SLP that Daniel DeLeon joined in 1890 was, politically speaking, almost invisible; it had less than 1,500 members nationwide, roughly 10 percent of whom were native-born Americans (Herreshoff 1967,

114; Hillquit 1910, 193). The same year, a single meeting of a single Nationalist Club, in San Francisco—one of at least 150 and perhaps as many as 500 "Bellamy clubs" formed across the continent in the early 1890s—had an attendance of "nearly 2000."[6]

It would be beside the point, therefore, to see in Bellamyism a "competitor" of Marxism, for there was hardly any American Marxism with which it could compete. In any case, many members of the SLP, especially English-speaking members, also were active in the Bellamy clubs.

In *Looking Backward*, where Bellamy derided the "followers of the red flag" (p. 251) he referred not to Marxists but to anarchists of the Johann Most school, or rather, to the caricature of Mostism publicized in the popular press in the aftermath of Haymarket. Bellamy rejected what he regarded as the anarchists' rhetorical violence and especially what seemed to him their naive, self-defeating belief that individual acts of terrorism could solve problems that were essentially social and economic. Characteristically, as he grew more familiar with Marxist and anarchist ideas, he absorbed many of them into his own already wide-ranging perspectives. All through the 1890s, in fact, Bellamy grew more and more radical. In 1891 *The New Nation* welcomed the news that the Chicago Nationalist Club endorsed the SLP candidates in the local elections (*NN* 21 Mar. 1891). Early the following year an editorial looked forward to "The Impending Russian Revolution": "Unless all signs fail, the history of the Russian revolution will soon be written upon one of the reddest pages of the human record. But dreadful in its course and circumstances as that revolution is likely to prove, who could wish it delayed?" (*NN* 2 Jan. 1892). In his weekly paper and in his last book, *Equality*, Bellamy's critique of capitalism gained in depth and precision, and he came to recognize the decisive role of the working class in the socialist transformation of society. All anticapitalist currents found support and encouragement in *The New Nation*. Few radical publications in U.S. history have been as nonsectarian as Bellamy's weekly. Along with contributions by Marxists, anarchists, Populists, feminists, trade unionists, Knights of Labor, single-taxers, and communitarians, it also featured advertisements for, and/or friendly reviews of, books and periodicals representative of these currents. A book especially well promoted in its pages was Marx's *Capital;* copies were offered with subscriptions. Benjamin Tucker's anarchist paper, *Liberty*, was a regular advertiser.

Bellamy exchanged polemics with representatives of other Left tendencies, but his severest criticism invariably was aimed at capitalism and its apologists. Far more radical than many democratic socialists of our own day, Bellamy not only was uncompromisingly hostile to the Democratic and Republican parties—which he saw as the two parties of capitalism—but strongly antireformist as well. "Others propose reforms," conservative philosopher William Torrey Harris wrote fearfully in 1889, "but Mr. Bellamy proposes revolution" (Goetzmann 1973, 196). Unlike the numerous reformers of his day whose role, consciously or unconsciously, was "to help capitalism obtain a longer lease of life by making it a little less abhorrent" (Bellamy 1897, 352), Bellamy affirmed the need for what he called a "revolutionary party" (p. 323, passim) fundamentally different from all other parties. He also foresaw that, as the revolution developed, the apparatus of the political state would have to be replaced by a purely economic administration. Since the goal was a society without classes, he argued that this new "state" would hardly qualify as a state at all—that "the prodigious simplification in the task of government" practically made government itself superfluous. "Almost the sole function of the administration now [in the year 2000] is that of directing the industries. . . . Most of the purposes for which government formerly existed no longer remain to be subserved" (Bellamy 1926 [1888], 207).

The closeness of such an orientation to that of Marxian socialism and revolutionary syndicalism helps explain why so many who regarded themselves as Bellamyists in the 1890s were able to consider themselves Marxists and revolutionary industrial unionists a decade later, without experiencing any sense of a break in the continuity of their lives and thought. In *Looking Backward* Bellamy had written disparagingly of "labor parties" (p. 253) but by the early nineties he recognized the Nationalist movement itself as a labor party—indeed, as "the only really practical labor party in the world" (Bellamy 1969 [1938], 90). Similarly, whereas he had formerly hesitated to call himself a socialist, he now defined his views not only as socialism but as "the most radical form of socialism" (p. 188). As the radical workers' movement grew, the Bellamyists grew with it, and they both evolved as Bellamy himself evolved: steadily leftward.[7]

The People's party was an important way station on this revolutionary road, and most of the future leaders of the Socialist party followed Bellamy through it. Charles H. Kerr, a young admirer of Bellamy's in the early 1890s, recalled years later: "I had . . . read *Looking Backward* and had been charmed by it, while I had failed to become interested in DeLeon's extremely unattractive version of Engels, and knew nothing whatever of the international socialist movement. Populism seemed to me the way toward the realization of Bellamy's beautiful dream, and I went into it with ardor" (Kerr 1904, 10).

By the turn of the century, Kerr was the foremost publisher of Marxist literature not only in the United States but throughout the English-speaking world. He later became a key figure in the extreme left wing of the Socialist party and a warm supporter of the Industrial Workers of the World (Roediger and Rosemont 1986, 249–51).

Kerr's trajectory was not unusual. Of course, to the editors of what Bellamy called the "plutocratic" press, populism was never anything more than another word for socialism and Bellamy was the evil genius lurking behind both. Disturbed by reports that *Looking Backward* was being studied by the poor western farmers who spearheaded the Populist revolt, the St. Louis *Post-Dispatch* editorialized that Bellamy "has sown the seeds of socialism in the rich soil of discontent, and the first practical manifestation of the socialistic spirit is the platform of the People's party" (Morgan 1944, 280).

Recognizing a nascent revolutionary tendency in the People's party, Bellamy and his coworkers did their best to develop it—to free it of monetary-reform illusions and thus to help keep its "first steps" in harmony with the "ultimate ideal" of abolishing wage slavery. There were hopeful signs. A *New Nation* editorial titled "Shall We Have to Export Socialism?" noted that "the recent platforms of the German Socialists [the Social-Democratic Party in Germany] . . . are pretty mild sort of talk compared with the utterances of our People's Party conventions" (*NN* 23 Sept. 1893). A year later Bellamy remarked that the People's party had adopted the nationalists' "practical programme of action to such an extent, that it sometimes is, wrongly, called the Nationalists' Party" (Bowman 1962, 448).

Populism as a significant independent movement ended with the capitulation of the People's party to William Jennings Bryan's Democrats in 1896. But its left wing—in which Bellamyists were a major force—drew conclusions from its demise radically opposed to the abject "lesser-evilism" upheld by the professional politicians who had captured the party leadership. Bellamy's own conclusions regarding this debacle were detailed in his last great work, *Equality,* published in 1897, the year before his death. Tuberculosis had forced him to withdraw from the day-to-day struggle early in 1894, when *The New Nation* ceased publication. But he continued to write occasionally for other periodicals, as well as to correspond with and receive visits from comrades throughout the country, and thereby played an appreciable role in many radicals' self-clarification as they pondered the question "What next?" posed by the Populist collapse. At the turn of the century Bellamyism itself, as an organized movement, hardly existed, but

168 FRANKLIN ROSEMONT

Bellamyists were in the forefront of just about every radical struggle. As we have seen, many of them helped form the new revolutionary party, avowedly socialist and based on the working class. Others, disillusioned with electoral politics, turned toward a new kind of labor unionism. A few tried their hand at both at the same time. Still others took up less political approaches to social change, such as the arts-and-crafts movement. As Bellamy himself said, "New issues demand new answers" (Bellamy 1898, 333).

To a much greater extent than is commonly acknowledged, the new forms, ideas, and methods assumed by radical and revolutionary currents in the late 1890s and early 1900s emerged under the sign of *Looking Backward* and *Equality*. Almost anywhere one looks in the radicalism of those years one finds strong traces of what Floyd Dell, a leading socialist intellectual of the 1910s, called Bellamy's "scientific utopianism" (Dell 1926, 145). Of course ideas from many other thinkers—from John Ruskin and Karl Marx to Peter Kropotkin and Elizabeth Cady Stanton—blended with Bellamy's in this inevitably eclectic development. Yet Bellamy's influence remained paramount. The prevailing tone and content, the very *flavor* of this *fin de siècle* "new left" were unmistakably his. Counterinstitutional rather than narrowly political or insurrectionary; imaginative and undogmatic, bridging the gulf between the "visionary" and the "practical"; emphatically feminist, nonviolent, egalitarian, marked by a strong moral sense, and aspiring to a "cooperative commonwealth"[8] rather than a "proletarian dictatorship"—Bellamyism is the word for American socialism during the decade and more that *Looking Backward* continued to outsell all other books in the field of social radicalism.[9]

It is symbolic of this flowering of Bellamyism after Bellamy that the undisputed leaders of the two socialist parties in the pre–World War I years—Debs of the SP and DeLeon of the SLP—both started out on their revolutionary careers under Bellamy's inspiration. Both, of course, had long since come to regard themselves as Marxists. It is a fact, however, that the Marxism of each of these men differs significantly from other Marxisms. Is it unreasonable to think that a thorough examination of their writings might reveal that at least some of the differences might have their source in Bellamy?

In the case of Julius A. Wayland, "the greatest propagandist of socialism that ever lived" (A. M. Simons, quoted in Quint 1964, 175), such an examination would only be gilding the lily. Wayland started out as a radical editor under Bellamy's influence in the early 1890s, and remained essentially a Bellamyist until vicious persecution drove him to suicide in 1912.[10] His widely read paper, *The Coming Nation*—a kind of successor to *The New*

Nation—began in Greensburg, Indiana, in 1893, with a motto calling for "a government of, by and for the people, as outlined in Bellamy's *Looking Backward*, abolishing the possibility of poverty" (Quint 1964, 183). Later, under the name *Appeal to Reason*, still regularly featuring texts by and about Bellamy, Wayland's paper attained the all-time largest circulation of any radical publication in U.S. history: a million or more copies a week (p. 197).

Upton Sinclair, American socialism's most prolific novelist, author of such classics as *The Jungle* and *The Flivver King*, remarked in 1910 that he became a socialist largely as the result of reading the *Appeal to Reason;* a half-century later he avowed that Bellamy "had a great influence on my thought and my life" (Brewer 1910, 160; Bowman 1962, dust jacket). Certainly Sinclair's extraordinary EPIC (End Poverty In California) movement of the mid-1930s was Bellamyist in inspiration. Interestingly, this mass movement drew on some forty years' accumulation of local California radical traditions extending back to the sixty-odd Bellamy clubs that had flourished all over the state in the 1890s. Members of these clubs joined branches of the Socialist party and rural food co-ops in the early 1900s, and later the "Plenty-for-All" stores, Progressive clubs, and the Utopian Society of the early 1930s; these in turn provided the immediate background for Sinclair's EPIC campaign, which, as Carey McWilliams put it, "furnished the reactionaries of the community with the biggest fright of their lives" (McWilliams 1946, 296). Bellamy's famous slogan, "Production for use, not profit," united all the links in this remarkable historic chain.

English-born Austin Lewis, a leader of the San Francisco Nationalist Club in the 1890s and editor of its paper, *The Weekly Nationalist*, became one of America's most inspired and original Marxist theorists; his book, *The Militant Proletariat* (1911) was among the earliest and remains one of the finest inquiries into the historic achievement of the IWW. Lewis, for whom William Morris's *News from Nowhere* seems to have provided a transition from Bellamy to Marx, was the first to translate several of Marx's and Engels's philosophical writings into English. A prominent member of the Socialist party's left wing in the 1910s, he was an important influence on his longtime friend Jack London (Lewis 1917; London 1968).

German-born Oscar Ameringer, "the Mark Twain of American Socialism," joined the movement shortly after reading *Looking Backward* around the turn of the century. Forty-three years later the great radical humorist recalled it lovingly in his autobiography (1983): "Yes, yes, *Looking Backward*. A great book. A very great book. One of the greatest, most prophetic books this country has produced. It didn't make me look backward, it made me look forward, and I haven't got over looking forward since I read *Looking Backward*" (p. 182).

Stuart Merrill, one of the "stars" of the Symbolist movement in French poetry, a close friend of Stéphane Mallarmé and translator of Baudelaire and Rimbaud into English and of William Morris and Oscar Wilde into French, was also a founder of the New York Nationalist Club in 1889, and remained a socialist the rest of his life. Born on Long Island, he grew up in France where his father, an abolitionist and Union Army veteran, was employed as legal advisor to the American legation. When his family returned to the United States in the 1880s, young Merrill was already a poet and a radical. He took part in Henry George's mayoral campaign and the defense of the Haymarket anarchists. As a spokesperson for the Bellamy movement, he organized public meetings and ran a "correspondence society" to distribute socialist literature. In the second issue of *The Nationalist* he summed up his view of the Bellamyist dialectic: "Upon the ruins of the competitive state will arise the Cooperative Commonwealth, with its system of equilibrated production and consumption. Then private interest will no more be hostile to public interest, but they will become identified. . . . The purest altruism will prove the truest egoism" (*N* [1889] 1: 2).

That he saw no contradiction between his politics and the practice of poetry he explained elsewhere: "Modern society is a badly written poem which one must be active in correcting. A poet, in the etymological sense, remains a poet everywhere, and it is his duty to restore some loveliness on Earth" (Lewisohn 1970, 49).

Merrill's anthology, *Pastels in Prose* (1890), prefaced by his and Bellamy's friend William Dean Howells, was the first collection of Symbolist prose poems in the United States and introduced English-language readers to such masters of black humor as Aloysius Bertrand and Villiers de l'Isle-Adam.

It may seem a long way from J. A. Wayland's "One-Hoss Philosophy" to Austin Lewis's sophisticated libertarian Marxism, and even a longer way from either or both of these to Stuart Merrill's international modernism. It is a sign of the breadth and scope of the Bellamy movement that it attracted such very different individuals. It would be easy to cite scores of other Bellamyists who later rallied to the red flag of socialist revolution.[11] But the few mentioned here (we shall meet others in our discussions of black radicalism, feminism, the IWW, and anarchism) suffice to highlight a crucial point: that in the United States, in the period 1895 to 1915, most of those who discovered a new approach to building the socialist movement, a new way of propagating the socialist ideal, or a new means of bringing

together heretofore separate components of the anticapitalist struggle—
that is, those who brought something new and original to the cause of
working-class emancipation—started out by making Edward Bellamy's
dream their own. One man's revolutionary imagination ignited many others.

"In this greatest of all revolutions":
Problems of Race and Gender

Bellamy considered himself and the Nationalist movement to be heirs of
the abolitionists and, for that matter, of the whole American radical tradition: the "Men of '76," the Declaration of Independence, Shays' Rebellion, the Unitarians and Transcendentalists, the early Utopians, the
women of Seneca Falls, and the early radical workers movement. He and
the Nationalist movement were, moreover, chief transmitters of this tradition—this complex of traditions—to the next generation of radicals in the
Socialist party and the IWW. Bellamy felt especially close to those who had
fought the good fight in one or more of these earlier struggles, and who then
took up Nationalism as the next step in the onward course of human
emancipation. *The New Nation* published several warm tributes to old-time
radicals such as antislavery agitator E. M. Chamberlin who, after the Civil
War, had formed the first labor party in Massachusetts and had remained
till the end an ardent supporter of "every honest effort to better the
condition of the workers and arouse them to a sense of their power and
possibilities." The article concludes: "It is an easy thing to be a champion
of the workers in these latter days of nationalism, when industrial reform is
in the very air; but it was a very different thing back in the '60s and '70s. All
honor to the men like Chamberlin, who in those dark, discouraging days,
held the fort for us" (*NN* 5 Mar. 1892).

The article noted that Chamberlin had been "a friend and co-worker of
Wendell Phillips," the most outstanding of those abolitionists who regarded the defeat of chattel slavery as but the prelude to the abolition of
wage slavery. From the end of the Civil War to the turn of the century the
name Wendell Phillips retained an enormous prestige on the Left, not only
in the United States but internationally; Karl Marx had only the highest
praise for the old antislavery crusader, and claimed him as a member of the
First International. Such was the esteem for Phillips in Bellamyist circles
that in 1888 muckraker Henry Demarest Lloyd, who would later pay a
large share of *The New Nation*'s bills (Destler 1963, 250), wrote to vener-
able labor journalist John Swinton (another supporter of Nationalism), that

Phillips's "discovery of the continuity of the abolition movement and the labour movement mark him as the greatest social thinker" (Lloyd 1912, 121).

The fact that writers on Bellamy and Bellamyism have overlooked the decisive impact of Bellamy's ideas on the foremost black socialist of the early twentieth century, George Washington Woodbey, who introduced countless black workers to the fundamentals of the socialist program, suggests how little is known of Bellamy's influence on black radicalism and the black labor movement. Woodbey, born a slave in Tennessee, was introduced to socialism by reading *Looking Backward* in 1896, and soon subscribed to the *Appeal to Reason*. An active Populist for several years, he joined the Socialist party early in the new century and quickly became a popular speaker and pamphleteer. In 1908 he was nominated for vice president on the Socialist ticket, as Debs's running mate. In 1912 he supported the I W W free-speech fight in San Diego, and two years later he ran as Socialist candidate for California state treasurer (Foner 1983, 6–10, 24, 28–30).

Woodbey's pamphlets, especially *What to Do and How to Do It, or, Socialism vs. Capitalism,* privately printed in 1903 and reprinted the same year in a large edition in *Wayland's Monthly,* and *The Distribution of Wealth* (1910), are replete with citations from the Old Testament prophets, Jesus, and Karl Marx, as well as from Frederick Douglass, John Brown, and Wendell Phillips, but they remain unmistakably Bellamyist in inspiration and outlook. The latter pamphlet's depiction of life in the future socialist society, in which we find workers dashing by in flying machines on their way to a few hours' delightful work in beautiful, luxuriously furnished factories whose spacious rooms are "decorated with the masterpieces of the painter and sculptor," is practically a summary of Bellamy's utopia (Foner 1983, 15, 19, 230). Woodbey was, in fact, one of the purest continuators of Bellamyist radicalism in the 1910s.

Further research will probably reveal that *Looking Backward* also served as an inspiration for such earlier black socialists as the Fourierist James T. Holly and Reverdy C. Ransom (in later years a bishop in the African Methodist Episcopal Church), whose writings on socialism reflect a typically Bellamyist approach and even vocabulary (Foner 1983, 269–89).

What black socialists clearly found appealing in Bellamy were his critique of capitalist inequality and injustice, and his persuasive picture of the coming universal brotherhood. It is noteworthy, however, that his published writings include no discussion of the specific problems of black Americans. Despite his veneration for the abolitionist heritage, Bellamy contributed nothing substantial to the theoretical clarification of the race issue. A letter to the editor of *The New Nation* noted that blacks were not mentioned in *Looking Backward*. Bellamy's reply acknowledged that "our correspondent is very possibly correct,"

> . . . but neither, probably, is the white man. For anything to the contrary that appears in the book, the people referred to in its pages, so far as we remember, might have been black, brown or yellow as well as white. Men, women and children are all the book discusses, and as to their rights and duties the author no more thought of dividing them into classes with reference to complexion, than as to height, width or weight.
>
> All men are brothers and owe one another the duties, and have, upon one another, the claims, of brothers. As to the colors of men, they have nothing to do with the matter. The standard of duty is not a chromatic one. Nationalists are color-blind. (*NN* 3 Oct. 1891)

Such a response, however inadequate it might seem to us today, was still in advance of much of what passed for Left views on the "race question" in the 1890s. The "color-blind" argument defined a widespread attitude that was still quite common a generation after Bellamy.

Equality informs us that race prejudice does not exist in the year 2000; sixty-year-old Dr. Leete knows of it only from the history books. The continued invisibility of black inhabitants of this utopia is disturbing, however, and Bellamy's pretense that any of these twenty-first-century Bostonians might just as well be black is simply not convincing. Dr. Leete's belief that the freed slaves had had a special need of Nationalism's "firm and benevolent" guidance, and that it served them as a "civilizing agent," reveals an attitude that can be called paternalistic at best and must have been offensive to black readers. And when it is further pointed out that the new system, in its early years, had "involved no more commingling of races than the old" capitalist system had, one cannot but conclude that Bellamy was not trying very hard to recruit blacks to the new movement. Elsewhere, however, he reiterated his confidence that the "conscious mutual interdependence" of the new society and "the intermarriage of all classes which will follow" would eventually "overcome antagonisms of race . . . which have been so dangerous" (Bellamy 1955, 124).

If Bellamy was not in the revolutionary vanguard of the struggle against racism, he went all the way on the "woman question." What Elizabeth Cady Stanton called "Edward Bellamy's beautiful vision of the equal conditions of the human family in the year 2000" (Stanton 1971, 135) made the author of *Looking Backward* one of the best known male feminists of the time. From the start the Bellamy movement was very much a feminist movement. Woman's emancipation was one of the major achievements of the revolution Bellamy dreamed of, and many celebrated veterans of the cause of women's rights took the lead in building the movement to realize the new utopia.

Among the first to rally to the Bellamy banner were Lucy Stone; Julia Ward Howe; Caroline Severance, founder of the New England Women's Club; and Addie Ballou, a supporter of Victoria Woodhull's Equal Rights party in 1872, who became the militant chief executive of the San Francisco Nationalist Club in the 1890s (Buhle 1981, 77–78). The president of the Women's Educational and Industrial Union, Abby Morton Diaz, a one-time Brook Farmer, pronounced *Looking Backward* "the book of the century" and helped organize the Boston Nationalist Club; her *Only a Flock of Women* (1893) is a classic of feminist Bellamyism (p. 79). Frances Willard, a noted temperance reformer and president of the National Council of Women, called Bellamy's book "a revelation" and became one of the movement's most zealous propagandists. Among her many recruits to the cause was revered social crusader Mary Livermore. Almost seventy when she was elected vice president of the Boston club in 1889, Livermore said she found in Bellamyism a program that surpassed as it encompassed all of her many other reform commitments (Buhle 1981, 80–81; Morgan 1944, 251).

Long before writing *Looking Backward* Bellamy had evinced a strong sympathy for the cause of women's rights, so it was perhaps only natural that his utopia should have been, as feminist historian Mari Jo Buhle has put it, "a virtual mirror image of women activists' own, decidedly sex-conscious dream of a just society" (p. 75). In the world of *Looking Backward*, women and men "now meet with the ease of perfect equals" (Bellamy 1926 [1888], 265). "Marriage, when it comes, does not mean incarceration for [women], nor does it separate them in any way from the larger interests of society, the bustling life of the world" (p. 260). Housework has been abolished, community dining is the norm, and maternity leaves are a matter of course.

Appealing as this picture of life in the year 2000 was for many women at the close of the nineteenth century, Bellamy soon recognized that his "paradise for womankind" (p. 120) still left much room for improvement. The real proof of his devotion to the cause of woman's emancipation may be seen in the changes that he made in his utopia in accord with the criticisms and suggestions of his feminist friends. *Looking Backward* had proposed, for example, an absurd "alumni" system of voting clearly at odds with the aspirations of Nationalist women, for whom the question of equal suffrage was fundamental. In subsequent Nationalist literature, alumni voting plays no role. In *The New Nation,* in *Equality,* and in tracts and speeches by other Nationalists, woman suffrage is a fixture of the Nationalist program.[12]

Unlike the apologists for patriarchy who masqueraded as Marxists in those days, and whose antifeminist rhetoric was scarcely distinguishable from the bourgeois policy of "keeping women in their place," Bellamy did not regard the women's movement as a threatening competitor but as an indispensable ally. As a *New Nation* editorial stated: "The existing forces of society, which we nationalists attack, are bound up with the suppression of women, and not till women come to their rights will men come to theirs. . . . The present worldwide agitation for the equality of the sexes is one of the main forces that is making necessary and inevitable the radical economic reorganization of society for which we work and wait. It is fitting that in this greatest of all revolutions, men and women should move abreast" (*NN* 21 Oct. 1893).

Bellamy's feminism continued to expand throughout the 1890s, and his utopia expanded along with it. Several of his *Talks on Nationalism*—"To a Woman's Rights Advocate," "To a Disciple of Malthus," and "To a Dress Reformer"—clarified important points that *Looking Backward* had left in doubt. In 1891 Bellamy's weekly paper argued that "while some men oppress other men, all men oppress women," and went on to defend women's "right to their own bodies" (*NN* 21 Nov. 1891). In *Looking Backward* Dr. Leete had boasted, with more than a hint of masculine egotism, that men had "given" women "a world of their own" (p. 259). *The New Nation,* however, stresses that one of nationalism's "distinguishing characteristics" is that "it claims all for woman that it claims for man, and . . . claims it for her in her own right and not by or through the favor of man" (*NN* 21 Nov. 1891).

Bellamy's last book shows how deeply the women's movement of the 1890s influenced his view of the coming revolution and the new society. Feminists had hailed *Looking Backward* as a book of their own, but the feminism of *Equality* is vastly deeper. In *Equality* he denounces, more bitterly than ever, "the utter hypocrisy underlying the entire relation of the sexes" in capitalist society, "the pretended chivalric deference to women on the one hand, coupled with their practical suppression on the other" (p. 129). In his new vision of utopia, woman's place is everywhere:

> . . . the elevation and enlargement of woman's sphere in all directions was perhaps the most notable single aspect of the Revolution. . . . Since the Revolu-

tion there has been no difference in the education of the sexes nor in the independence of their economic or social position, in the exercise of responsibility or experience in the practical conduct of affairs. . . . They are no longer, as formerly, a peculiarly docile class, nor have they any more toleration for authority, whether in religion, politics or economics, than their brethren. In every pursuit of life they join with men on equal terms. (Pp. 263–64)

In *Looking Backward* we were told that "under no circumstances" was a woman "permitted to follow any employment not perfectly adapted . . . to her sex" (p. 257), but in *Equality* "there is not a trade or occupation . . . in which women do not take part" (p. 43). In *Equality* women are no longer at war with their bodies; they have overthrown the tyranny of fashion and now wear simpler clothes, as feminist dress reformers had long urged. Married women do not take their husbands' names. "Absolute sexual autonomy" is guaranteed. Sexuality is no longer a taboo subject. Several years earlier a *New Nation* feature had taken up the question of reproductive rights, affirming that under Nationalism "It will be for women to say how many children shall come into the world" (*NN* 3 Feb. 1894). *Equality* concludes with a more detailed discussion of this subject. "Prior to the establishment of economic equality by the great Revolution," we are reminded, "the non-childbearing sex was the sex which determined the question of childbearing." In the new society, however, women are "absolutely free agents in the disposition of themselves" (p. 412). Elsewhere in the book we learn that childbirth is now painless and that, thanks to the new conditions of equality, parents at last are worthy of their children.

A headline from *The New Nation*, "The War for Woman's Independence Must Become Socialistic" (28 Oct. 1893), was a cardinal tenet of Bellamy's feminism. As the movement declined in the late nineties, the struggle for feminist socialism assumed new forms. With the passing of Mary Livermore, Lucy Stone, Frances Willard, and others of the "old guard," younger women who had taken part in Bellamyist agitation—including Florence Kelley, Imogene Fales, and Corinne Brown—came to regard themselves as Marxists and found their way to the Socialist party. Charlotte Perkins Gilman was also active in the SP for a time but never accepted its Marxian orientation. A leading California Nationalist in the 1890s and widely regarded as the most influential feminist theorist in the early decades of the new century, she consistently rejected all varieties of Marxism and remained a more or less orthodox Bellamyist socialist till her death in 1935 (Buhle 1981, 79; Hill 1980, 170–71; Riegel 1963, 166).

One of the most remarkable figures in a movement crowded with remarkable figures, Gilman in a very real sense was the truest Bellamyist of them all, not merely because of her fidelity to Bellamy's socialism, but because her own life and work followed a path so similar to his. Like Bellamy, she was an imaginative writer, deeply introspective, with an interest in psychopathology; her early tale, "The Yellow Wallpaper," is a classic of horror with feminist implications. Like Bellamy, she followed through these implications, providing her own feminist-socialist critique of capitalist civilization in *Woman and Economics* (1898) and her own fantastic, hilarious, feminist utopia in *Herland* (1915). Both of these books are recognizably Bellamyist, yet they add to Bellamy's vision as much and even more than they borrow. In responding imaginatively to Bellamy's challenge, Gilman grasped the animating spirit of Bellamy's method.

A hundred years after *Looking Backward*, women earn fifty-nine cents for every dollar earned by men, and so mild a reform as the Equal Rights Amendment has failed to pass. Is Bellamy's feminism too far ahead of our time?

"One great union": Bellamyism and the IWW

Long after all but the faintest local traces of the organized Nationalist movement had vanished, Bellamy was an important influence on the largest and most revolutionary workers' organization the United States has ever seen: the Industrial Workers of the World (IWW), known as Wobblies, founded in Chicago in 1905. Although this influence has not been explored by historians, it has been readily acknowledged by Wobblies themselves.[13]

Hints that new revolutionary tremors would soon be running through the American working class were not rare in the increasingly proletarianized Bellamyist publications of the 1890s. The leading role of a newly united labor movement was asserted as early as 1892 in the Nationalist novel *Philip Meyer's Scheme: A Story of Trades-Unionism*, by Archibald McCowan (writing as "Luke A. Hedd"), a work vigorously promoted by *The New Nation*. Another Nationalist novel, James A. Galloway's *John Harvey: A Tale of the Twentieth Century* (1897), shows the "long discordant" labor movement uniting in "one great union" that becomes the decisive force in the revolution. Whether future Wobblies read this story which thus announces one of their own favorite watchwords we do not know, although the fact that it was published by Charles H. Kerr, already the leading radical publisher in the country, suggests the likelihood that some did. There is not the slightest doubt, however, that many Wobblies had read Bellamy's work.

The influence of *Looking Backward* on two prominent founders of the IWW, Eugene Debs and Daniel DeLeon, has already been noted. Another early Wobbly with former Bellamyist connections was an old Knight of Labor, George Speed, a resident of the Bellamy-influenced Kaweah utopian colony in California, a member of the SLP, and for many years an associate of Jack London (London 1968, 183).

The celebrated IWW orator, Elizabeth Gurley Flynn—whose mother, incidentally, had belonged to the Concord, New Hampshire, Bellamy Club—wrote vividly in her autobiography of the "profound impression" *Looking Backward* had made on her at the age of fifteen:

> The book portrayed an ideal society, due to the abolition of banks, landlords and capitalists. It was an imaginative description of what a socialist America could be like, with collective ownership of all natural resources and industries and full utilization of machinery, technical knowledge and the capacities of her people. It appealed to me as practical and feasible. . . . It was a biting criticism of capitalism . . . a convincing explanation of how peaceful, prosperous and happy America could be under a socialist system of society. (Flynn 1976, 49–50)

Within a year of reading Bellamy, Flynn joined the IWW and soon became its best known woman organizer.

Ralph Chaplin, by the 1910s a leading IWW editor, cartoonist, and songwriter, had several years earlier drawn a cover and illustrations for the Charles H. Kerr Company's "Pocket Library of Socialism" edition of Bellamy's *Parable of the Water Tank*. In 1915 Chaplin wrote the famous IWW song, "Solidarity Forever," long since adopted as the anthem of the entire American labor movement. In view of the supreme resonance of the notion of solidarity in the world of *Looking Backward* and *Equality*, might Chaplin's lyrics have been inspired, in part, by Bellamy's great dream?

Another well-known Wobbly interested in Bellamy was poet/editor/ organizer Covington Hall, renowned for unionizing lumberjacks in the deep South in the 1910s. As late as 1945, in a discussion of Bellamy's contention that ruling classes learn nothing from their predecessors' fates and that "the capitalist class will prove no exception," Hall went on to insist that "everything that has happened in the last generation, and is now happening, proves Bellamy right beyond contradiction" (Hall 1945).

Wobbly Irving Abrams, who was also active in the anarchist and free-thought movements, went as far as to proclaim *Looking Backward* one of "the bibles" of his generation of radicals (Abrams 1987, 34). Certainly Bellamy's books were in the library of every one of the hundreds of IWW halls around the United States and in the IWW Work People's College in

Duluth, Minnesota. Only Jack London and Upton Sinclair might have had a wider Wobbly readership in the first two decades of this century. Even in the mid- and late 1920s, when the newer trends in American radicalism had consigned Bellamy to oblivion, the IWW press continued to cite him as an important source. A long appreciation of *Looking Backward* appeared in the IWW newspaper *Industrial Worker* on November 17, 1926. The following year, two Wobbly authors, in a full-length chronicle of the "class war" in America, declared that

> the vision of a triumphant working class is the abolition of all classes, the equalizing of all peoples in a state of society something very like that pictured by Edward Bellamy forty years ago in *Looking Backward* and its sequel, *Equality*. . . . What we want is a new social system based on social equality of all, with every member of society doing a useful part and enjoying the full benefit of his work. That *everyone* includes the present capitalists as well as workers. There will be no capitalists, no employer and employed, no wage system; all will be workers, that is, performers of some useful function in society, and all will get the full benefit of what they do. (Delaney and Rice 1927, 166)

IWW organizer Fred Thompson, one-time general secretary-treasurer, many times editor of its weekly paper, and long recognized as the union's official historian, affirmed that Bellamy "had made a strong impression on American labor" (F. Thompson 1955, 16), that *Looking Backward* was "a good introduction to radical ideas," and that well into the 1930s "everybody read it" (F. Thompson 1987). Elsewhere he recalled that the poem, "To Labor," by Charlotte Perkins Gilman—who also wrote the anthem of the AFL Women's Trade Union League (Tax 1980, 95)—was a favorite of IWW soapboxers in the 1920s and 1930s (Bird et al. 1985, 217).

A later-generation Wobbly, Jenny Velsek, recalls receiving *Looking Backward* in 1940 as a gift from her fiancé, Charles Velsek. Both had been members of the IWW for several years, and Charlie had been chairman of the union's General Executive Board. Jenny Velsek found the book "amazing" and "impressive"; she and Charlie discussed it together at length. And she adds: "Lots of Wobblies read it" (Velsek 1987).

In *Standing Fast*, a fine evocative novel of American radicalism from the 1930s through the 1960s, Harvey Swados told of a young worker whose radicalism was sparked by an old IWW seaman who urged him to read *Looking Backward* (Swados 1970, 58). It so happens that the young worker in the novel was based on a real-life radical, Stan Weir, who confirms that this incident really took place in his youth. The Wobbly seaman was Fred Liere, a Dutch immigrant also well known in the Seamen's Union of the

Pacific. Weir remembers discussing Bellamy with "half a dozen" IWW seamen. "Those old Wobblies were not dogmatic," he recalls. "They didn't care much about theoretical subtleties. What they wanted was to get their fellow workers interested in radical ideas." In literature, Weir points out, they promoted "anything that would jog people's minds and make them think. *Looking Backward* was just perfect for that" (Weir 1987).

Most remarkable of all, perhaps, is the case of Walter Nef, principal organizer of the largest and in many ways most effective and most impressive IWW affiliate, Agricultural Workers' Organization No. 400, the pioneering union of America's migratory farm workers. Of German-Swiss background, Nef has been called "one of the most efficient organizers the IWW ever had" (Renshaw 1967, 135, citing Wobbly Charles Ashleigh). Before turning to agriculture he worked on construction and in a sawmill on the northwest coast, took part in the Spokane free-speech fight of 1909–10, and organized lumber workers in Minnesota (Foner 1981, 73, 224n). After serving several years as the AWO's general secretary and "guiding genius" (Dubofsky 1969, 345)—during which Wobbly harvest hands won substantial wage increases, shorter hours, and working conditions much superior to those endured by farm workers today—he headed the large IWW local in Philadelphia. One of the 101 IWWs convicted of obstructing the war effort in 1918, Nef spent many hard years in prison for his beliefs.

Although he regarded himself as an equalitarian socialist even before he joined the IWW, it was only much later in life that Nef discovered Bellamy's books. He immediately recognized in *Looking Backward* and *Equality* the theoretical basis for the ideas that had animated his whole life's work. In his last years, in the 1940s—when the IWW "One Big Union" had shrunk to a very small organization—Nef continued agitating for Bellamyism through his mimeographed *Equalitarian Bulletin* (McGuckin 1987).[14]

Wobblies appreciated Bellamy's merciless indictment of capitalist iniquity as much as socialists did, but they especially liked his emphasis on the social and economic, rather than political, character of the Revolution, and on the industrial structure and egalitarianism of the new society. Time and again we find IWW pamphleteers summing up the Wobbly conception of social transformation in terms that Bellamy himself liked to use: "Machine production, the social consciousness of humanity, and the industrial form of social organization: these are the bases of the new society. These are the guarantees of Industrial Democracy" (Woodruff n.d., 40).

Forty years after he helped found the IWW, C. E. "Stumpy" Payne, somewhat less self-assuredly but still within a clearly Bellamyist frame-work, reflected on the possibilities of an "industrial republic":

> With the passing of democracy went all the old forms of maintaining it. New ones must be built. The shape of those new instruments begins to emerge, though they are not yet clear. But they cannot be the forms of the past. The new forms must fit the new conditions. Modern industry is a vast complicated web of interdependent units, woven together by the dependence of each upon all the others. . . . A prime necessity of the new forms . . . is that every person shall fully realize his value to others, and his dependence on all others for his exis-tence. . . . Industry must be operated and controlled by those who understand it [i.e., the workers]. (Payne 1945, 3–4)

J. A. Wayland remarked in the early 1890s that "The whole West is permeated with 'Bellamyism'" (*NN* 24 Dec. 1891). Another observer from those days reported that, throughout the West, Bellamy's books "were bought as fast as the dealers could supply them" (Elizabeth Higgins, quoted in Hicks 1961, 132). Considering the importance of the West in the IWW's origins and development, it seems fair to conclude that Bellamy may have influenced IWW thinking even more than the Wobblies them-selves may have realized. "By organizing industrially," says the last line of the famous IWW Preamble, "we are forming the structure of the new society within the shell of the old." Isn't this conception much closer to Bellamy than to Marx, LaSalle, Proudhon, Bakunin, the early utopians, the Bolsheviks, the anarchosyndicalists, or any other revolutionary cur-rent?

"Liberty is the first and last word": *Bellamy and the Anarchists*

Because Bellamy is so often dismissed as a "state-socialist"—indeed, as "the archetypal state-socialist" (Tod and Wheeler 1978, 111)—and there-fore as fundamentally and irredeemably authoritarian, it is worthwhile to examine Bellamy's connections with those revolutionists who called them-selves anarchists, and whose principal aim was the abolition of the state and of all forms of coercion.[15]

As noted earlier, Bellamy's criticism of the "followers of the red flag" in *Looking Backward* was aimed at the already-stereotyped anarchist bogey-man of the day, Johann Most, editor of the New York German-language anarchist paper, *Freiheit*. A former member of the Reichstag, Most was a gifted revolutionary pamphleteer, renowned in the German-speaking world especially as a humorist and as the author of some of the best-loved German workers' songs. In the mainstream English-language press, however, he was known only as the wild-eyed apostle of "propaganda by the deed," as detailed in his notorious pamphlet, *The Science of Revolutionary Warfare* (1885), an urban guerrilla manual that included recipes for bombs and poisons (Avrich 1984, 61–67, 164–65).

It is doubtful that Bellamy knew Most's work first-hand. *Looking Backward*'s hostile glance at anarchists relied on standard caricatures from the commercial press and revealed no familiarity with the movement or its theories. The rise of the Nationalist movement, which expanded Bellamy's awareness of other currents of social radicalism, also convinced him of the impossibility of relying on the mainstream press for information on these currents. When the Burlington, Vermont, *Free Press* declared that Bellamy himself was "no better than an anarchist of the Herr Most school" (*NN* 14 Nov. 1891), it may well have stimulated his curiosity about anarchism as much as his disgust with "plutocratic" journalism.

Anarchists, meanwhile, had become interested in the best-selling radical book of the time. The most famous anarchist in the world, Peter Kropotkin, criticized *Looking Backward* in a long, four-part series featured on the front page of the anarchist weekly *La Révolte*, published in Paris, in 1889. Clearly impressed by the book's phenomenal circulation ("one finds it on sale at every railway station"), the author of *Mutual Aid* found a number of things to admire in Bellamy's novel: its forceful arguments for the abolition of wages and of money, for example, and its emphasis on the new society's freedom of choice in pursuing occupations. Although he was disturbed by the book's reflection of what he called "authoritarian prejudices," Kropotkin added that Bellamy's concessions to authoritarianism are "absolutely useless in [Bellamy's] own system." "Whatever the faults of this little book," he concluded, it has "rendered the immense service of suggesting some ideas and offering material for discussion to all those who truly seek the social Revolution" (Kropotkin 1889; Nettlau 1981, 403).

Another reviewer was the prominent Italian anarchist, Saverio Merlino. Highly critical of Bellamy's plan for social reconstruction and of his "materialism," Merlino was nonetheless enthusiastic about the author's powerful critique of capitalist society, his literary artistry, and his extraordinary imagination. Interestingly, Merlino argued that Bellamy had unconsciously made use of essentially anarchist ideas while believing that he opposed them. In Merlino's later review of *News from Nowhere* by William Morris (whom Merlino regarded as an anarchist), he conceded, in a comparison of the two books, that *Looking Backward* had greater dramatic intensity and a stronger hold on the reader's interest (Bowman 1962, 307–8, 344; Merlino 1891, 225).

Among American anarchists, the individualists—whose principal organ was Benjamin Tucker's *Liberty,* published in New York—were perhaps most hostile to the new collectivist utopia (Martin 1970, 227). Here and there, however, Bellamyists and individualists seem to have got on fairly well. According to the Denver, Colorado, *Individualist,* for example, "the Denver nationalists are worthy of much praise, because of the freedom of expression allowed to all phases of the social question at their meetings" (*N* 2 [8 July 1890]:342).

The fact that the secretary of the Denver Nationalist Club, Arthur Cheesewright, had long been active in defending the Haymarket anarchists—his "Haymarket Defense Song" appeared in 1887 (Roediger and Rosemont 1986, 117)—may have facilitated good relations between the two groups. The Haymarket defense and amnesty campaign was the major labor defense effort of the nineteenth century. After four of the defendants were hanged in 1887, three others languished in prison until Illinois Governor John P. Altgeld pardoned them in 1893. Many Bellamyists were active in this campaign, most notably Clarence Darrow, the young vice president of the Chicago Nationalist Club (*NN* 13 June 1891). When Governor Altgeld at last issued his famous pardon—an act greeted with howls of derision by editors of dailies across the land—Bellamy's weekly hailed the gesture, adding that "it should have been done long ago" (*NN* 29 July 1893).

Bellamy never succeeded in seeing eye to eye with the anarchists, but his attitude toward them changed noticeably during the 1890s. *The New Nation*'s occasional polemics on the subject tend to be comradely in tone. In December 1891 the paper reprinted an article by British socialist and animal-rights advocate Henry S. Salt that boldly declared that "anarchy . . . is the goal where extreme communist and extreme individualist even nowadays meet, and where both parties will unite their forces in the future" (*NN* 12 Dec. 1891). A few weeks later it featured an article on Karl Marx by well-known anarchist C. L. James of Eau Claire, Wisconsin (*NN* 9 Jan. 1892). A front-page editorial in February 1892, titled "Nationalism Logically Implied in Individualism," argued that "there is no anarchist on earth who holds more absolutely to the principle of self-direction in self-regarding matters than does *The New Nation*" (*NN* 13 Feb. 1892). When Emma Goldman spoke of anarchism as "a social system without government of any kind," Bellamy's paper cited definitions of "system" from

Webster's dictionary to show that this was "a contradiction in terms" (*NN* 21 Oct. 1893). But *The New Nation* also declared Henry Olerich's anarchist utopia, *A Cityless and Countryless World,* "well worth reading." Subtitled "An Outline of Practical Co-operative Individualism," the book was said to show how "an exceedingly elaborate social system, extending to very min-ute details of personal habits, can be carried out without any force except voluntary cooperation" (*NN* 10 June 1893).

Bellamy's ecumenical attitude toward other radicals was shared by many anarchists in the 1890s. In the preface to his book, *Why Government at All?* (1892), Chicago anarchist William H. Van Ornum expressed his eagerness "to secure the cooperation of all schools of social reformers" (p. vi). Although his carping criticism of what he termed the "absurdities" and "fallacies" of Bellamy and others precluded such cooperation, the failure of his own peculiar proposal—that anarchists should run for major offices on a platform promising only to abolish government—may have led him to reconsider his tactical approach. Two years later we find his *Money, Cooperative Banking and Exchange* among ten pamphlets of "Reform Literature" available postpaid from *The New Nation* (*NN* 27 Jan. 1894). Two years after that, in his *Fundamentals of Reform,* a call for a united front of anarchists, nationalists, socialists, and single-taxers, Van Ornum urged one and all to abandon their divisive labels, for "we are frittering away our strength in mutual destruction instead of mutual and helpful construction" (Avrich 1978, 152).

A *New Nation* editorial sympathetically explaining the reasons for a new wave of anarchist bombings in Europe was reprinted by Lucy Parsons, one of the best-known labor agitators of the time and widow of Haymarket martyr Albert R. Parsons, in her Chicago paper, *Freedom; A Revolutionary Anarchist-Communist Monthly;* in a short preface she called it "a correct and intelligent version of the situation across the waters . . . in such striking contrast to what our capitalistic press would have us believe. . . . Mr. Bellamy's deductions and conclusions meet with our hearty endorsement" (*Freedom* June 1892; Roediger and Rosemont 1986, 155–56).

Bellamyists and anarchists continued to intermingle throughout the decade. The celebrated Nationalist lecturer Charlotte Perkins Gilman con-tributed poems to numerous anarchist periodicals. Voltairine de Cleyre, whom Emma Goldman called "the greatest woman Anarchist of America" (Avrich 1978, 4), contributed poems to *The Pennsylvania Nationalist.* Wil-liam Francis Barnard—the "Anarchist Poet" in Hutchins Hapgood's novel of turn-of-the-century Chicago radicalism, *The Spirit of Labor*—had a poem in *The New Nation* (1 July 1893).

Some anarchists even became Bellamyists. Albert Currlin, former editor of the Chicago *Arbeiterzeitung* (which, under his predecessor, Haymarket martyr August Spies, was the largest German-language daily in the city), was organizing Nationalist clubs in California in 1889 (Burbank 1966, 202). At a meeting of the San Francisco club the following year, Currlin's speech on the eight-hour movement "was cheered repeatedly and made a profound impression" (Haskell 1890, 13). Another anarchist-turned-Bellamyist was C. S. Griffin, a collaborator on Albert Parsons's *Alarm* who later wrote a collection of Nationalist essays (Morgan 1944, 436).

At least one prominent Bellamyist went on to become a prominent anarchist: William C. Owen. Born in India and raised in England, Owen emigrated to the United States in 1882 and went to California, where he served as secretary of the International Workmen's Association in 1885. In May 1889 he helped organize Los Angeles Nationalist Club No. 1, the inaugural meeting of which was held in his house. In April of the following year he presided over the state convention of Nationalist clubs, at which the California Nationalist party was formed, and from May to November he edited the party's official organ, the *Weekly Nationalist* (Haskell 1890). Later, in New York, he helped form a socialist group that shared the political views of William Morris, published a book on Herbert Spencer, wrote a laudatory review of Marx's *Capital* for *The New Nation*, and met the Italian anarchist Saverio Merlino. Now regarding himself as an anarchist, Owen translated "as best I could, everything by Kropotkin on which I could lay my hands," and began an extensive collaboration on the international anarchist press. From 1910 to 1916 he devoted himself primarily to the cause of the Mexican Revolution, as editor of the English section of Ricardo Flores Magon's paper, *Regeneración*, published in Los Angeles. Late in 1916, hunted by the police as a "subversive," Owen returned to England, where he remained until his death a tireless anarchist activist and pamphleteer (Becker 1986, 13–15).

Unfortunately for the historian of radical ideas and movements, none of those who passed from anarchism to Bellamyism or vice versa seem to have left us an account of their reasons for doing so. Moreover, little is known of the effect such ideological and organizational comings-and-goings may have had on Bellamy's own thinking. But we do know the criticism that anarchists made of *Looking Backward*, and that it was substantially the same as that made by the Marxist William Morris in his oft-quoted review in *The Commonweal*, journal of the Socialist League (22 Jan. 1889). Bellamy probably read the review, and we know that he read Morris's more detailed "response" to his utopia—Morris's own utopian novel, *News from No-*

where—for it is reviewed at length in *The New Nation*, almost certainly by Bellamy himself (*NN* 18 Apr. 1891).[16] An examination of Bellamy's later writings, especially *Equality*, the author's definitive last word on his social philosophy, should enable us to determine what effect, if any, libertarian criticism had on the final shaping of his utopia.

Anarchists who differed vehemently among themselves on many matters agreed on their criticisms of *Looking Backward*. Whether Marie-Louise Berneri, a prominent anarchist of a later generation, read all that her predecessors had to say on the subject we do not know, but her *Journey Through Utopia* expresses the substance of their comments in a detailed anarchist critique that can be summarized as follows:

> 1. Bellamy's proposed industrial system is authoritarian and statist, as evidenced especially by its militarylike regimentation, use of compulsion, and absence of political rights.
>
> 2. His utopia is not truly a classless society, for an "industrial aristocracy" of "managers" enjoys special privileges and power (Berneri 1982, 250).
>
> 3. Bellamy "takes little note of the differences in the psychological make-up of individuals" and there is no place in his utopia for "conscientious objectors"— that is, those who would prefer not to participate in it (Berneri 1982, 254, 249).

Now there are numerous passages in *Looking Backward* stating the precise opposite of every one of these criticisms. Assertions alone, however, prove as little in literature as in life. William Morris's objection, that what Bellamy tells us about his utopia is not necessarily upheld by the "impression" the reader receives from his account of it, is not entirely unfounded. There are, indeed, glaring contradictions: assured that jails no longer exist, twenty-eight pages later we are astonished to learn that there are still jailers! We may accept Bellamy's contention that, in this utopia, "there is far less interference of any sort with personal liberty" than under the system of wage slavery, but his recurring military motif does not help convince us that his system is "entirely voluntary" (Bellamy 1926 [1888], 116). Whatever Bellamy's intentions, the organizational structure of his utopia, as originally presented, strikes the modern reader as woefully bureaucratic.

Bellamy himself evidently reached this conclusion, for in *Equality* the industrial army and all its trappings have virtually disappeared. *Looking Backward* had abolished the army and navy, more or less in passing, but now Dr. Leete emphasizes that "the soldier has had his day, and passed away forever with the ideal of manhood which he represented" (p. 210). Instead of the military imagery that disfigured *Looking Backward*, Bellamy's later writings are brightened by libertarian imagery. Social classes are "prisons for their inmates," Bellamy writes, and the aim of the Revolution is to "break the bars and set the prisoners free" (Bellamy 1969 [1938], 130). "Full, free, untrammeled": that is life in the year 2000, mentally and physically, individually and socially (Bellamy 1897, 119). When Julian West assumes that "no doubt there is a compulsory side" to the new social organization, Dr. Leete replies: "Not at all. . . . If our system cannot stand on its merits as the best possible arrangement for promoting the highest welfare of all, let it fall." And he adds: "As to compelling anyone to work against his will by force, such an idea would be abhorrent to our people" (p. 41). In the new society, "no sort of constraint [is] brought to bear upon . . . anybody" (p. 360). "Liberty," says Dr. Leete, "is the first and last word of our civilization" (p. 262).

Political rights and democracy, treated so cavalierly in *Looking Backward,* are guaranteed in the later writings.[17] "We don't propose a paternal government, but on the contrary to establish democracy more perfectly than ever by making the people economically as well as politically equal" (Bellamy 1969 [1938], 58). Bellamy realized that he had nothing in common with the elitist intellectuals of his time who "went so far as to say that the democratic experiment had proved a failure when, in point of fact, it seems that no experiment in democracy, properly understood, had as yet ever been so much as attempted" (Bellamy 1897, 21). So expanded is the democracy in his revised utopia that public officials "are liable to have their powers revoked at any moment by the vote of their principals; neither is any measure of more than merely routine character ever passed by a representative body without reference back to the people . . . " (p. 274). The whole population of the United States is "organized so as to proceed almost like one parliament if needful. . . . You [in the capitalist nineteenth century] used to vote perhaps once a year. . . . We [in the year 2000] vote a hundred times perhaps a year, on all manner of questions" (p. 275).

Government exists only "in the sense of a coordinating directory of associated industries" (p. 409). "We enjoy the exhilaration of conducting the government of affairs directly" (p. 275). Referring to the philosophers' ancient dream that humankind might sometime be able "to live without law," Dr. Leete explains "that condition, so far as concerns punitive and coercive regulations, we have practically attained. As to compulsory laws, we might be said to live almost in a state of anarchy" (p. 409).

With the abolition of wage slavery and social classes, the revolution achieved "the final destruction of all forms of advantage, dominion or privilege" (p. 376). It is true that something in the way of privilege still exists, for some people in the year 2000 work fewer hours than others. Those who enjoy the shortest hours are not officials, however, but those who perform the hardest and most unpleasant work. Since officials are subject to immediate recall, there is little chance that a new "managerial class" will arise. As an added safeguard, Bellamy assures us that workers in the year 2000 unquestionably retain the right to strike, "and if the provocation were great enough, I should hope they would strike, and succeed, too" (Bellamy 1969 [1938], 89).

In *Equality* as in *Looking Backward*, everyone between the ages of twenty-one and forty-five does his or her share of the work—not, Bellamy insists, through compulsion, but in the new spirit of solidarity that has replaced the competitive and exploitative spirit of the plutocratic age. After an initial three-year period of working at a wide variety of jobs, all are free to choose the work they like best. The new organization of labor not only respects but actually depends on individual differences: "The personal eccentricities of individuals in great bodies have a wonderful tendency to balance and mutually complement one another, and this principle is strikingly illustrated in our system of choice of occupation and locality" (Bellamy 1897, 39).

In one of his "Talks on Nationalism" Bellamy argued that "the whole system" of his utopia was "necessarily, by its essential principle, committed to encouraging the utmost possible development of the individuality of every person . . . " (Bellamy 1969 [1938], 39). *Equality* greatly expands on this theme. In the new society,

> Nobody owes anybody, or is owed by anybody, or has any contract with anybody (Bellamy 1897, p. 34).
>
> Equality creates an atmosphere which kills imitation, and is pregnant with originality, for everyone acts out himself, having nothing to gain by imitating anyone else (p. 61).
>
> While we insist on equality we detest uniformity, and seek to provide free play to the greatest possible variety of tastes (p. 31).

But what about those who, despite all enticements, still want no part of this utopia? *Equality* provides for "conscientious objectors." Dr. Leete explains that the new society "had no need or use for unwilling recruits" (p. 361). We shall see in a moment why the doctor speaks in the past tense: "If anyone did not wish to enter the public service and could live outside of it without stealing or begging, he was quite welcome to. The books say that the woods were full of self-exiled hermits for a while, but one by one they tired of it and came into the new social house. Some isolated communities, however, remained outside for years" (p. 361).

This explanation is not entirely satisfying, however, for we cannot help wondering about the fate of the poor recalcitrants who may have resorted to stealing or begging. Elsewhere in *Equality* we learn that this society that can "almost" be called anarchy is still burdened with police. We are assured that their number is very small—less for the whole country than formerly for Massachusetts alone—but we are never told why they are felt to be necessary at all, or what it is they do as their share of the public service.[18]

Similarly, *Equality*'s many new details regarding the organization of production and distribution, from the workplace on up, raise almost as many new questions as they answer old ones. When it is explained, for example, that "the regulation of the conditions of work in any occupation is effectively, though indirectly, controlled by the workers in it" (p. 56) the qualifier "indirectly" inevitably arouses misgivings. Few anarchists would favor Bellamy's "unitary industrial administration," which, however simple and democratic Bellamy intended it to be, remains highly centralized, economically at least. Such a conception, however, is not far from plans advanced by some anarchosyndicalists, and is very close to the IWW's One Big Union.

It is curious how few of Bellamy's critics, anarchist or otherwise, have discussed the consistent nonviolence of his utopian vision. Distracted, perhaps, by the industrial army, they have failed to notice that the "greatest and most bloodless of revolutions" (Bellamy 1926, 285) has created a society completely free of real military institutions, military weapons, war, and the possibility of war. If the state consists, in its essentials, of "special bodies of armed men, prisons, etc.," as Lenin defined it (Lenin 1943, 10), or "permanent violence," in the words of the anarchist Malatesta (Richards 1977, 58), then Bellamy's utopia has no state.

In his review of Morris's *News from Nowhere*, Bellamy tried to clarify his agreement and disagreement with the anarchists: "In the sense of a force to restrain and punish, governmental administration may no doubt be dispensed with in proportion as a better social system shall be introduced; but in no degree will any degree of moral improvement lessen the necessity of a strictly economic administration for the directing of the productive and distributive machinery. This is a distinction which anarchists too commonly overlook" (*NN* 14 Feb. 1891).

Anarchists might not recognize such a society as anarchy, but surely it qualifies as a democracy—more truly democratic, perhaps, than any real society that has ever existed, and incomparably more democratic than the "government by bayonets" (Bellamy 1897, 319) that Bellamy saw emerging in the United States of the 1890s. In this sense, the "impression"—to use William Morris's word—given by *Equality* is very different from that of *Looking Backward*.

The point, of course, has not been to prove that Bellamy became an anarchist—which he did not—but rather to show that his utopia evolved steadily in a libertarian direction, and that anarchist criticism played a role in this development. This is remarkable enough, considering the antianarchist hysteria that prevailed in the decade after Haymarket. Let it not be forgotten that Bellamy was also criticized—denounced, reviled, and ridiculed are perhaps more accurate words—by innumerable apologists for capitalism and its government: by journalists, clergymen, educators, politicians, bankers, philosophers, lawyers, economists, and military men. But he never took their criticism seriously: "The cause of the capitalists was so utterly bad . . . that there was literally nothing that could be said for it that could not be turned against it with greater effect" (p. 402). The only criticism he found challenging came from the extreme Left, and especially from anarchists and feminists.

Significantly, his positive response to this challenge, exemplified by the growing libertarian and feminist tendency of his later work, made his utopia more consistent with the fundamentally emancipatory moral/psychological outlook elaborated in his preutopian writings. It could therefore be said that Bellamy was psychologically predisposed in favor of libertarian and feminist criticism. Bellamy's was not, in any case, an "authoritarian personality." On the contrary, revolt against authority marked him from childhood on. A preacher's son, with other preachers among his ancestors, he was infinitely prouder of a rather different reputed forebear: the notorious pirate Samuel Bellamy, who, moreover, was known to have expressed views that have been described as "distinctly socialistic" (Philip Gosse, quoted in Morgan 1944, 9–10).[19] From his teens, when the future author of *Looking Backward* wrote that "to break laws without the least regard to their quality, just because they are laws; to defy and overlook restraint just because it is restraint—these are among the most ineradicable instincts of human nature" (Morgan 1944, 80), to his last years when he struggled against death to complete his picture of a future society that he wanted to be "almost anarchy," his work is brimful of antiauthoritarian impulses and implications. It is notable that the glorification of leadership played no role in his revolution, in his utopia, or in the movement his utopia inspired. Organizationally, the Bellamy movement—a loose federation of autonomous local groups—could easily pass for anarchist. That Bellamy was no ordinary "state-socialist" was conceded by Marie-Louise Berneri when she observed that *Looking Backward* "allows a greater degree of personal freedom than most other utopias based on the same [i.e., statist] principles" (Berneri 1982, 249). Had she read *Equality* she would have found an even greater degree of personal freedom and much less statism.

Such had been, in fact, the conclusion of Peter Kropotkin who, shortly after its publication, hailed *Equality* as a work "much superior" to *Looking Backward* and as

> a decidedly admirable criticism of the capitalist system. Bellamy in this book, which I recommend to everyone to read, does not criticize capitalism from the moral, but from the economic point of view. He shows that this is the most absurdly uneconomic system of production. Bellamy does not go into metaphysics as does Marx; neither does he appeal to sentiment. In order to show the evils of capitalism he takes the point of view of Proudhon, the only one which, in my opinion, was really scientific. . . . From this he deduces all the vices of the capitalistic system, and analyzes them so admirably that I know of no other Socialist work on the subject that equals Bellamy's *Equality*. (Kropotkin 1898, 42)

The anarchist who, in 1889, had bemoaned the "authoritarian prejudices" of *Looking Backward,* now, nine years later, exclaimed

> What a pity that Bellamy has not lived longer! He would have produced other excellent books. I am positive that were Bellamy to have met an Anarchist who could have explained to him our ideal, he would have accepted it. The authoritarianism which he introduced into his Utopia was useless there and contradictory to the very system. It was simply a survival, a concession, a tribute to the past. (Kropotkin 1898, 42)

Kropotkin's argument is convincing. The fact that Bellamy later altered or abandoned so many particulars of the social organization described in *Looking Backward* indicates that these particulars—the industrial army and others—should be seen as accidental excrescences rather than the essence of his thought. For him, such details were at best parts of a "provisional plan" that was, in its entirety, "subject to radical modifications" or even "complete abandonment, according to circumstances" (Bellamy 1897, 350). These were things that could be argued about endlessly, things that ultimately would be resolved in practice. What was beyond argument, for Bellamy, were his moral/psychological first principles and their "logical consequences" on the social plane: that the repressive system of competition and exploitation—capitalism, or wage slavery—must be replaced by a nonrepressive system of cooperation and solidarity.

That these first principles and their socialist consequences are the real essence of Bellamyism is further indicated by the fact that *Equality* was not a repudiation, or even a correction, but rather an *expansion* of *Looking Backward:* "Since [*Looking Backward*] was published what was left out of it has loomed up as so much more important than what it contained that I have been constrained to write another book" (p. iii). While the underlying aspiration remained the same, his revolutionary perspectives had broadened and deepened, and so had his image of utopia. The real continuators of Bellamyism in the next generation also recognized the sequel as an evolution rather than a break. For Eugene Debs, J. A. Wayland, Charlotte Perkins Gilman, and the Wobblies, Edward Bellamy was always the author of *Looking Backward* AND *Equality*.

"Blending with the face of nature in perfect harmony": *Bellamy, Radical Ecology, and Animals' Rights*

Of all the myriad distortions of Bellamy over the past century, none has been more persistent or wider of the mark than the delusion that he was an incorrigible urbanist with a fanatical faith in technology for technology's sake. Freeing the machinery of production from the profit system and placing it in the service of real human needs seemed to him a task of special urgency for humankind, but he was sharply critical of the so-called benefits of industrial progress under capitalism: "What few beggars there had been in America in the first quarter of the nineteenth century went afoot, while in the last quarter they stole their transportation on trains drawn by steam-engines, but there were fifty times as many beggars" (Bellamy 1897, 237). He detested cities, lived his whole life as a villager, and loved nothing so much as to hike through the forest and by the sea, "to chance all awed and silent upon those secret places of the woods, those room-like nooks whose air is warm with the sense of something living there . . . to lie beneath the pines and listen to the song of eternity in their branches" (from the unfinished novel "Eliot Carson," quoted in Morgan 1944, 155).

Such lines, and they are far from rare in his work, remind us not only that Bellamy was a contemporary of John Muir, the "Yosemite Prophet"; Frank Hamilton Cushing, who signed himself "1st War Chief of Zuni, U.S. Ass't Ethnologist"; and Prentice Mulford, tireless pursuer of "God in the Trees, or the Infinite Mind in Nature," but also that he shared these authors' particular rejection of capitalist civilization's inherent rapacity and greed, as well as their love of wildness in all its forms. Decades-old misconceptions notwithstanding, the author of *Looking Backward* and *Equality* was much closer to this long-lost current of American wilderness radicalism than to the technocrats and New Dealers with whom he often continues to be classified by careless critics.

"I wouldn't give much for a country where there are no wildernesses left," says a character in one of his tales, published ten years before *Looking Backward* (Bellamy 1898, 218). From the rapturous opening pages of "The Religion of Solidarity" (1874) to the culmination of his whole life's thought in *Equality*, Bellamy's ardor for wilderness is a reverberant theme.

Capitalist expansion in the 1880s and 1890s brought continent-wide environmental devastation. During this period the Indians out West were finally "pacified." Wholesale slaughter of once-vast bison herds continued unabated. At the behest of powerful cattlemen, wolves were massacred by the thousands. As the lumber industry desolated the forests, the always-rare ivory-billed woodpecker was driven to the brink of extinction. The passenger pigeon, once so common that flocks of them literally darkened the skies, was hunted so relentlessly that all of a sudden, or so it seemed, no one ever saw them anymore; the last one died in 1914 (Matthiessen 1964, passim).

Bellamy, who could spend hours "admiring the trembling leaves" on trees (Morgan 1944, 91), was not one to take such calamities lightly. Only socialism, he argued, could put a stop to the double exploitation of the working class and the natural environment, reconciling humankind and the rest of the planet. Radical environmentalism, the militant defense of wilderness, was an important part of Bellamyist agitation. We find *New Nation* articles protesting "the reckless cutting of timber" (*NN* 14 Feb. 1891) and "the wretched state of our forests," promising that "when nationalism is finally adopted . . . there can be no doubt [that our forests] will be guarded more zealously than a gold mine" (*NN* 2 May 1891). Another *New Nation* text, "The Bird Victims of Bedloe's Island," noted with savage irony that the Statue of Liberty was responsible for the death of countless birds (*NN* 31 Oct. 1891). In an article protesting the genocide of Alaskan Eskimos, Bellamy's paper approached the perspective of today's radical ecologists in its perception of the complex interrelatedness of human society and the natural environment. The article denounces "the slaughter and destruction of whales," and of "the walrus [who] once swarmed in great numbers in those northern seas. But commerce wanted more ivory, and the whalers turned their attention to the walrus, destroying thousands annually for the sake of their tusks." The wild reindeer, too, "with the advent of improved breech-loading fire-arms . . . are both being killed off and frightened away." Thus the "slow starvation and extermination" of the Eskimos proved to be a direct result of capitalist attack on their food supply (*NN* 13 June 1891).

The environmental dimension of Bellamy's critique of capitalism was evident in *Looking Backward*. What first impresses Julian West about the new Boston, for example, is "the complete absence of chimneys and their smoke" (p. 41). However, like so many other features of his utopia that he himself finally regarded as essential, ecological considerations played a much larger role in *Equality*. In this return trip to the year 2000 we find that America's cities have shrunk to such an extent that they are no longer recognizable as such. Most people have moved to the country, and while "localities where population . . . remains denser than in other places" still exist, "their populations are small fractions of what they were" (p. 293). In one of his earlier "Talks on Nationalism," Bellamy had already argued that, with socialism, the total human population would decrease substantially as enlightened and carefree people had fewer children (Bellamy 1969 [1938], 122).

The new society has banished pollution altogether, not only from the air but from the waterways: "Nothing that can defile is allowed to reach the sea or river nowadays" (Bellamy 1897, 68). In the year 2000 we find human activity no longer at war with the environment but, on the contrary, "blending with the face of Nature in perfect harmony" (p. 296). One result of the new conditions is that, along with noise and dust, disease is largely a thing of the past. Another result has been that "the feeling of solidarity asserted itself not merely toward men and women, but likewise toward . . . animals" (p. 286). Horses are no longer exploited as "beasts of burden" (p. 297). "Soon after the Revolution," moreover, "the use of animals for food discontinued" (p. 285). Under capitalism, Dr. Leete explains, meat-eating "was just like our economic system. Humane persons generally admitted that it was very bad and brutal, and yet very few could distinctly see what the world was going to replace it with" (p. 287). After the revolution, however, "the new conception of our relation to the animals appealed to the heart and captivated the imagination of mankind" (p. 286).

Bellamy's new ecological emphasis is especially evident in his account of "The Reforesting." A few miles outside of Boston, where Julian West and Dr. Leete were traveling by air-car, the last survivor of nineteenth-century capitalism is struck by the grandeur and beauty of the woods below. "How far does this park extend?" he asks, and the doctor replies, "to the Pacific Ocean" (p. 296). In Bellamy's utopia, wilderness is not only preserved but vastly enlarged. "It was found after the Revolution that one of the things most urgent to be done was to reforest the country" (p. 297). In the year 2000 there are five to ten times as many trees as there had been at the close of the last century of capitalism. Although Bellamy favored roadways to make heretofore remote areas accessible to travelers, his whole approach was one of cooperating with rather than "conquering" nature. Indeed, "in the mountainous regions . . . where Nature has furnished effects which man's art could not strengthen, the method has been to leave everything absolutely as Nature left it" (p. 296).

It is characteristic of Bellamy that he chose, as the emblem of his utopia, the windmill, a nonpolluting and even non-waste-producing energy-conserving device that figures prominently in today's search for appropriate technologies. For Bellamy, the windmill symbolized the simplicity, solidarity, and freedom of life in the new utopia: "The mill stands for the machinery of administration, the wind that drives it symbolizes the public will, and the rudder that always keeps the vane of the mill before the wind, however suddenly or completely the wind may change, stands for the method by which the administration is kept at all times responsive and obedient to every mandate of the people, though it be but a breath" (p. 273).

"Only the beginning": Bellamy's Importance for Today

Bellamy's love of wilderness, his recognition of the vital human need for wilderness, and his choice of a device so common yet so strange as the windmill as the ensign of his utopia, bring us back to our starting point: the author of Looking Backward and Equality was above all a man of the imagination. If imagination is the wilderness of the mind, and wilderness the imagination of the Earth, Bellamy's solidarity embraces both, and both are essential to the revolution he desired.

Those of his contemporaries who understood him best never doubted the centrality of imagination in his life and thought. "In Edward Bellamy," wrote William Dean Howells, "we were rich in a romantic imagination surpassed only by that of Hawthorne" (Bellamy 1898, xiii). Charlotte Perkins Gilman was moved especially by Bellamy's "largeness of thought" and his "daring imagination" (Hill 1980, 171), qualities so pronounced that even a critic as severe as the anarchist Merlino was happy to concede them. As his tales show, the fantastic was the very air that Bellamy breathed. An admirer of *Alice in Wonderland*, he influenced *The Wizard of Oz* (Aaron 1961, 105; Baum and Macfall 1961, 69; Hearn 1973, 18, 75).

Such evidence is hard to reconcile with the dismal caricature of Bellamy as a malevolently militaristic, high-tech corporate statist that continues to dominate the critical literature, but it harmonizes well with the increasingly libertarian, eros-affirmative, feminist, nonviolent, presurrealist, and environmentalist we have encountered in our survey of Bellamy's evolving utopia.

The exalted role of imagination in Bellamy's outlook contrasts sharply with the low position it holds in American intellectual life today, and the contrast helps account for the prevailing indifference and even hostility toward Bellamy on the part of so many critics in recent years. Nothing threatens what Bellamy called the "fatuous self-complacency" (Bellamy 1926 [1888], 310) of totalitarianism and conformism so much as the imagination. As American culture has grown more totalitarian and conformist it has turned against those who have dared to dream of something else, something better. And Bellamy did not only dream; he acted accordingly. In declaring that the true name of "free enterprise" is slavery—that was the word he used, again and again—and in devoting his energies and resources to the revolutionary cause, he knew he was violating America's most sacred taboo. A hundred years later he is still paying the price for this unpardonable transgression.

A favorite strategy of those who uphold the status quo has always been to argue that, bad as things are, the proposed alternatives are worse. The currently fashionable variant of this smug cynicism pretends that revolutionary socialism is an outdated ideological relic of nineteenth-century industrial society, and utterly without meaning in the age of automation and television. Naive at best, such criticism is especially laughable when directed against Bellamy, who predicted automation and television as well as socialist revolution.

Were Bellamy to return today for a look around he would no doubt be astonished to find that the American people still tolerated that "source and sum of all villainies," capitalism (Bellamy 1897, 352). But he probably would be surprised at little else, and least of all by the fact that the problems he had found to be inherent in this system had multiplied ten-thousandfold.

He who had warned that there could be no "worse threat to the world's future" than "capitalism under a consolidated plutocracy" (p. 175) would not be surprised that war and the threat of more war has become constant;

that over half of America's national budget is now used for war preparations; and that the United States and other large nations, between them, have stockpiled enough bombs to destroy the world thousands of times over.

Having long ago concluded that capitalism's "central principle" was "the supremacy of capital and its interests, as against those of the people at large" (p. 13), he would not be surprised that, since the achievement of the eight-hour day in the early 1900s, there has been no significant reduction in the hours of labor, that a large proportion of this century's legislation has been designed to paralyze the organized labor movement, and that union busting has become a major U.S. industry.

He who had devoted an entire chapter of *Equality* to the question of "How the Profit System Nullified the Benefit of Inventions" would not be surprised to find that the innovations he himself foretold—such as radio, television, helicopters, and shopping malls—are used today as instruments of social control. As one of the first to have cried out against the devastation of America's forests and wilderness, and one who recognized this devastation as the direct and inevitable result of capitalism's need for ever-greater profits, he would not be surprised that a hundred years of industrial expansion had destroyed all but a tiny fraction of our old-growth forests and subjected a large part of America's surviving wilderness to the most egregious and damaging commercial exploitation. Similarly, he who had shown that the massacre of wild and domestic animals by the food industry and by vivisectionists was yet another horror endemic to a social system that places profits above all else would be sickened, no doubt, but hardly surprised by the systematic abuse and torture that characterize today's massive "factory farms" and "experimental laboratories."

The very headlines of today's daily newspapers would seem to Bellamy depressingly similar to those of his return-to-1887 nightmare in the closing pages of *Looking Backward*. An eventful century has passed, but the key words are all still there: "impending war . . . military credits . . . the unemployed . . . strikes . . . government preparing to repress outbreaks . . . wholesale evictions . . . fraud . . . embezzlement . . . misappropriation . . . speculators . . . shocking corruption . . . systematic bribery . . . business crisis . . . burglaries . . . a woman murdered . . . suicide . . . destitution among women wage-workers . . . startling growth of illiteracy . . . more insane asylums wanted"—and of course orations and editorials aplenty on the "moral grandeur" of the civilization that has made all this possible (Bellamy 1926 [1888], 307–8).

It might take him a while to learn the meaning of some specifically modern terms, but such things as planned obsolescence, the traffic death toll, carcinogens, nuclear waste, Star Wars, napalm, the CIA, disinformation, and capital flight would hardly convince him that he was wrong to describe capitalism as "the irreconcilable enemy of democracy, the foe of life and liberty and human happiness" (Bellamy 1897, 330).

Certainly Bellamy would not be surprised to see how most legislative reforms passed since his time—unemployment compensation, public housing, social security, Medicare, OSHA, and countless others—had failed to achieve their purpose and in some cases, because of bureaucratic maneuvering and corruption, had served only to aggravate the very problems they had been designed to alleviate: "No constitutional devices or cleverness of parliamentary machinery could have possibly made popular government anything but a farce, so long as the private economic interest of the citizen was distinct from and opposed to the public interest, and the so-called sovereign people ate their bread from the hand of capitalists" (pp. 273–74).

Distrustful as he always was of any "socialism" that was not nourished by poetry and guided by moral imperatives, Bellamy would not be surprised to find that the nations that call themselves socialist today retain so many of the features he most abhorred in capitalism: money, wages, buying, selling, banks, laws, prisons, an immense military apparatus—indeed, a whole system based on "the universal intimidation of the employed by the employer" (p. 400). Like many revolutionary theorists of today, Bellamy probably would conclude that this kind of "socialism" is in fact essentially capitalist.

Neither would it surprise him that America's own one-dimensional Marxists, who have never forgiven him for not sharing every jot and tittle of their own ideology, long ago joined in a "popular front" with unabashedly procapitalist liberals and conservatives, old and neo, to uphold the ruling opinion that he and his utopia can be safely disposed of with such epithets as "mechanical" and "middle class."[20]

Politically, socially, economically, ecologically, intellectually, and morally, the situation of America and the world today would hold few surprises for Edward Bellamy. One could say, perhaps, and not untruly, that vindication of his role as a prophetic critic of capitalism is small consolation for us who have to live in conditions he deplored as the worst of all possible slavery. With the year 2000 so close upon us, Bellamy's vision of a life of equality, solidarity, and freedom is still but a dream of a tomorrow indefinitely postponed—a tomorrow that, indeed, in many ways seems further away today than it did a hundred years ago. And yet, in spite of—or

because of—the seeming dimness of the prospects before us, could anything be more urgent here and now than the renewal of such a vision?

Bellamy's utopia was intended above all as a contribution to a discussion
of the future of human society, and this is a discussion we must all resume in
earnest if life is to continue on this planet. With his good-humored spirit of
self-correction and open-ended inquiry, Bellamy never pretended that he
had found all the answers or even that the answers he did find were the best
for all time. That the future society must be based on the principles of
equality and cooperation he regarded as "absolutely beyond question," but
he was no less insistent that "the details of such a cooperative organization
may be greatly varied consistently with these principles" (Bellamy 1937,
179). We have seen that he dispensed with many details of *Looking Backward* in his later writings, and it would not surprise him that the experience
of the last hundred years had rendered still others obsolete. Not long after
his death, for example, the word nationalism took on a narrow, chauvinistic
meaning completely antithetical to his own. Already in the 1890s Bellamy's
socialism had grown increasingly *inter*nationalist, and in *Equality* he refers
not to nationalism or nationalists but rather to the "revolutionary party"
and the "revolutionary movement." We know today, too, that nationalization—an experiment untried in Bellamy's time—is far more likely to
reinforce the capitalist system than to undermine it. Of course Bellamy's
concept of nationalization was inseparable from his concept of industrial
democracy—a means by which workers can effectively control their own
lives—and therefore had next to nothing in common with the Lassallean or
Stalinist notions of total state control with which many critics have nonetheless confused it. But the word is no longer used in the sense that Bellamy
intended, and proponents of workers' self-management today, fully sharing
Bellamy's "irreconcilable opposition alike to governmental and capitalist
paternalism" (Bellamy 1937, 129), would never advocate nationalization.

We might mention, finally, that Bellamy never really "solved" the
problem of work—but then, who has? Surely this is one of those "important points" that, as he put it, "may be safely left to the future to settle"
(p. 180). What he wanted, in any case, was not to organize work but rather
to reduce it and even to abolish it. "The object of life is to live," he confided
to a diary in his youth. "We are not to work but to live, to live the fullest,
freest, most developed life we can" (Aaron 1961, 97). This youthful sentiment helped define his utopia: "It is not our labor," Dr. Leete explains in
Looking Backward, but life's "higher and larger activities . . . that are
considered the main business of life" in the year 2000 (p. 196). Entirely in

line with these priorities—priorities shared by all true poets—was Bellamy's remark, just before he died, that socialism was not "the end of human progress," but "only the beginning" (Morgan 1944, 420).

If Bellamy's direct participation in the radical ferment of the nineties led him to set aside certain details of his original utopia, it also inspired him to add much that was new. The growing libertarian, working-class, feminist, and ecological dimensions of his later writings not only complement the profound indictment of capitalism set forth in *Looking Backward*—a critique rarely if ever surpassed in American literature—but also prefigure much of what is best and most hopeful in the radicalism of today. No Bellamyist movement, as such, has existed for many years, but Bellamy's is still a living legacy.

Eugene Debs, Charlotte Perkins Gilman, and all those old-time socialists, feminists, and Wobblies were right after all: Edward Bellamy was the outstanding pioneer of American socialism, one of this country's most resounding voices against injustice, inequality, exploitation, poverty, and war, a brave comrade fully deserving of the high place they reserved for him among the honored spokespersons for a better world. That he has been so neglected and even despised in recent years speaks volumes about the intellectual backwardness and moral cowardice of our own time.

To read Edward Bellamy today is still to look forward. America and the world have a long way to go before they catch up to the great and lonely dreamer of Chicopee Falls.

Notes

1. The fact that Mumford never even managed to get Julian West's name right (he makes it Julius) and that in his plot summary West "reawakens to the world of 1887 as soon as the institutions of 2000 have been described"—which of course is not true—makes one wonder if he took the trouble to read Bellamy's novel at all. When *The Story of Utopia*, originally published in 1922, was reissued forty years later, he acknowledged that his entire study—a 315-page critique of some forty works—was characterized above all by its "incompleteness and superficiality," and that it was, "from a scholarly point of view, almost an affront to decency"; indeed, he confessed that he conceived the book, "did all the necessary reading for it," and wrote it in a little over one month (Mumford 1969, 9). An oftentimes lucid and penetrating critic of modern technology and authoritarian social structures, Mumford unfortunately seems never to have reexamined Bellamy's work in later years; in *The Myth of the Machine: The Pentagon of Power* (1970), he merely recapitulated his earlier superficial attack.

2. In his Springfield *Union* editorial "Feudalism of Modern Times" (3 Nov. 1873), Bellamy noted that "it is the dream of socialism to introduce democracy into

the industrial world also, but whether it be realizable, experience only can show."
See also his militant editorial, "Overworked Children in Our Mills," in the Springfield *Union* (5 June 1873). In other of his preutopian writings he discussed the Brook
Farm community, denounced the inhumanity of Australian prison camps, and
defended the workers' right to organize unions (Morgan 1944, 105, 108).

3. Except where otherwise noted, this section is based on material in Ginger
(1965).

4. "K. A. Koskin, a member of the Petersburg Soviet in 1905, related that the
novel was read with interest during the first Russian revolution by the workers of
the city and particularly by those at the Putilov Works, which was famous for its
revolutionary traditions. Koskin recalled that the appealing portrayal of the radiant
future and the social tendencies of Bellamy's Utopia won the hearts of the workers"
(Bowman 1962, 73).

5. Some of the most important of *The New Nations*'s many articles and editorials
on strikes are "The Great [Coal] Miners' Strike" (2 May 1891); "Lessons of the
Indianapolis Street Car Strike" (5 Mar. 1892); "The Stone-Cutters' Strike with its
Nationalist Moral" (28 May 1892); "Lawful Strikers against Lawless Corporation," on the Buffalo railroad strike (3 Sept. 1892); a whole series on the Homestead
strike (July through October 1892); and "The Danbury Hatters Make a Plain
Point" (16 Dec. 1893).

6. The peak number of clubs is commonly accepted to be 165 (Franklin 1938,
754; Quint 1964, 82). One of the last issues of *The Nationalist*, however, noted that
"over 500" clubs had been formed (*N* 3, no. 2 [Sept. 1890]: 114).

7. Interestingly, Frederick Engels's low opinion of the Bellamy movement's
original organ, *The Nationalist*—that "there is not much in it" and that it was
"superficial and shallow . . . but full of conceit" (Marx and Engels 1953, 229)—
was shared by Bellamy, who, incidentally, had no part in this journal's production.
Highly critical of its "self-appointed" editors, he declared that it "never amounted
to much" (Morgan 1944, 273). It is not clear that Engels ever saw an issue of
Bellamy's own paper, *The New Nation*, or even that he read *Looking Backward*.

8. The felicitous phrase, "cooperative commonwealth," widely used by socialists of all tendencies well into the new century, was popularized by Danish-born
Laurence Gronlund in his 1884 book of that title, and seems to be Gronlund's sole
enduring contribution to American radicalism. Although Aaron (1961, 114) and
Quint (1964, 78) assert that Gronlund "unquestionably" and "undeniably" influenced Bellamy, neither offers any evidence. Bellamy, however, expressly denied
that he had read Gronlund before writing *Looking Backward* and went on to stress
his "radical differences" with him. Objecting especially to the autocratic, non-
egalitarian, and antifeminist features of Gronlundian socialism, he concluded that
Gronlund's vision of the new society was "wholly opposed" to his own (*NN* 2 May
1891). Gronlund, for his part, in his last book, lashed out at Bellamy's "grievous,"
"unsound," and "unsafe" teachings and above all at the antihierarchical conception of the new social organization described in *Equality*. Genuinely horrified by
Bellamy's admonition to workers, "Do ye for yourselves that which is now done by
the capitalists," that is, organize production and distribution without the mediation
of "management," Gronlund likened Bellamy to such arch-villains as Marx and the
anarchists (Gronlund 1898, 95–97, 345–46).

9. Bellamy's writings continued to circulate widely as socialist propaganda at
least through World War I. Charles H. Kerr published Bellamy's speech, *Plutocracy
or Nationalism—Which?*, in the "Pocket Library of Socialism" pamphlet series, of
which many hundreds of thousands of copies were distributed; a preface by Kerr
himself praised the "clear insight into the trust problem which it showed at a time
when the problem had not yet taken shape in the minds of the people at large," and
concluded that "however far this address misses an apprehension of the methods by
which socialism must come, it is a noble and convincing plea for the socialist ideal"
(Bellamy 1900, 3–4). Also included in the "Pocket Library of Socialism" was *The
Parable of the Water Tank*, a chapter from *Equality*. The *Parable*, moreover, was "the
most popular and frequently reproduced" text in J. A. Wayland's *Appeal to Reason*
(Quint 1964, 197). Gaylord Wilshire's *Why a "Workingman" Should Be a Socialist*,
was originally issued as Nationalist propaganda in 1890; reprinted many times, "by
1903 its total printing was three million" (Kipnis 1952, 465).

   10. "One evening [Wayland] placed a brief note in his copy of *Looking Backward*, then blew his brains out with a revolver. The note read: 'The struggle under
the capitalist system isn't worth the effort. Let it pass.' One of the most colorful and
capable figures in the American socialist movement had given up the fight" (Ginger
1949, 332).

   11. Other Bellamyists who became prominent in the Socialist party include
J. Mahlon Barnes, Corinne Brown, Jesse Cox, Imogene Fales, Job Harriman,
Robert Howe, Florence Kelley, Algernon Lee, Henry R. Legate (Bellamy's assis-
tant on *The New Nation*), C. H. Matchett, Lucian Sanial (a veteran of the Paris
Commune), and Gaylord Wilshire (Quint 1964, 83–84; Johnson 1974, 21; Morgan
1944, 270; *NN* 7 Mar. 1891). Many other socialists, such as Scott Nearing, Norman
Thomas, novelist Caroline Pemberton, and Heywood Broun, founder of the Newspaper Guild, acknowledged Bellamy as a major influence on their lives (Nearing
1972, 29; Bowman 1962, 212; Pemberton 1902, 202; Broun, in Bellamy 1926
[1888], iv). Socialists of other countries were similarly appreciative. Among the
outstanding figures of the Second International who were admirers of Bellamy were
the Frenchman Jean Jaurès, the Russian Maxim Gorky, and the leader of the
socialist women's movement in Germany, Klara Zetkin, who translated *Looking
Backward* in 1890 and wrote a long introduction for a new edition in 1914 (Bowman
1962, 154–55). The celebrated British artist and socialist, Walter Crane, struck up a
"spontaneous friendship" with Bellamy in Boston in 1891 (Dickason 1953, 183).
Crane's article, "Why Socialism Appeals to Artists," appeared in *The New Nation*
16 Jan. 1892.

   12. For example, Addie Ballou addressed the San Francisco Nationalist Club on
April 7, 1890 as follows:

   I believe that if Nationalism is put in practice this inequality and injustice will
   be done away with—and now the hour of equality and justice seems upon us—
   women have a voice in Nationalism. They have told us that politics are not fit for
   a woman to take part in, but we will make them fit; we have come to the day
   when women can work with a will, and we are here to stay until equality and
   justice reign. . . . If no one will protect nor provide work for women, they must

protect themselves. If your intelligent Mayor cannot relieve the suffering and distress in this city . . . put a woman in his place. The reason they have not done something for us I can tell you in three words—'women can't vote'. . . . We are going to keep on thundering on Nationalism as our only relief, and it is my belief that we will succeed. (Haskell 1890, 17)

13. In the IWW's official history, Fred Thompson cites "such books as Bellamy's *Looking Backward*" among the sources of Wobbly thought (Thompson 1955, 16). Quint discerned "a strong syndicalist spirit" in *Looking Backward* (Quint 1964, 76), and Philip Foner has argued that the IWW's "vision of a new society suddenly brought within reach shared more of the charismatic dreams of Edward Bellamy than the theories of Marx and Engels" (Foner 1965, 143), a view shared by Dubofsky (1969, 167). None of these authors, however, discusses the subject further. Although it does not specifically consider Bellamy's impact, Sal Salerno's dissertation (1986), which focuses on the heretofore neglected anarchist and syndicalist influences, is the best study of the Wobblies' ideological diversity.

14. Biographical information on Nef is scarce, and much of what has appeared in print is incorrect; Fink (1974), for example, has him dying in the 1930s. Nef's 1940s Bellamyist activity is noted in passing in Bowman (1962, 111). I have relied primarily on discussions with Henry McGuckin, Jr., of San Francisco, whose father was an IWW organizer and a close friend of Nef's for decades. McGuckin recalls that Nef lived for some time in the McGuckin home and that the *Equalitarian Bulletin* was printed in their basement (McGuckin 1987).

15. I would like to thank Paul Avrich and Heiner Becker for several suggestions that proved helpful in writing this section.

16. This review of *News from Nowhere* begins by declaring Morris "one of the greatest of living poets" and the book "exceedingly well worth reading." Two mild criticisms of Morris's utopia are made. First, "We are given no suggestion as to how any form of administration extending beyond town limits is conducted, as, for instance, the railroad. . . . As to the industrial system . . . Mr. Morris is provokingly silent." Second, "It is quite excusable for an Englishman to select England as the locality of his 20th century Eden; but we object to his describing America as being at that time so far behindhand in social progress as to be an object of pity." Upton Sinclair may have been right when he suggested that Morris was prejudiced against Bellamy's utopia for the simple reason that it was written by an American (Sinclair 1925, 238). E. P. Thompson, Morris's most outstanding interpreter in our own time, has noted that in *News from Nowhere* the great pre-Raphaelite's "opposition to *Looking Backward* led him to willful exaggeration, more than once" (Thompson 1977, 693).

17. *Looking Beyond* by Ludwig A. Geissler of New Orleans, one of many sequels to *Looking Backward* by Bellamy's fellow Nationalists, enlarged the democracy of the year 2000 as early as 1891. Among other innovations Geissler introduced direct election of officials by the rank and file. In his preface he stressed that Bellamy had "never made pretension of being a prophet or dictator, decreeing laws for future generations"; moreover, whether society is to be transformed "by independent groups with voluntary cooperation or by centralization, the future will tell"

(Geissler 1891, 3). The book can be regarded as a sequel not only to *Looking Backward* but to "The Blindman's World" as well. The Martians in Bellamy's tale expressed only aversion for the earth, but in *Looking Beyond* our planet receives a friendly signal from Mars, and the era of interplanetary communication and cooperation begins. *Looking Beyond* was enthusiastically reviewed in *The New Nation* as "one of the brightest and best" contributions to "the literature of the year 2000" (*NN* 21 Nov. 1891).

18. On the occasion of an unemployed demonstration early in the 1890s, *The New Nation* remarked that "the police did not interfere and as usual, when the police do not interfere, there was no disturbance of the peace" (*NN* 21 Jan. 1893).

19. In 1717 Capt. Bellamy excoriated those who "submit to be governed by laws which rich men have made for their own security. . . . They villify us, the scoundrels do, when there is only this difference: they rob the poor under cover of law, forsooth, and we plunder the rich under protection of our own courage" (Myers 1910, 1: 50). Young Bellamy could have read the pirate's entire speech in any number of works, most notably the classic *General History of the Pyrates* by "Charles Johnson" (Daniel Defoe), and the anonymous *Lives and Bloody Exploits of the Most Noted Pirates*.

20. As it happens, the most influential misreading of Bellamy in recent years is the work of a self-proclaimed Marxist, Arthur Lipow, who manages to see in Bellamy a precursor not only of "modern bureaucratic liberalism" but also of Stalinism and even of fascism (Lipow 1982, x, xi, 137). Lipow's defective summary of Bellamy's ideas is focused, almost to the exclusion of all else, on what he regards as Bellamy's "authoritarianism," a term he uses incessantly in his book. However, nearly all the contemporaries of Bellamy whom he cites as critics of this alleged authoritarianism turn out to be archconservatives and reactionaries whose criticism of Bellamy was meant to apply to all socialism. Nowhere does Lipow discuss Bellamy's relationship to libertarianism, or anarchism. The IWW is only mentioned once, disparagingly, in a footnote. The involvement of women in the Bellamy movement is also relegated to a footnote (six lines), and Bellamy's own feminism is ignored altogether. Lipow has much to say about the industrial army but says nothing about Marx's advocacy of it in the *Communist Manifesto*. He fails to mention Bellamy's nonviolence and the fact that no real military power exists in Bellamy's utopia. The superficiality of Lipow's study is exemplified by its time-frame. The bulk of the book is concerned with the three years, 1888 to 1890; the entire decade of the 1890s, far more significant for a study of Bellamy's influence, is skimmed over in a brief final chapter. Worst of all is Lipow's conclusion that Bellamy's "major legacy" belongs to the "antidemocratic reaction," an outrageous thesis in support of which he offers only the meagerest, most questionable evidence.

"It seems almost incredible," Bellamy wrote in *Equality*, "that the obvious and necessary effects of economic equality could be apprehended in a sense so absolutely opposed to the truth" (p. 391).

Works Cited

Aaron, Daniel. 1961. *Men of Good Hope: A Story of American Progressives*. New York: Oxford University Press.

Abrams, Irving S. 1988. *Haymarket Heritage: Memoirs.* Edited by Phyllis Boanes and Dave Roediger. Chicago: Charles H. Kerr.
Adamic, Louis. 1935. *Dynamite: The Story of Class Violence in America.* New York: Viking.
Adams, Frederick Upham. 1897. *President John Smith: The Story of a Peaceful Revolution.* Chicago: Charles H. Kerr.
Altgeld, John Peter. 1986. *Reasons for Pardoning the Haymarket Anarchists.* Introduction by Leon M. Despres. Chicago: Charles H. Kerr.
Ameringer, Oscar. 1983. *If You Don't Weaken.* Foreword by Carl Sandburg. Introduction by James Green. Norman: University of Oklahoma Press.
Avrich, Paul. 1978. *An American Anarchist: The Life of Voltairine de Cleyre.* Princeton: Princeton University Press.
———. 1984. *The Haymarket Tragedy.* Princeton: Princeton University Press.
Baum, Frank Joslyn, and Russell P. Macfall. 1961. *To Please a Child: A Biography of L. Frank Baum.* Chicago: Reilly & Lee.
Becker, Heiner. 1986. "W. C. Owen: 1854–1929." *Freedom,* Centenary Edition, London: Freedom Press. 13–15.
Bellamy, Edward. 1897. *Equality.* New York: Appleton.
———. 1898. *The Blindman's World and Other Stories.* Prefatory sketch by William Dean Howells. Boston: Houghton Mifflin.
———. 1900. *Plutocracy or Nationalism—Which?* Preface by Charles H. Kerr. Chicago: Charles H. Kerr.
———. 1926 [1888]. *Looking Backward, 2000–1887.* Introduction by Heywood Broun. Reprint. Boston: Houghton Mifflin.
———. 1937. *Edward Bellamy Speaks Again.* Kansas City, Mo.: Peerage Press.
———. 1955. *Selected Writings on Religion and Society.* Edited by Joseph Schiffman. New York: Liberal Arts Press.
———. 1962 [1900]. *The Duke of Stockbridge: A Romance of Shays' Rebellion.* Reprint. Cambridge: Harvard University Press.
———. 1969 [1880]. *Doctor Heidenhoff's Process.* Reprint. New York: AMS Press.
———. 1969 [1938]. *Talks on Nationalism.* Reprint. Freeport: Books for Libraries.
———. n.d. *The Parable of the Water Tank.* Chicago: Charles H. Kerr.
Berneri, Marie-Louise. 1982. *Journey Through Utopia.* Foreword by George Woodcock. London: Freedom Press.
Bird, Stewart, Dan Georgakas, Deborah Shaffer. 1985. *Solidarity Forever: An Oral History of the IWW.* Chicago: Lake View Press.
Bleich, David. 1964. "Eros and Bellamy." *American Quarterly* 16 (Fall): 445–59.
Bliss, W. D. P. 1910. *Encyclopedia of Social Reform.* New York: Funk & Wagnalls.
Blumberg, Dorothy Rose. 1964. " 'Dear Mr. Engels': Unpublished Letters, 1884–1894, of Florence Kelley to Friedrich Engels." *Labor History* 5, no. 2 (Spring): 103–33.
Bordin, Ruth. 1986. *Frances Willard: A Biography.* Chapel Hill: University of North Carolina Press.
Bowen, J. C., and Estelle M. Stewart. 1929. *History of Wages in the United States from Colonial Times to 1928.* Washington: U.S. Department of Labor.
Bowman, Sylvia, et al. 1962. *Edward Bellamy Abroad: An American Prophet's Influence.* New York: Twayne.

Breton, André. 1978. *What Is Surrealism? Selected Writings.* Edited and introduced by Franklin Rosemont. New York: Monad Press.

Brewer, George D. 1910. *"The Fighting Editor," or, Warren of the Appeal.* Chicago: Charles H. Kerr.

Brommel, Bernard J. 1978. *Eugene V. Debs: Spokesman for Labor and Socialism.* Chicago: Charles H. Kerr.

Buhle, Mari Jo. 1981. *Women and American Socialism, 1870–1920.* Urbana: University of Illinois Press.

Burbank, David T. 1966. *Reign of the Rabble: The St. Louis General Strike of 1877.* New York: Augustus M. Kelley.

Debs, Eugene V. 1903. "Reminiscences of Myron W. Reed." *The Comrade* 3, no. 2 (November).

———. 1908. *Debs: His Life, Writings and Speeches.* Introduction by Mary E. Marcy. Chicago: Charles H. Kerr.

Delaney, Ed, and M. T. Rice. 1927. *The Bloodstained Trail: A History of Militant Labor in the United States.* Seattle: Industrial Worker Committee.

Dell, Floyd. 1926. *Intellectual Vagabondage: An Apology for the Intelligentsia.* New York: George H. Doran.

Destler, Chester McArthur. 1963. *Henry Demarest Lloyd and the Empire of Reform.* Philadelphia: University of Pennsylvania Press.

Dickason, David Howard. 1953. *The Daring Young Men: The Story of the American Pre-Raphaelites.* Bloomington: Indiana University Press.

Dubofsky, Melvyn. 1969. *We Shall Be All: A History of the Industrial Workers of the World.* New York: Quadrangle.

Engels, Frederick. 1887. *The Condition of the Working Class in England in 1844.* Translated by Florence Kelley. New York: John W. Lovell.

Fink, Gary M., ed. 1974. *Biographical Dictionary of American Labor Leaders.* Westport, Conn.: Greenwood.

Flynn, Elizabeth Gurley. 1976. *The Rebel Girl: An Autobiography. My First Life, 1906–1926.* New York: International.

Foner, Philip S. 1965. *History of the Labor Movement in the United States.* Volume 4: *The Industrial Workers of the World, 1905–1917.* New York: International.

———. 1981. *Fellow Workers and Friends: IWW Free-Speech Fights as Told by Participants.* Westport, Conn.: Greenwood.

———, ed. 1983. *Black Socialist Preacher: The Teachings of Rev. George Washington Woodbey and His Disciple Rev. George W. Slater, Jr.* San Francisco: Synthesis Publications.

Franklin, John Hope. 1938. "Edward Bellamy and the Nationalist Movement." *New England Quarterly* 11, no. 4: 739–72.

Galloway, James A. ("Anon Moore"). 1897. *John Harvey: A Tale of the Twentieth Century.* Chicago: Charles H. Kerr.

Gavett, Thomas W. 1965. *Development of the Labor Movement in Milwaukee.* Madison: University of Wisconsin Press.

Geissler, Ludwig A. 1891. *Looking Beyond: A Sequel to "Looking Backward" and An Answer to "Looking Further Forward" by Richard Michaelis.* London: William Reeves.

Gilman, Charlotte Perkins. 1966. *Women and Economics: A Study of the Economic Relation between Men and Women as a Factor in Social Evolution*. New York: Harper.

———. 1973. *The Yellow Wallpaper*. Afterword by Elaine R. Hedges. Old Westbury: Feminist Press.

———. 1979. *Herland*. Introduction by Ann J. Lane. New York: Pantheon.

Ginger, Ray. 1949. *The Bending Cross: A Biography of Eugene Victor Debs*. Rutgers: Rutgers University Press.

———. 1965. *Altgeld's America: The Lincoln Ideal Versus Changing Realities*. Chicago: Quadrangle.

Goetzmann, William H., ed. 1973. *The American Hegelians: An Intellectual Episode in the History of Western America*. New York: Knopf.

Gompers, Samuel. 1948. *Seventy Years of Life and Labor: An Autobiography*. 2 vols. in 1. New York: Dutton.

Gronlund, Laurence. 1898. *The New Economy: A Peaceable Solution to the Social Problem*. Chicago: Herbert S. Stone.

Hall, Covington. 1945. "Comment by Covami." *Industrial Worker*, 1 September.

Haskell, Burnette G. 1890. Family Collection. *Accounts of Meetings of the San Francisco Nationalist Club*. Bancroft Library, University of California, Berkeley.

Hearn, Michael Patrick. 1973. *The Annotated Wizard of Oz*. New York: Clarkson N. Potter.

Henry, Marjorie Louise. 1927. *La Contribution d'un Américain au symbolisme français: Stuart Merrill*. Paris: E. Champion.

Herreshoff, David. 1967. *American Disciples of Marx: From the Age of Jackson to the Progressive Era*. Detroit: Wayne State University Press.

Hicks, John D. 1961. *The Populist Revolt: A History of the Farmers' Alliance and the People's Party*. Lincoln: University of Nebraska Press.

Hill, Mary A. 1980. *Charlotte Perkins Gilman: The Making of a Radical Feminist*. Philadelphia: Temple University Press.

Hillquit, Morris. 1910. *History of Socialism in the United States*. New York: Funk and Wagnalls.

Johnson, Oakley C. 1974. *Marxism in the United States before the Russian Revolution, 1876–1917*. New York: Humanities Press.

Kapp, Yvonne. 1976. *Eleanor Marx*. Vol. 2. New York: Pantheon.

Kelley, Florence. 1986. *The Autobiography of Florence Kelley: Notes of Sixty Years*. Edited and introduced by Kathryn Kish Sklar. Chicago: Charles H. Kerr.

Kerr, Charles H. 1904. *A Socialist Publishing House*. Chicago: Charles H. Kerr.

Kipnis, Ira. 1952. *The American Socialist Movement, 1897–1912*. New York: Monthly Review.

Kropotkin, Peter. 1889. "Le Vingtième Siècle." Review of *Looking Backward*. Serialized in *La Révolte* (Paris), Nov. 20, Dec. 14, Dec. 21, and Dec. 28.

———. 1898. "Edward Bellamy." *Freedom* (London) 12 (July): 42.

Lenin, V. I. 1943. *State and Revolution*. New York: International.

Lewis, Austin. 1917. Review of *"News from Nowhere."* *Internationalist Socialist Review*, May, 686.

Lewisohn, Ludwig. 1970. *The Poets of Modern France*. Port Washington, N.Y.: Kennikat.

Lipow, Arthur. 1982. *Authoritarian Socialism in America: Edward Bellamy and the Nationalist Movement*. Berkeley: University of California Press.

Lloyd, Caro. 1912. *Henry Demarest Lloyd (1847–1903): A Biography*. New York: Putnam's.

Lloyd, Henry Demarest. 1894. *Wealth against Commonwealth*. New York: Harper.

London, Joan. 1968. *Jack London and His Times: An Unconventional Biography*. Seattle: University of Washington Press.

Marcuse, Herbert. 1962. *Eros and Civilization: A Philosophical Inquiry into Freud*. New York: Vintage.

Martin, James J. 1970. *Men against the State: The Expositors of Individualist Anarchism in America, 1827–1908*. Colorado Springs: Ralph Myles.

Marx, Karl, and Frederick Engels. 1953. *Letters to Americans: 1848–1895*. New York: International.

———. 1986. *The Communist Manifesto*. Chicago: Charles H. Kerr.

Matthiessen, Peter. 1964. *Wildlife in America*. New York: Viking Compass.

McCowan, Archibald ("Luke A. Hedd"). 1892. *Philip Meyer's Scheme: A Story of Trades-Unionism*. New York: Ogilvie.

McGuckin, Henry E., Jr. 1987. Interviews with author. February 5 and 10.

McMurry, Donald L. 1929. *Coxey's Army: A Study of the Industrial Army Movement of 1894*. Boston: Little Brown.

McWilliams, Carey. 1946. *Southern California Country: An Island in the Land*. New York: Duell, Sloan & Pierce.

Merlino, Saverio. 1891. "Chronique des livres." Review of *Looking Backward*. *La Société Nouvelle* (Paris-Brussels) 2 (August): 222–25.

Morgan, Arthur E. 1944. *Edward Bellamy*. New York: Columbia University Press.

Morton, A. L. 1968. *The English Utopia*. Berlin: Seven Seas.

Mumford, Lewis. 1969. *The Story of Utopia*. New York: Viking.

———. 1970. *The Myth of the Machine: The Pentagon of Power*. New York: Harcourt.

Myers, Gustavus. 1910. *History of the Great American Fortunes*. Vol. 1. Chicago: Charles H. Kerr.

Nearing, Scott. 1972. *The Making of a Radical: A Political Autobiography*. New York: Harper.

Nettlau, Max. 1981. *Die erste Blutezeit der Anarchie, 1886–1894*. Vaduz: Topos verlag.

O'Sullivan, Vincent. "Stuart Merrill." In *Dictionary of American Biography*.

Payne, C. E. 1945. *Industrial Government*. Usk, Wa.: C. E. Payne.

Pemberton, Caroline. 1902. "How I Became a Socialist." *The Comrade* 1, no. 9 (June): 202.

Quint, Howard H. 1964. *The Forging of American Socialism: Origins of the Modern Movement*. Indianapolis: Bobbs-Merrill.

Renshaw, Patrick. 1967. *The Wobblies: The Story of Syndicalism in the United States*. Garden City: Doubleday.

Richards, Vernon. 1977. *Errico Malatesta: His Life and Ideas*. London: Freedom Press.

Riegel, Robert E. 1963. *American Feminists*. Lawrence: University Press of Kansas.

Roediger, Dave, and Franklin Rosemont. 1986. *Haymarket Scrapbook*. Chicago: Charles H. Kerr.

Rosemont, Franklin. 1980. "Free Play and No Limit: An Introduction to Edward Bellamy's Utopia." In *Surrealism and Its Popular Accomplices*, edited by Franklin Rosemont. San Francisco: City Lights.

Salerno, Sal. 1986. "The Early Labor Radicalism of the IWW: A Sociological Critique." Ph.D. diss., Brandeis University.

Shannon, David A. 1967. *The Socialist Party of America: A History*. Chicago: Quadrangle.

Sinclair, Upton. 1925. *Mammonart: An Essay in Economic Interpretation*. Pasadena: The Author.

Sotheran, Charles. 1915. *Horace Greeley and Other Pioneers of American Socialism*. New York: Mitchell Kennerley.

Stanton, Elizabeth Cady. 1971. *Eighty Years and More: Reminiscences 1815–1897*. Introduction by Gail Parker. New York: Schocken.

Swados, Harvey. 1970. *Standing Fast*. Garden City: Doubleday.

Tax, Meredith. 1980. *The Rising of the Women: Feminist Solidarity and Class Conflict, 1880–1917*. New York: Monthly Review.

Thompson, E. P. 1977. *William Morris: Romantic to Revolutionary*. London: Merlin.

Thompson, Fred. 1955. *The IWW: Its First Fifty Years*. Chicago: The Industrial Workers of the World.

———. 1987. Interview with author. February 9.

Tod, Ian, and Michael Wheeler. 1978. *Utopia*. New York: Harmony Books.

Van Ornum, William H. 1892. *Why Government at All?* Chicago: Charles H. Kerr.

Velsek, Jenny. 1987. Interview with author. February 8.

Wayland, Julius A. 1912. *Leaves of Life: A Story of Twenty Years of Socialist Agitation*. Girard: Appeal to Reason.

Weir, Stan. 1987. Interview with author. February 8.

Woodruff, Abner E. n.d. *The Evolution of Industrial Democracy*. Chicago: IWW Publishing Bureau.

Bellamy and
Looking Backward:
A Selected Bibliography

NANCY SNELL GRIFFITH

Edward Bellamy was a prolific writer. Before the publication of *Looking Backward*, he published several novels, twenty-three short stories—most in leading magazines of the day—and innumerable editorials and reviews in the Springfield *Union* and other local papers. When the popularity of *Looking Backward* resulted in the formation of the Nationalist party, he contributed many pieces to Nationalist newspapers.

The bibliography that follows is a selected one, dealing mainly with discussions of *Looking Backward*. It is divided into three sections:

1. A list of the first editions of Bellamy's major works, with a brief description of each. As a matter of interest, I have included Bellamy's explanation of his reasons for writing *Looking Backward*.

2. A very brief list of the most significant general works dealing with Bellamy's life and work. Many of these works have been reprinted; these subsequent editions have not been included.

3. A selected bibliography of the most important criticism of *Looking Backward*, with an attempt to include materials on many aspects of the book: religion, education, and the role of women; its relationship to the utopian tradition as a whole; comparisons to the works of other writers; discussion of its literary characteristics, including its relationship to science fiction; and criticism of Bellamy's economic system. I have also included some comments on *Looking Backward* and Nationalism by Bellamy's contemporaries; while they are in some cases less scholarly, they present an interesting contemporary perspective. Among these are charges that Bellamy plagiarized all or part of the book, and answers to these charges. Introductions to the various editions of *Looking Backward* have been omitted; they would of course be useful in any research on the subject.

Unpublished materials, such as dissertations and conference proceedings, have been omitted. For these, as well as for more detailed listings of Bellamy's other works and criticism of them, see: Nancy Snell Griffith, *Edward Bellamy: A Bibliography* (Metuchen, N.J.: Scarecrow, 1986). This bibliography also includes a more extensive list of works on Bellamy's life, a discussion of his imitators, lists of his journalistic works, and a much more comprehensive list of works on *Looking Backward* and Nationalism.

Works by Bellamy

The Blindman's World and Other Stories. Prefatory sketch by William Dean Howells. Boston and New York: Houghton Mifflin, 1898. A collection of Bellamy's short stories, which are imaginative and speculative, often centered on strange phenomena and bizarre situations. Howells compared Bellamy's imaginative fiction to that of Hawthorne, but other critics disagreed.

Dr. Heidenhoff's Process. New York: D. Appleton, 1880. A psychological and fantastic tale centered around the effects of guilt on those who have transgressed. Seen by critics of the time as imaginative and ingenious, although somewhat depressing, and compared by some to the work of Hawthorne.

"The Duke of Stockbridge." Serialized in the Berkshire *Courier* (Great Barrington, Mass.) 45, no 1 (1879). Later published, much revised by Francis Bellamy, as *The Duke of Stockbridge: A Romance of Shays' Rebellion*. New York: Silver Burdett, 1900. Joseph Schiffman's 1962 edition is an attempt to return to Bellamy's original. A historical romance about Shays' Rebellion, the novel is notable chiefly for its accurate portrayal of the life and times of western Massachusetts in the eighteenth century. Many critics have seen in it the first expression of Bellamy's social conscience.

Edward Bellamy Speaks Again! Kansas City: Peerage Press, 1937. A collection of speeches and articles on Nationalism. Contains Bellamy's explanations of why and how he wrote *Looking Backward*.

Equality. New York: D. Appleton, 1897. A sequel to *Looking Backward*, intended to answer its critics. Although it appealed to many Nationalists and other reformers, most readers saw it as a tiring tract because of its long didactic passages and decreased emphasis on the romance form.

Looking Backward, 2000–1887. Boston: Ticknor, 1888. Bellamy's most popular work, a picture of an ideal society based on the equality of all and achieved by evolution rather than revolution. It prompted many reactions and served as the basis for the Nationalist movement.

Miss Ludington's Sister: A Romance of Immortality. Boston: James R. Osgood and Co., 1884. A woman attempts to communicate, through a medium, with her dead "sister," who is in truth her younger self.

Demonstrates Bellamy's theory of serial selves. William Dean Howells compared Bellamy's writing in this book to that of Hawthorne, but other critics disagreed, finding the book pleasant, flimsy, and sentimental.

"The Religion of Solidarity" (originally written in 1874), with a discussion of Edward Bellamy's philosophy by Arthur E. Morgan. Yellow Springs, Ohio: Antioch Bookplate Co., 1940. Bellamy's exploration of his relationship to the infinite; contains ideas about brotherhood and equality that were to appear again in his later work.

Selected Writings on Religion and Society. Edited and with an introduction by Joseph Schiffman. New York: Liberal Arts Press, 1955. Includes "The Religion of Solidarity," as well as excerpts from *Looking Backward, Equality, Talks on Nationalism,* and Bellamy's unpublished journals.

Six to One: A Nantucket Idyl. New York: G. P. Putnam's Sons, 1878. Bellamy's first published novel, issued anonymously in a limited edition. Six female healers combine forces to restore the health of a New York newspaperman who has come to Nantucket for a rest. Although some critics have searched for deeper meanings, most have considered this book to be a light summer romance.

Talks on Nationalism. Chicago: Peerage Press, 1938. Collection of "Talks on Nationalism," originally published in the *New Nation.*

"Why I Wrote *Looking Backward.*" In *America as Utopia,* edited by Kenneth M. Roemer, New York: Burt Franklin, 1981, 22–27. A combination of two different essays written by Bellamy in 1889 and 1894 on his reasons for writing *Looking Backward.*

General Works

Bowman, Sylvia E. *Edward Bellamy.* Boston: Twayne Publishers, 1986. An analytical study of Bellamy that deals with his life; his principles as expressed in *Looking Backward,* the *New Nation,* and some of his earlier writings in the Springfield *Union;* his ideas for implementing the new society, and the socioeconomic and intellectual life it would foster; and the influence of *Looking Backward* on later political and social movements.

———. *The Year 2000: A Critical Biography of Edward Bellamy.* New York: Bookman Associates, 1958. Part 1 is a chronological study of Bellamy's life and the influences on him that produced *Looking Backward.* Part 2 explores Bellamy's ideas as expressed in *Looking Backward, Equality,* and various of his articles. Includes a valuable bibliography of books and articles by and about Bellamy, listing many unsigned articles that Bowman identified as his.

————, et al. *Edward Bellamy Abroad: An American Prophet's Influence.* New York: Twayne, 1962. A collection of essays by Bowman and numerous other writers cataloging the influence of Bellamy and *Looking Backward* in twenty-eight countries. Includes an international bibliography of works by and about Bellamy, as well as reactions to him.

Lipow, Arthur. *Authoritarian Socialism in America: Edward Bellamy and the Nationalist Movement.* Berkeley: University of California Press, 1982. A study of Nationalism's intellectual roots that proposes that Bellamy's ideas are not unique, but fit into the context of post–Civil War reform movements. Lipow sees both Bellamy and the Nationalists as changing during the 1890s, becoming more democratic and less authoritarian. Lipow believes that for the most part, however, Bellamy's ideas do not reflect working-class socialism, in that his reforms come from above, not below.

MacNair, Everett W. *Edward Bellamy and the Nationalist Movement, 1889– 1894: A Research Study of Edward Bellamy's Work as a Social Reformer.* Milwaukee: Fitzgerald, 1957. A study of the nature of the Nationalist movement, who participated and what it accomplished. Includes an extensive list of the various Nationalist clubs, their members, and their publications. Also includes a useful discussion of all of Bellamy's fiction.

Morgan, Arthur E. *Edward Bellamy.* New York: Columbia University Press, 1944. A chronological study of Bellamy's life and work, combined with a study of his philosophy. The author treats Bellamy as an incisive social philosopher, possessing "a ranging and universal type of personality" (p. viii). Based largely on unpublished papers and manuscripts and on information obtained from Bellamy's family.

————. *The Philosophy of Edward Bellamy.* New York: King's Crown Press, 1945. Morgan traces Bellamy's philosophy of life through his published and unpublished writings and notebooks, paying particular attention to his attitudes toward fate, happiness, and religion, and his relationship to the philosophy of India. Bellamy's "Religion of Solidarity" is reproduced as "his principal effort to state his ultimate philosophy" (p. 4).

Thomas, John L. *Alternative America: Henry George, Edward Bellamy, Henry Demarest Lloyd and the Adversary Tradition.* Cambridge, Mass.: The Belknap Press of Harvard University Press, 1983, pp. 27–43, 83– 101, 152–72, 234–77+. Thomas illustrates the connection between these authors' books and their lives, their worlds of ideas and of political action. Deals with Bellamy's life, early works, and social ideas as expressed in his notebooks and articles in the Springfield *Union*. Also discusses *The Duke of Stockbridge*, his novellas and short stories, "Eliot Carson," *Looking Backward*, and *Equality*.

Looking Backward

Armytage, W. H. G. "Bellamy and the Mechanical Millennarians." Chapter in *Yesterday's Tomorrows: A Historical Survey of Future Societies*. London: Routledge and Kegan Paul, 1968. *Looking Backward* influenced *News from Nowhere* and *A Connecticut Yankee*. Discusses various reactions to the book, including the theological debate it prompted and its influence on popular science writing.

Beauchamp, Gorman. *"The Iron Heel* and *Looking Backward:* Two Paths to Utopia." *American Literary Realism, 1870–1910* 9 (1976): 307–14. Compares the two works, in order to "establish the similarities and define the differences between the two schools of socialist thought, the bourgeois and the Marxist, both of which posited utopia ahead, but divided radically over the path that must be taken to reach it" (p. 308).

Becker, George J. "Edward Bellamy: Utopia, American Plan." *Antioch Review* 14, no. 2 (June 1954): 181–94. Bellamy's basic idea was economic equality; he felt that changes in the material environment could affect human nature. Includes a discussion of Nationalism and criticisms of Bellamy's ideas by his contemporaries.

Berneri, Marie-Louise. "Edward Bellamy: *Looking Backward.*" Chapter in *Journey through Utopia*. London: Routledge and Kegan Paul, 1950. A discussion of the main ideas of *Looking Backward*. The romance form appealed to popular taste, while Bellamy's approach to economic problems was clear and practical. There is no room for nonconformists in Bellamy's society, and no means to alter the system politically.

Bleich, David. "Eros or Bellamy." *American Quarterly* 16, no. 3 (Fall 1964): 445–59. An analysis of *Looking Backward* using Freud's theories and pointing out Bellamy's similarities to Marcuse. "Bellamy's novel is an affirmation of the pleasure principle in a world ruled by the reality principle . . . it is a vision of a world . . . in which life becomes art, in which work and play are identified . . . [it] is a wish that aims at eliminating the need for wishes" (p. 457).

Boller, Paul F., Jr. "Edward Bellamy's Collectivistic Freedom." Chapter in *Freedom and Fate in American Thought: From Edwards to Dewey*. Dallas:

SMU Press, 1978. Bellamy saw freedom as societal rather than as individual. He was in revolt against Calvinism and favored economic equality, the equality of women, and economic well-being as the basis of spiritual growth.

Dombrowski, James. "Edward Bellamy; Religion in Utopia." Chapter in *The Early Days of Christian Socialism in America.* New York: Columbia University Press, 1936. Bellamy was important in "developing social consciousness in religion" (p. 84). Discusses the religious themes of *Looking Backward,* the ministers who supported Nationalism, and the relationship between Nationalism and Christian Socialism.

Fellman, Michael. "The Evolution of Order: Edward Bellamy's Nationalist Utopia." Chapter in *The Unbounded Frame: Freedom and Community in Nineteenth Century American Utopianism.* Westport, Conn.: Greenwood Press, 1973. Bellamy's concept of reform depends on evolution rather than on revolution: man becomes perfect through changing his environment, producing a morally perfect future. Includes a biographical sketch and a discussion of Bellamy's ideas as represented in his other works. Then concentrates on *Looking Backward* and the resulting Nationalist movement.

Filler, Louis. "Edward Bellamy and the Spiritual Unrest." *American Journal of Economics and Sociology* 8, no. 3 (April 1949): 239–49. Compares Brook Farm and *Looking Backward,* to show that Bellamy is the successor to the idealists of the 1840s. Discusses the spiritual unrest of the 1880s and how it influenced Bellamy.

Franklin, John Hope. "Edward Bellamy and the Nationalist Movement." *New England Quarterly* 11, no. 4 (December 1938): 739–72. After a discussion of Bellamy's personal philosophy and its embodiment in *Looking Backward,* focuses on the development of the Nationalist movement itself and Bellamy's involvement in it.

Gilman, Nicholas P. "Nationalism in the United States." *Quarterly Journal of Economics* 4 (October 1889): 50–76. A brief biographical sketch of Bellamy and a discussion of his earlier works. Includes a description of *Looking Backward* and the resulting formation of the Nationalist clubs, which were more literary than political. The world of *Looking Backward* is impossible with human nature as it is.

Grimes, Alan Pendleton. "Edward Bellamy." Chapter in *American Political Thought.* New York: Holt, 1955. Bellamy's goal in *Looking Backward* is "discrediting the old capitalistic ethic and ennobling the morality of social cooperation" (p. 337). The capitalistic system was wrong not only on moral grounds, but also on economic ones, because it led to waste.

Bellamy focused on the economic order rather than on the political one, because he felt that if the economic problems were solved—and equality were a reality—everything else would fall into place.

Gutek, Gerald. "An Analysis of Formal Education in Edward Bellamy's *Looking Backward.*" *History of Education Quarterly* 4, no. 4 (December 1964): 251–63. While Bellamy's idea of universal education would produce a greater sense of community, his educational philosophy was only a partial one, and needed further development.

Hansot, Elisabeth. "Edward Bellamy's *Looking Backward* and *Equality.*" Chapter in *Perfection and Progress: Two Modes of Utopian Thought.* Cambridge: MIT Press, 1974. Compares Bellamy to his classical predecessors. Discusses Bellamy's use of economic equality as the basis of his society; his portrayal of human nature and motivation; the static character of his society; and how his ideas serve as a critique of the present.

Hayden, Dolores. *The Grand Domestic Revolution.* Cambridge: MIT Press, 1981, 135–49. Bellamy's arrangements for domestic work in *Looking Backward* influenced actual reforms through the Nationalist party and other organizations. Bellamy concentrates on reorganizing domestic space and the physical environment through architecture and city planning. He still keeps gender distinctions as to who does what kind of work.

Henderson, Harry B. "Bellamy, Cable, James, Adams, Crane. . . . " Chapter in *Versions of the Past: The Historical Imagination in American Fiction.* New York: Oxford University Press, 1974. Utopias, such as *Looking Backward,* are "only the historical novel inverted" (p. 199). An understanding of the historical novel, as typified by *The Duke of Stockbridge,* can help in analysis of *Looking Backward.*

Hicks, Granville. "Struggle and Flight." Chapter in *The Great Tradition: An Interpretation of American Literature since the Civil War.* New York: Macmillan, 1933. *Looking Backward* is the literary expression of the growing forces of revolt in the United States at the time. The fictional form used by Bellamy resulted in the common man's exposure to the ideas of socialism. It is ironic that the bettering of the working man's lot under Bellamy's scheme comes through the enlightened middle class, and is presented in the book by professional men.

Hobson, J. A. "Edward Bellamy and the Utopian Romance." *Humanitarian* 13 (September 1898): 179–89. *Looking Backward* is an excellent example of the utopian romance, in that it expresses what is best about the present society and depicts a new society that grows logically out of it. Examines the main attributes of the book and compares it with other "modern" utopias, including Morris, Hertzka, and Ruskin.

[Howells, William Dean.] "Editor's Study." *Harper's* 77 (June 1888): 154–55. Bellamy used romance to present a view of the future. *Looking Backward* is "a book which in the sugar-coated form of a dream has exhibited a dose of undiluted socialism, which has been gulped by some of the most vigilant opponents of that theory without a suspicion of the poison they were taking into their systems" (p. 154).

Jehmlich, Reimer. "Cog-work: The Organization of Labor in Edward Bellamy's *Looking Backward* and in Later Utopian Fiction." In *Clockwork Worlds: Mechanized Environments in SF*, edited by Richard D. Erlich et al., 27–46. Westport, Conn.: Greenwood, 1983. A discussion of "which aspects of modern working life the individual author thinks most detrimental and what alternatives he suggests; whether or not his diagnosis and therapy reflect attitudes toward work common to his time" (pp. 27–28). There are parallels between Bellamy and Marx in their analysis of working conditions under a capitalist economy, but Bellamy is more optimistic, relies less on violence, and appeals more to the masses.

Kasson, John F. "Technology and Utopia." In his *Civilizing the Machine; Technology and Republican Values in America, 1776–1900*. New York: Penguin, 1977, 191–202, 227–28, 230–33. *Looking Backward* is an attempt to create a technological society under popular control rather than in the hands of a few, a "freeing of technology from the inefficiencies of capitalism" (p. 228). This was part of a larger American effort to "integrate technology and republican values" (p. 230), to narrow the gap between them.

Ketterer, David. "Utopian Fantasy as Millennial Motive and Science-Fictional Motif." *Studies in the Literary Imagination* 6, no. 2 (Fall 1973): 79–103. A discussion of *Looking Backward* as science fiction. Utopian science fiction is "a semantic impossibility" (p. 95) resulting from a confusion of mere quantitative changes (science fiction) with qualitative social change (utopianism).

Khanna, Lee Cullen. "The Reader and *Looking Backward*." *Journal of General Education* 33, no. 1 (Spring 1981): 69–79. *Looking Backward* was the most successful of the era's many utopian novels because of Bellamy's skill as a writer of fiction. "The book continues to engage readers . . . because at a deeper structural level it involves them in a process—a game—of discovery" (pp. 69–70). Bellamy used contrasting metaphors and forced the reader to question his own identity.

Khouri, Nadia. "Clockwork and Eros: Models of Utopia in Edward Bellamy and William Morris." *C.L.A. Journal* (College Language Association) 24, no. 3 (March 1981): 376–99. A study of *Looking Backward* and *News from Nowhere* as a function of their historical contexts. Analyzes "in what sense a utopian arrangement simultaneously recalls the society which it negates and develops political configurations whereby it is capable of truly transcending the reality it criticizes" (p. 379).

Leach, William. "Looking Forward Together: Feminists and Edward Bellamy." *Democracy* 2, no. 1 (1982): 120–34. Many American feminist groups adhered to Nationalist and socialist ideas of equality, individual fulfillment, education, rational love, rational dress, and cooperation. Though Bellamy's system called for individual freedom, it was based on paternalism and showed a lack of intimacy and passion in the relationship between the sexes.

Levi, Albert William. "Edward Bellamy: Utopian." *Ethics* 55, no. 2 (January 1945): 131–44. A discussion of the influence and success of *Looking Backward*, concentrating on its relationship to the social and economic conditions of its time, particularly the growth of large corporations and the increase in union activities and strikes.

Loubere, Leo. *Utopian Socialism: Its History since 1800*. Cambridge, Mass.: Schenkman, 1974, 131–58. A discussion of how such writers as Bellamy and Morris dealt with economic organization, work, government, education, and women's issues. Bellamy represents "the more statist and centralized society" in "the tradition of Babeuf, Cabet and Blanc" (p. 131).

Madison, Charles A. "Edward Bellamy, Social Dreamer." *New England Quarterly* 15, no. 3 (September 1942): 444–66. Focuses on the real-life basis for Bellamy's social philosophy. *Looking Backward* and its social tenets were not mere accidents but grew out of the steady development of Bellamy's social conscience.

McHugh, Christine. "Abundance and Asceticism: Looking Backward to the Future." *Alternative Futures* 1, no. 3–4 (Fall 1978): 47–58. *Looking Backward* is still relevant—it combines affluence and abundance with asceticism, and is "free from excesses of consumerism, materialism, and personal indulgence" (p. 48). The book reflects the "myth of the garden" and the theme of abundance, a theme that has often been discarded by modern futurists. Religious values were very important in shaping the society of moderation in *Looking Backward*.

———. "Midwest Populist Leadership and Edward Bellamy: 'Looking Backward' into the Future." *American Studies* 19, no. 2 (Fall 1978): 57–

74. Explores the agrarian response to Bellamy's vision of economic equality, especially his influence on the Populist movement.

Meier, Paul. "Sources and Influences: Edward Bellamy." Chapter in *William Morris: The Marxist Dreamer*. Vol. 1. Atlantic Highlands, N.J.: Humanities Press, 1978. Compares and contrasts *Looking Backward* and *News from Nowhere*, particularly in the authors' attitudes toward socialism and mechanization. Morris wanted to write an anti-Bellamy utopia and refused to see any merit in *Looking Backward* besides its criticism of capitalism, yet he owes Bellamy a great debt. Both authors are humanists, one abstract, the other concrete.

Morgan, Arthur. *Plagiarism in Utopia: A Study of the Continuity of the Utopian Tradition, with Special Reference to Edward Bellamy's "Looking Backward."* Yellow Springs, Ohio: Author, 1944. Bellamy's notebooks, early editorials, and letters show that he did not plagiarize from MacNie, Bebel, Gronlund, or Cabet. American utopias are interrelated and are linked to the utopias of the past.

Morris, William. "Looking Backward." *Science Fiction Studies* 3, no. 3 (November 1976): 287–90. Reprinted from *The Commonweal* 5 (June 22, 1889): 194–95. Morris objects to *Looking Backward* as dangerous— some people may accept it as really possible and be attracted to it; others may dislike it and thus turn away from socialism altogether. Bellamy's vision is limited—his picture of utopia is essentially personal and reflects his own temperament.

Mumford, Lewis. *The Story of Utopias*. New York: Boni and Liveright, 1922, 159–69. Bellamy sees "labor organization and distribution of wealth" as "the key to every other institution in his utopia" (p. 161). While Bellamy makes a great contribution through his passion and generosity, his system is mechanical and impersonal.

Negley, Glenn Robert, and John Max Patrick. "Edward Bellamy, 1850–1898." Chapter in *Quest for Utopia: An Anthology of Imaginary Societies*. New York: Schuman, 1952. A discussion of Bellamy's "philosophy of social structure and organization" and "the method of changing social structure which he proposes" (p. 77). Bellamy is an economic materialist, who sees the possibility of change through the evolutionary reform of institutions.

Olson, Theodore. "Bellamy: Corporate Solidarity and Organic Change." Chapter in *Millennialism, Utopianism and Progress*. Toronto: University of Toronto Press, 1981. Bellamy is linked to earlier utopians like Mercier, Saint-Simon, and Fourier. *Looking Backward* shows the perfect society as growing inevitably and automatically from the imperfect present, and the emphasis is on the city and the industrial system. Discusses developmental logic and rectilinear progress as depicted in *Looking Backward*.

Parrington, Vernon L. *American Dreams: A Study of American Utopias.* Providence, R.I.: Brown University Press, 1947, 57–97. Three utopian works preceded *Looking Backward* and were similar to it: MacNie's *Diothas*, Dodd's *Republic of the Future*, and Thomas's *Crystal Button*. Thus it is a mistake to view Bellamy as an isolated innovator. Includes a review of Bellamy's life and work, focusing on a discussion of the ideas in *Looking Backward* and reactions to it. Considers *Equality* as Bellamy's answer to his critics.

———. "Edward Bellamy and *Looking Backward*." Chapter in *Main Currents in American Thought*. Vol. 3. New York: Harcourt, Brace, 1930. A discussion of the ideas and influence of *Looking Backward* and *Equality*. Bellamy is an idealist, a believer in man's inherent goodness. His long-term influence was slight, but he stands as "a testimony [that there] were some who were concerned for a juster social order" (p. 315).

Parssinen, T. M. "Bellamy, Morris and the Image of the Industrial City in Victorian Social Criticism." *The Midwest Quarterly* 14, no. 3 (Spring 1973): 257–66. Bellamy's society differs from that of Morris: Bellamy set his utopia in a refined industrial city; Morris, feeling that the city was corrupting, rejected it for a nonurban setting.

Patai, Daphne. "Utopia for Whom?" *Aphra* 5, no. 3 (Summer 1974): 2–16. Bellamy allowed women in the work force, saw marriage as a love relationship rather than an economic one, and believed in equal education, but he still was paternalistic, kept women psychologically dependent, and maintained gender distinctions in job assignment.

Pfaelzer, Jean. "A State of One's Own: Feminism as Ideology in American Utopias 1880–1915." *Extrapolation* 24 (Winter 1983): 311–28. *Looking Backward* is the first example of the contrast between "a progressive political agenda and a traditional characterization of women" (p. 315). While Bellamy changed the conditions of women's lives, he did not change their roles or personalities—their existence was still intended to serve and enhance that of men.

———. *The Utopian Novel in America, 1886–1896: The Politics of Form.* Pittsburgh: University of Pittsburgh Press, 1984, 26–51, 70–73, 87–92. *Looking Backward* is a combination of the romantic fable and the manifesto, in which Julian West is saved by love and re-education. Discusses the literary qualities of the work, as well as Bellamy's use of technology and the industrial army and his depiction of women. Includes consideration of Nationalism, as well as a comparison of Bellamy and Howells.

Quint, Howard. "Bellamy Makes Socialism Respectable." Chapter in *The Forging of American Socialism*. Columbia: University of South Carolina Press, 1953. Bellamy popularized socialism by making it interesting to the common man. Discusses Nationalism and how it is related to Marxism.

Rhodes, Harold V. "Bellamy: The Socialist Utopian." Chapter in *The Methodology of Utopian Political Theory*. Tucson: University of Arizona Press, 1967. Discusses the historical background of *Looking Backward*, and cites both the social and moral bases for its writing. Bellamy was very influential, but his methodology was faulty: through discounting revolution and governmental action, he left himself with no possible means of achieving utopia.

Roemer, Kenneth M. "Contexts and Texts: The Influence of *Looking Backward*." *Centennial Review* 27, no. 3 (Summer 1983): 204–23. Describes the extent of *Looking Backward*'s popularity, and places it within the historical context of the day. Then focuses on "the internal characteristics of the text that may help us to understand" its popularity (p. 206).

———. "Sex Roles, Utopia and Change: The Family in Late Nineteenth-Century Utopian Literature." *American Studies* 13, no. 2 (Fall 1972): 33–49. Although Bellamy depicts a society in which women are economically equal to men and serve at all levels of society, women are "still primarily defined in relation to [their] children and husbands" (p. 39).

———. "Utopia and Victorian Culture, 1888–99." Chapter in *America as Utopia*. New York: Burt Franklin, 1981. Late nineteenth-century utopian writers were influenced by the mainstream of Victorian ideas, particularly ideas about technology, morality, Christianity, order, and the promise of the future. Discusses *Looking Backward* and *Equality*.

Rooney, Charles J. *Dreams and Visions: A Study of American Utopias, 1865–1917*. Westport, Conn.: Greenwood, 1985. Utopian authors of this period, including Bellamy and some of his imitators, saw a variety of social problems and proposed a variety of solutions. *Looking Backward* and other Nationalist utopias are very ordered types of socialist utopias, where the present political apparatus is dismantled, equality is paramount, and all workers share equally in the wealth.

Rosemont, Franklin. "Free Play and No Limit: An Introduction to Edward Bellamy's Utopia." *Cultural Correspondence*, nos. 10–11 (Fall

1979): 6–16. Relates *Looking Backward* to Bellamy's sources, the historical context in which it was written, and Bellamy's earlier fiction. All of Bellamy's works exhibit the recurring themes of the "supersession of memory," "reintegration of the personality," "transcendence of time," and "need for wilderness."

Saccaro-Battisti, Giuseppa. "Changing Metaphors of Political Structures." *Journal of the History of Ideas* 44 (January/March 1983): 31–54. A discussion of the use of political metaphors in utopian and science fiction works. Divides the metaphors in *Looking Backward* into two types: those depicting the decaying society of the nineteenth century, and those depicting the perfect society of the year 2000.

Sadler, Elizabeth. "One Book's Influence: Edward Bellamy's 'Looking Backward.'" *New England Quarterly* 17 (December 1944): 530–55. Deals with Nationalism, lists Bellamy imitators and other utopians, and includes some discussion of books and articles on Bellamy.

Samuels, Warren J. "A Centenary Reconsideration of Bellamy's *Looking Backward*." *American Journal of Economics and Sociology* 43 (April 1984): 129–48. *Looking Backward* had an impact on the development of the welfare state and also influenced many thinkers, including Thorstein Veblen. Bellamy dealt with the fundamental questions of economic organization, indeed, of economic belief and social values. His system, however, was centralized and static.

Segal, Howard P. *Technological Utopianism in American Culture.* Chicago: University of Chicago Press, 1985, 3–7, 19–31, 47–55, 99–100. Concentrates on twenty-five literary utopias, written between 1883 and 1933, whose societies were based on technological progress. Discusses the reasons why Bellamy's book was so much more popular and influential than the others and describes the uses made of technology in the new societies.

Shipley, Mrs. John B. (Marie A. Brown). *The True Author of "Looking Backward."* New York: John B. Alden, 1890. Lists many parallel passages to show that Bellamy's scheme was "taken intact from . . . 'Woman in the Past, Present and Future'" by Bebel, and his romance came from "A Far Look Ahead" (preface).

Shurter, Robert L. "The Writing of *Looking Backward.*" *The South Atlantic Quarterly* 38, no. 3 (July 1939): 255–61. Bellamy's life and background is the basis for *Looking Backward*. The timing of its publication was opportune, and its popularity changed Bellamy's life.

———. *The Utopian Novel in America, 1865–1900.* New York: AMS Press, 1973. After a definition of utopia, a survey of English utopian literature prior to 1888, and a discussion of early utopian literature in America, the author concentrates on Edward Bellamy, his predecessors and sources, *Looking Backward*, the reactions to it, Nationalism, and other American utopias of the period. Bellamy "gave the clearest expression to the reform ideas of the generation" (p. 282). Includes interesting autobiographical material sent to Shurter by Bellamy's daughter.

Smith, Goldwin. "Prophet of Unrest." *Forum* 9 (August 1890): 599–614. Reprinted in Goldwin Smith. *Essays on Questions of the Day, Political and Social.* New York: Macmillan, 1893, 38–56. Questions the basic features of Bellamy's society; his scheme is improbable, unrealistic, and out of line with human nature.

Suvin, Darko. "Anticipating the Sunburst: Dream, Vision or Nightmare?" Chapter in *Metamorphoses of Science Fiction.* New Haven: Yale University Press, 1979. Revised version appears in Kenneth M. Roemer, ed. *America as Utopia.* New York: Burt Franklin, 1981, 57–77. *Looking Backward* is part of the late nineteenth-century socialist vision that served as a "solution to both the ideational and the formal problems of nineteenth-century SF" (p. 171). Bellamy "links . . . two strong American traditions: the fantastic one of unknown worlds and potentialities, and the practical one of organizing a new world" (p. 177).

Taylor, Walter Fuller. "Edward Bellamy." Chapter in *The Economic Novel in America.* Chapel Hill: University of North Carolina Press, 1942. Includes a biographical sketch of Bellamy, focusing on the origin of his ideas about social reform. Discusses *Looking Backward*, concentrating on the plot, its criticisms of capitalism, its portrait of utopia, and the resulting Nationalist movement.

Thomas, John L. "Utopia for an Urban Age: Henry George, Henry Demarest Lloyd, Edward Bellamy." In Donald Fleming and Bernard Bailyn, eds., *Perspectives in American History* 6 (1972): 135–63. A study of *Looking Backward* in light of city planning. Bellamy focused on regional village groupings rather than on large industrial cities. Late nineteenth-century utopians were "intent on perpetuating an environment wholeness" (p. 163).

Towers, Tom H. "The Insomnia of Julian West." *American Literature* 47, no. 1 (March 1975): 52–63. *Looking Backward* is a romance, rather than a political or economic blueprint for change. "Such an examination of *Looking Backward* leads to the conclusion that Bellamy was less concerned with the operation of the new society than with the familiar Romantic idea of the realized self" (p. 53).

Trimmer, Joseph F. "American Dreams: A Comparative Study of the

Utopian Novels of Bellamy and Howells." *Ball State University Forum* 12, no. 3 (Summer 1971): 13–21. The utopian writings of these two novelists show "the workings of the American intellect during a time of social and economic crisis" (p. 13). Bellamy is more concerned with ideology, while Howells's work is more aesthetic, more an idyll.

Walden, Daniel. "Edward Bellamy and William Dean Howells: The Infinity Beyond." *Journal of Human Relations* 12, no. 3 (1964): 325–34. Howells and Bellamy responded differently to the evils of the day. "Where Howells' possible solution . . . was 'complicity' [each man involved in the lives of others], Bellamy wrote of the idea of 'solidarity' [brotherhood or unity of all men]" (p. 330).

———. "The Two Faces of Technological Utopianism: Edward Bellamy and Horatio Alger, Jr." *Journal of General Education* 33, no. 1 (Spring 1981): 24–30. *Looking Backward* is the "first fully developed example of technological utopianism" (p. 24), in which technology is "safe, aesthetically pleasing, and productive of all the finer aspects of civilized life" (p. 26). Contrasts Bellamy's forward-looking attitude with Alger's fusion of the past with the present.

Wilson, R. Jackson. "Experience and Utopia: The Making of Edward Bellamy's *Looking Backward.*" *Journal of American Studies* 11, no. 1 (April 1977): 45–60. Bellamy's utopia was not forward-looking and industrially centered, but reflected his "unwillingness or inability to confront the industrial city." His Boston resembled "nothing so much as Bellamy's own home town of Chicopee Falls" (p. 45).

Winters, Donald E. "The Utopianism of Survival: Bellamy's *Looking Backward* and Twain's *A Connecticut Yankee.*" *American Studies* 21, no. 1 (Spring 1980): 23–38. Twain was attracted to Bellamy and *Looking Backward.* Discusses *A Connecticut Yankee* as a utopian work, using Robert Jay Lifton's survivor paradigm.

Wolfe, Don Marion. "Utopian Dissent and Affirmation: Howells, Bellamy and George." Chapter in *The Image of Man in America.* New York: Crowell, 1970. A brief biographical sketch and discussion of *Looking Backward.* To Bellamy, man is naturally good. Society can mold man, who is plastic, into a noble form; material well-being will result in a better spiritual life.

Contributors

SYLVIA E. BOWMAN, professor emeritus of Indiana University, is author of *The Year 2000: A Critical Biography of Edward Bellamy* (1958, 1979) and editor and author of *Edward Bellamy Abroad* (1962). Her latest book, *Edward Bellamy*, was published as volume 500 in Twayne's United States Authors Series, which Professor Bowman founded in 1960 and for which she served as Editor-in-Chief until 1976.

MILTON CANTOR, professor of history at the University of Massachusetts in Amherst, is the author of, among other works, *Max Eastman* (1970) and *The Divided Left: American Radicalism, 1900–1975* (1978). He also edited *American Workingclass Culture: Explorations in American Labor and Social History* (1979), *Black Labor in America* (1969), and, with Bruce Laurie, *Class, Sex, and the Woman Worker* (1977).

NANCY SNELL GRIFFITH, a librarian in the Music Department at Davidson College in North Carolina, received her B.A. in English and German from Dickinson College, where she worked with Bellamy scholar Joseph Schiffman. She is the author of *Edward Bellamy: A Bibliography* (1986) and co-author of *Albert Schweitzer: An International Bibliography* (1981).

LEE CULLEN KHANNA, professor of English at Montclair State College, has published articles on the utopian fiction of Edward Bellamy and Thomas More as well as on contemporary utopian novels. Her current project, *Utopia and Gender: New Worlds, New Texts,* places recent utopian fiction in the contexts of earlier utopian speculation, feminist theory, and new directions in literary theory.

DAPHNE PATAI, professor of women's studies and of Spanish and Portuguese at the University of Massachusetts in Amherst, is the author of *The Orwell Mystique: A Study in Male Ideology* (1984), *Myth and Ideology in Contemporary Brazilian Fiction* (1983), and *Brazilian Women Speak: Con-*

temporary Life Stories (1988). She is currently at work on the British utopian writer Katharine Burdekin.

JEAN PFAELZER, associate professor of English and American studies at the University of Delaware, is the author of *The Utopian Novel in America, 1886–1896: The Politics of Form* (1985), and of many articles on utopian fiction and on gender. Currently she is editing a special issue of *American Transcendental Quarterly* on nineteenth-century utopianism and is writing a critical biography of Rebecca Harding Davis.

KENNETH M. ROEMER, professor of English and graduate adviser at the University of Texas at Arlington, is the author of *The Obsolete Necessity: America in Utopian Writings, 1888–1900* (1976) and the editor of two books—*America as Utopia* (1981) and *Approaches to Teaching Momaday's "The Way to Rainy Mountain"* (1988)—and of the Society for Utopian Studies newsletter, *Utopus Discovered*. His current Bellamy research is supported by a Senior Scientist Fellowship from the Japan Society for the Promotion of Science.

FRANKLIN ROSEMONT has written in the fields of surrealism, American popular culture, and labor history. Author of *André Breton and the First Principles of Surrealism* (1978), he has also edited Breton's *What Is Surrealism? Selected Writings* (1978), as well as volumes by dancer Isadora Duncan, U.S. socialist editor Mary E. Marcy, and IWW cartoonist Ernest Riebe. His most recent books are *Haymarket Scrapbook* (co-edited with David Roediger, 1986) and *Apparitions of Things to Come: Edward Bellamy's Tales of Mystery and Imagination* (1988).

HOWARD P. SEGAL, associate professor of history at the University of Maine, and director of the Technology and Society Project, has written extensively on technology and American utopianism. He is the author of *Technological Utopianism in American Culture* (1985) and co-author of *Technology in America: A Brief History* (1988) and is now at work on a study of experiments in decentralized technology in modern America.

SYLVIA STRAUSS, professor of history at Kean College, N.J., is the author of *"Traitors to the Masculine Cause": The Men's Campaign for Women's Rights* (1982), and numerous articles on feminism. She is the coordinator of the Women's Studies Program at Kean College and in 1987 was awarded a grant from the New Jersey Department of Higher Education to integrate gender, class, and race issues into the general education courses at Kean College.

W. WARREN WAGAR, distinguished teaching professor of history at the State University of New York at Binghamton, is a founding member of the

Society for Utopian Studies. His books include *H. G. Wells and the World State* (1961); *The City of Man: Prophecies of a World Civilization in 20th-Century Thought* (1963); *Good Tidings: The Belief in Progress from Darwin to Marcuse* (1972); *World Views* (1977); and *Terminal Visions: The Literature of Last Things* (1982).